AN A TO Z OF KING ARTHUR AND THE HOLY GRAIL

SIMON COX'S A TO Z SERIES

AN A TO Z OF
KING ARTHUR
AND THE
HOLY GRAIL

SIMON COX
AND MARK OXBROW

with additional material by
Ed Davies, Susan Davies, Mark Foster and Jacqueline Harvey

MAINSTREAM
PUBLISHING

EDINBURGH AND LONDON

First published in Great Britain in 2007 by
MAINSTREAM PUBLISHING COMPANY (EDINBURGH) LTD
7 Albany Street
Edinburgh EH1 3UG

ISBN 9781845960759

All photographs courtesy of Mark Oxbrow unless otherwise stated

A catalogue record for this book is available from the British Library

Typeset in Apollo and Hamilton

Printed and bound in Great Britain by
William Clowes Ltd, Beccles, Suffolk

ACKNOWLEDGEMENTS

For steadfast endeavour and duty above and beyond, the indispensable Susan Davies deserves a special mention, along with a medal! The various contributors were, as always, brilliant: Jackie Harvey, one of the best researchers in the business; Mark Foster, writer, researcher, friend and genius designer; Ed Davies for his sharp insight and constant wit.

In the US, Jennifer Clymer remains brilliant three times; M.J. Miller still knows that it's all about me; Mark Finnell and Tina Gloss-Finnell for great evenings and conversation; Eric for the biscuits; Derek and Don for being the coolest people; Ken and MPTF.

Thanks to Robert Kirby and Katie at PFD; Catherine Cameron; Bill, Fiona and Amy at Mainstream; special thanks to our editor, Claire Rose, for nurturing this series of books.

At home, Horst, Yul and Charlie for the calming influence; Lorenzo for being cute. All in Marina Court for the encouragement and friendship; Mark Freitag for DIY miracles! The boys of Blue Ginger, Ali and Shuhel and their amazing chef, for the Chicken Tenga – brain food!

Thanks to my co-author, Mark Oxbrow, for being the Arthurian colossus that he is, and to his wife Jill for keeping him focused; Ian and Viv Robertson for kindness and friendship – another Fringe?

I am indebted to the friends and family members who have helped and encouraged constantly. Mum and Dad on Gozo; Mark and Claire; the Welsh crew, Uncle Allan, Aunt Betty and cousin David; Neil and Alison Roberts, along with Imogen and Joe, for great visits and constant smiles; Jane and Alexander; Andy Gough and Filip Coppens, great researchers.

Music is the bread that I feed on. I work with a constant set of complex and wonderful sounds ringing in my ears. I couldn't get by without: Kamelot, Epica, After Forever, Abydos, Vanden Plas, Leaves Eyes, Journey, Harlan Cage, Lacuna Coil, Stream of Passion, Lunatica, Opeth.

Simon Cox

For Jill and the bump (should appear before this reaches paperback). With lots of love to Fleur, Gran, Mum, Dad, Lewis and Craig. Love to John and Pam, Stephanie, Geoff and Ratha, Great Aunties Margaret and Garland, Auntie Audrey, Freda and James and their bump! Big love to Simon and Susan (you rock!), Ian and Vivienne, Pat and Charlie, Gordon Strachan, Claudine and Hervé Glot, Maggie from Hocus Pocus for reminding me to believe in magic and Chris Thornborrow for the adventure of painting Avalon.

Huge thanks and many well-earned drinks to all the lovely folk at Mainstream. Thanks to the staff of the National Library of Scotland, the Mitchell Library, the British Library, Rosslyn Chapel, Glastonbury Abbey, King Arthur's Great Halls in Tintagel, le Centre de l'Imaginaire Arthurien at Comper in Brocéliande and the Musée du Louvre.

A massive thank you to Judy Shoaf, the wonderful moderator of Arthurnet, and to all the scholars and enthusiasts who make it such a lively and illuminating list. Big thanks to Ewan McIntosh and Morgane. All the best to Prof. Tolkien, John Duncan, Norris J. Lacy, Alan Lupack and Barbara Tepa Lupack, Basil Clarke, Richard Barber, John Boorman, Nicol Williamson and the Pythons. Finally a word of thanks to Chrétien, Marie, Wolfram, Robert, Geoffrey, Malory, Taliesin, the Gawain poet and all the anonymous poets, scribes and storytellers who have kept the stories of Arthur alive.

Mark Oxbrow

CONTENTS

INTRODUCTION

In this book in Simon Cox's A to Z series, the stories of King Arthur and the Holy Grail are examined and explained. Alongside the companion guides to Ancient Egypt, Atlantis and the occult, it is intended to inform and to excite further study. The team that puts these books together (for it is a team, including researchers, writers, editors and publishers) are very pleased with the outcome and hope this book, and indeed the whole series, may in time become a recognised reference work for the student of mysteries and historical enigmas.

King Arthur is a historical icon, a figure of reverence and awe for many and one whose very existence is simply taken for granted by a large proportion of the population. Arthur, his deeds and his quest for the Holy Grail have become archetypes that resonate with us right down to the present time. If ever a delivering hero was needed, it is now. Arthur is the king we all want, the king we all aspire to be and a figure of such true soul, purpose and spirit that he has become the mythical hero par excellence.

Over a thousand years ago, the bards recited poems of Arthur. Their Arthur was not a wise king. His warriors were not knights in shining suits of armour. If the Arthur of history existed, he was a Dark Age warlord, a merciless leader of battles who commanded his men as they fought against invading armies and whose bloody deeds were recounted in great halls.

Within six centuries, he had become King Arthur, ruler of the legendary realm of Logres. The Dark Age warrior was now a wise and valiant king who bore the magical sword Excalibur and kept the finest court of knights and ladies in all Europe. His adviser was the wizard Merlin, his sister was the enchantress Morgan le Fay and his queen was the beautiful, unfaithful Guinevere.

Arthur was destined to be king. He was raised in secret until, at the age of 15, he drew the sword from the stone and was hailed as king. King Arthur led his lords and men to victory against all enemies. He founded the wondrous city of Camelot and gathered his knights at the Round Table, where all men were equal. The gallant deeds of Sir Gawain, Sir Lancelot, Sir Percival and Sir Galahad were recorded by scribes in medieval manuscripts and recited by troubadours in castles around Europe. In the end, Arthur and his kingdom fell in a single, terrible battle against his treacherous son Mordred.

Woven into the legends of King Arthur is the story of the Grail. In the last years of the twelfth century, a French Arthurian romance composed by Chrétien de Troyes captured the imaginations of lords and ladies, knights and poets. In the years that followed, Chrétien's *Perceval, or the Story of the Grail* was adapted, altered and continued. The mystery of the Holy Grail deepened as later writers claimed that it was the cup used by Jesus at the Last Supper, the vessel that caught the blood of Christ on the Cross and a magical stone that fell from the heavens. Pure knights sought the secrets of the Grail as the quest became a spiritual act.

The Arthurian tales of Merlin, Guinevere and the Knights of the Round Table inspired Victorian writers and artists to create poems, paintings, books, plays, murals, tapestries and stained glass. The Round Table is found today in parliaments, peace talks and assembly rooms around the world. Novelists, playwrights and filmmakers have turned to the stories of King Arthur and the Holy Grail to create multimillion-dollar movies, hit Broadway musicals, Las Vegas shows and blockbuster novels.

Thousands of books have been written about the Holy Grail. It has been the focus of academic studies, literary novels, pulp fantasies, operas, comic books, conspiracy theories, TV documentaries and a million websites, and the darling of Hollywood. It has been claimed that the 'real Holy Grail' can be found in Glastonbury, Nanteos in Wales, Rosslyn, Genoa, Valencia and New York. It has also been suggested that the Holy Grail is in reality a symbol of the sacred feminine, of Mary Magdalene and the holy bloodline of Jesus. A 'Holy Grail' has become the description of choice for unobtainable goals and ultimate expressions. Newspaper headlines note that 'Antigravity is the Holy Grail of Science' and journalists write about 'Coca-Cola's Holy Grail', the 'Holy Grail of snowball fighting' and so on. The quest for the Holy Grail has come to symbolise the search for perfection, wisdom or self-knowledge. Most Arthurian scholars agree that the Grail as it is perceived now never existed, that it was simply a literary invention, a fictional object conjured up by the first Grail poet, Chrétien de Troyes.

In the summer of 2006, Mark Oxbrow and his wife Jill were holidaying in Paris. They meandered through the galleries of the Musée du Louvre, gazing at magnificent works of art and antiquities from the four corners of the world. In the Richelieu Wing, they saw some of the treasures of medieval France – the Sword of Charlemagne and the Eagle of Abbot Suger. Mark noticed a French fourteenth-century ivory casket carved with scenes from Chrétien's *Story of the Grail*: Perceval kneeling before the knights in the forest, fighting the Red Knight and appearing at King Arthur's court. Then they found one of the treasures of the Abbey of Saint Denis. The Patène de Serpentine is a golden platter, a sacred vessel set with precious gems and natural pearls; it was one of a thousand wonders in the museum. It can be seen in the picture section of this book.

In the months that followed, Mark wrote about the *Story of the Grail* and researched the history of the Patène de Serpentine. Everything he learned about the Patène showed that it was an important holy vessel of the French court. At the time when Chrétien de Troyes was composing the first Grail romance, it bore the holy Mass wafer in the sacred ceremonies of the queens of France. Chrétien's patrons were the daughter of the King of France and the guardian of the heir to the French throne. The Patène de Serpentine is a real medieval treasure that perfectly matches every detail Chrétien de Troyes gives us about the Grail. What's more, part of it dates to the time of Christ. Has the real Holy Grail finally been found?

Simon Cox and Mark Oxbrow
February 2007

ARTHUR, KING OF THE BRITONS

Tales of Arthur have been told for over a thousand years. Centuries before the crusaders fought in the Holy Land, Christopher Columbus sailed to the New World or William Shakespeare wrote his plays, the deeds of Arthur were being recounted by bards and storytellers.

The earliest surviving mention of Arthur is in a Welsh poem known as *Y Gododdin*, composed following the Battle of Catraeth *circa* AD 600. In *Y Gododdin*, the bard Aneirin tells us that a warrior known as Gwawrddur had killed his enemies and left their dead bodies to the ravens 'though he was not Arthur'. By the seventh century, Arthur was remembered as a mighty warrior without equal. His name needed no explanation; anyone who heard Aneirin's poem would have known of the valour of Arthur.

But who was Arthur? The historical Arthur is a shadowy and controversial figure. Early histories and chronicles tell us that Arthur was not a king at all. He fought alongside the kings of the Britons but was himself described as a 'dux bellorum' – a 'leader of battles'. When the Romans finally left Britain in the fifth century, the Britons had to defend themselves against invasions by the Saxons, Angles, Jutes, Picts and Scots. The real Arthur was remembered as the great military commander who led the Britons in a Dark Age war against the invaders. He is said to have fought a series of decisive battles against the enemies of the Britons. From the fragments of historical evidence, various theories about the identity of Arthur have been put forward. It has been suggested that he was a Welsh war leader, a Bronze-Age warrior, a northern Briton who had trained as a Roman cavalry soldier, the descendant of a Sarmatian Roman soldier, a Roman general turned emperor, or a king or war leader of the ancient Scottish kingdom of Dál Riata.

Around AD 1135, over five hundred years after the historical Arthur would have lived, a Welsh cleric named Geoffrey of Monmouth immortalised the king. In his book *Historia Regum Britanniae, The History of the Kings of Britain*, Geoffrey gathered together the legends and tales of Arthur and reworked them to create the basis of the story of King Arthur as we know it today. At the time, Geoffrey's work was strongly criticised, described as fiction and fantasy, but *The History of the Kings of Britain* became hugely popular and led to the flourishing of Arthurian literature in the Middle Ages.

Writers and poets from across Europe wrote of King Arthur and of the valiant deeds of his knights. In France, Chrétien de Troyes introduced the Grail quest to the legends of Arthur. The French clerk Robert de Boron sanctified the Grail, identifying it with the vessel Christ used at the Last Supper. The German minnesinger, or poet, Wolfram von Eschenbach composed an alternative version of the story of the Grail. In England, the poet Wace introduced the Round Table. With each new writer, the story of King Arthur grew and changed. New characters such as Lancelot, Galahad and the Swan Knight Lohengrin were introduced, and King Arthur and his Knights of the Round Table became chivalrous knights in shining armour who lived at the magnificent castle of Camelot and battled giants, dragons and wicked knights. In the Middle Ages, Arthur was transformed from a war leader famed for cutting down his enemies to an idealised medieval king who brought peace and wisdom to his realm.

In the fifteenth century, Sir Thomas Malory wrote his epic *Le Morte d'Arthur*, which collected and retold the Arthurian legends in what would effectively become the definitive version. Malory's tales of King Arthur and the Knights of the Round Table would influence later writers, poets and artists including Alfred, Lord Tennyson, Mark Twain, T.H. White, T.S. Eliot, William Morris, Edward Burne-Jones and Dante Gabriel Rossetti.

While the details differ from book to book, what the tales have in common has allowed the development of a standard narrative of the life of King Arthur. It was an enchantment woven by the wizard Merlin that led to the birth of Arthur. Uther Pendragon, the King of the Britons, gathered together all the lords and knights of his kingdom for a great feast one Easter. Among the nobles was Gorlois, the Duke of Cornwall. Gorlois brought his wife, the fair Igraine, to court, and King Uther was seized by an unbearable lust as soon as he saw her. When the king's passion became clear, Gorlois took his wife and fled to Cornwall, hiding Igraine in Tintagel Castle and preparing for war. King Uther pursued the Duke and laid siege to Tintagel.

The castle lay on a rocky peninsula that jutted out into the sea. It was said that three men could defend it against a whole army. Uther, overwhelmed by his lust, pleaded with Merlin to aid him. Merlin used his magic to transform Uther into the image of Gorlois so that he could ride unchallenged into the castle and be with Igraine in her bedchamber. That night, a child was conceived.

As morning broke, Gorlois was killed, and Igraine was persuaded to marry the father of her child. But Uther was a broken man; he died before Arthur was born, believing he had failed as a king. As the waves crashed on the rocky shore at Tintagel, Igraine bore a son. Once the child was weaned, Merlin appeared and took the boy from his mother. Igraine was left to grieve for her dead husbands and her lost son with her daughter, Morgan le Fay, Arthur's half-sister.

Merlin had Arthur fostered in the household of the noble Sir Ector. The young Arthur grew up alongside Kay, Sir Ector's son, learning the rules of knighthood and chivalry. At this time, Britain was a divided land without a king. The petty kings and lords fought among themselves while the people waited for the true king who would pull the sword from the stone. The sword in the stone lay in a churchyard in London, and while many knights and kings had tried to pull it free, none had succeeded. The sword pierced a blacksmith's anvil and a huge stone. Where so many mighty knights had failed, the boy Arthur succeeded. He grasped the hilt and pulled the sword from the stone; as he held the sword aloft, Arthur was proclaimed king.

In the years that followed, King Arthur gathered the finest knights together to fight the enemies of the Britons. When his sword was broken, Arthur was given the magical sword Excalibur by the Lady of the Lake. He gained the allegiance of the many kings and lords of Britain and built a mighty castle known as Camelot. There he had Merlin create the Round Table, where his knights could meet as equals. The kingdom of Britain knew peace, and Arthur's rule was fair and just. His lands were plentiful and his people were content. Arthur's thoughts turned to love, and he made the maiden Guinevere his queen. Arthur's best friend, the noble Sir Lancelot, became Queen Guinevere's champion, but a secret passion grew between Lancelot and the queen. In time, it would tear apart the Round Table and lead to the fall of Arthur.

At Pentecost, as King Arthur and the Knights of the Round Table were gathered at a feast, they witnessed a miraculous vision of the Holy Grail. Arthur asked his knights to seek out the sacred object, and so began the quest for the Holy Grail. Sir Percival, Sir Gawain, Sir Lancelot and Sir Galahad are the knights most associated with the Grail quest. Sir Percival met the Fisher King and saw the Grail in a wondrous procession within the Castle of the Grail. Sir Gawain crossed the Sword Bridge and survived the deadly Perilous Bed. Sir Lancelot was entrapped by magic and became the lover of Elaine of Corbenic, thinking she was Guinevere. Elaine was the daughter of the Grail King Pelles, a descendant of Joseph of Arimathea. Lancelot and Elaine had a son, Galahad, who would become the perfect knight, finally achieving the Grail and being crowned king of the city of Sarras.

The story of King Arthur ends in tragedy. Arthur's other half-sister Morgause appeared at Camelot and seduced the king. She conceived a child whom she named Mordred. Morgan le Fay plotted Arthur's downfall so that Mordred would become king. Through Morgan's intrigues, the love affair of Lancelot and Guinevere came to light and the queen was accused of treason. She was condemned to be burned at the stake, but at the last moment Sir Lancelot rode in and rescued Guinevere from the flames. Lancelot fought his way through his fellow knights to reach her, killing Sir Gawain's brothers. Guinevere survived but, overcome with shame and remorse, she left Lancelot and Arthur, and chose a life of seclusion in a nunnery. King Arthur pursued Sir Lancelot and, as war raged between them, the treacherous Mordred tried to usurp his father's throne.

In one final, terrible battle, King Arthur and the loyal Knights of the Round Table faced Mordred and his army. At Camlann, the field of battle was filled with the dead and dying as father and son fought to the death. Arthur was mortally wounded by Mordred but was able to kill the usurper as they fell. Tennyson described this last battle in his 'Morte d'Arthur':

> So all day long the noise of battle roll'd
> Among the mountains by the winter sea;
> Until King Arthur's table, man by man,
> Had fallen in Lyonnesse about their Lord,
> King Arthur: then, because his wound was deep,

The bold Sir Bedivere uplifted him,
Sir Bedivere, the last of all his knights,
And bore him to a chapel nigh the field,
A broken chancel with a broken cross,
That stood on a dark strait of barren land.
On one side lay the ocean, and on one
Lay a great water, and the moon was full.

Sir Bedivere knelt by Arthur's side as the king lay dying. Arthur commanded Bedivere to cast Excalibur into the water. Twice Sir Bedivere hid the sword and told Arthur he had thrown it into the water. Twice Arthur rebuked the knight for his lies. A third time Sir Bedivere went to the water's edge. He took Excalibur and threw the sword as far into the water as he could, and a hand rose above the water and caught it, brandished it, then vanished with it beneath the waves. When Sir Bedivere returned to the fallen king, he told him what he had seen. Arthur was borne away to the mystical Isle of Avalon by three queens in a dark barge. There, he was tended by his half-sister Morgan le Fay and the enchantresses of Avalon. Some say that Arthur eventually died of his wounds.

In the twelfth century, the monks of Glastonbury Abbey in Somerset claimed to have discovered the grave of Arthur and his queen. They dug down between two stone pyramids and unearthed an ancient lead cross bearing the name 'Rex Arturius'. Beneath the cross was the hollowed-out trunk of an oak tree, which held the remains of a tall man and a woman.

The Welsh, descendants of Arthur's Britons, long believed that Arthur was not dead and buried. There was a Welsh saying, 'Unwise, a grave for Arthur', that recorded the common belief that Arthur still lived and would one day return to lead the Britons against their enemies in their hour of greatest need.

Some say that Arthur still rests on the enchanted Isle of Avalon and, in legends told across Britain, King Arthur and his knights lie sleeping within a hollow hill awaiting the call to ride into battle. The legendary King Arthur is a tragic hero who still lives on, 'the once and future king'.

King Arthur is one of the most famous figures in all of human history; he is known the world over. Literally thousands of books have been written about the adventures of Arthur and the Knights of the Round Table. The Arthurian legends appear in paintings and stained-glass artworks created by some of the world's finest artists. Arthur's story has been told in countless movies, musicals, pageants and shows, TV series, cartoons, plays, comic books, computer games and websites. King Arthur gives his name to theme parks, roller-coaster rides and tourist attractions, pizza parlours, toys, games and a million other products. He has also become an iconic figure for the mystical new-age movement. Places associated with Arthur, including Glastonbury and Stonehenge, have become the centres of modern pilgrimages as people embark on their own Grail quests. The legendary Arthur has taken on a sacred and magical significance that the Dark Age warrior could never have dreamed of.

SEE ALSO: Battles of Arthur; Camelot; Excalibur; Guinevere; Knights of the Round Table; Lancelot; Merlin; Mordred; Morgan le Fay; Round Table; Sword in the Stone

AVALON

When Arthur was mortally wounded by his son Mordred at the Battle of Camlann, he was borne away to the Isle of Avalon. On the mystical island Arthur's wounds were tended by Morgan le Fay and the enchantresses of Avalon.

Avalon appears as early as AD 1135, in Geoffrey of Monmouth's *History of the Kings of Britain*. Geoffrey tells us that Arthur's sword was forged on the island and that when 'the renowned king Arthur himself was mortally wounded' he was taken 'to the isle of Avallonis to be cured of his wounds'.

In his *Vita Merlini* (*Life of Merlin*), Geoffrey describes the island in more depth. He calls Avalon 'Insula Avallonis' and 'Insula Pomorum', the 'Isle of Apples', describing it as a wondrous isle where the trees in the orchards bore both apples and blossom at the same time, and the fields did not need farmers to plough them, as nature herself made the crops grow. The Isle of Apples was also called the Fortunate Island. The island produced plentiful crops and grapes, and people lived for a hundred years or more there. Avalon was an island of maidens where nine sisters lived. This sisterhood was led by Morgan le Fay. Morgan was said to exceed her sisters in the art of healing and had the magical ability to change her shape and to fly – to 'cut the air on new wings'. In Layamon's *Brut*, Arthur tells Constantine, the son of Cador, the earl of Cornwall, that the queen of Avalon was Argante,

> . . . a fey most fair,
> And she will make sound all my wounds,
> And make me whole with healing potions;

The magical Isle of Apples has much in common with other legends of an earthly paradise, including the story of the Garden of Eden, where the Tree of the Knowledge of Good and Evil and the Tree of Life grew. Avalon was one of many fabled islands, phantom islands that appear on maps and in legends of the sea, such as Hy-Brasil, St Brendan's Island, Terra Australis, the Isle of Demons and the fabled Atlantis of which the Greek philosopher Plato wrote, an ancient island civilisation that vanished beneath the waves.

In Greek mythology, the Garden of the Hesperides was inhabited by nymphs who sang enchanting songs and watched over wondrous trees bearing golden apples that granted immortality. Gaia gave the trees to the goddess Hera as a wedding present. The ancient Greek poet Hesiod said that the Hesperides were the daughters of Nyx, the goddess of Night. The apple trees grew in a garden surrounded by a high wall and guarded by a many-headed dragon named Ladon. One of the labours of Heracles was to retrieve the golden apples from the Garden of the Hesperides.

The heroes of ancient Irish tales voyaged to the enchanted Blessed Isles: Tir-na-n-oge, the Land of the Ever-Young; Tir Tairgire, the Land of Promise; Tirfo Thuinn, the Land Beneath the Waves; Mag Mell, the Plain of Joy; Tir Nam Beo, the Land of the Living; Mag Mor, the Great Plain; Tirn Aill, the Other World. Tir na nIngnad, the Land of Wonders, was noted for its wild apples and 'fair fragrant apple trees'. The Isle of Arran was known as Emhain Abhlach, the Island of the Apple Trees. Manannan mac Lir, the ancient shape-shifting Irish God of the Sea, was the guardian of the Blessed Islands.

The Irish poem *The Voyage of Bran Mac Febal*, written some time around the seventh century, relates the adventures of Bran, son of Febal, who sailed across the sea to the Land of Women. When Bran had been at sea for two days and two nights, he met Manannan mac Lir, riding in a chariot coming towards him over the waves. The following extract, taken from Kuno Meyer's nineteenth-century translation, describes the islands of the faerie realm:

> A branch of the apple-tree from Emain
> I bring, like those one knows;
> Twigs of white silver are on it,
> Crystal brows with blossoms . . .

AVALON

An ancient tree there is with blossoms,
On which birds call to the Hours.
'Tis in harmony it is their wont
To call together every Hour . . .

Without grief, without sorrow, without death,
Without any sickness, without debility,
That is the sign of Emain —
Uncommon is an equal marvel.

A beauty of a wondrous land,
Whose aspects are lovely,
Whose view is a fair country,
Incomparable is its haze . . .

Along the top of a wood has swum
Thy coracle across ridges,
There is a wood of beautiful fruit
Under the prow of thy little skiff.

A wood with blossom and fruit,
On which is the vine's veritable fragrance,
A wood without decay, without defect,
On which are leaves of golden hue.

The Island of Avalon is also related to Annwn, the Welsh otherworld, a realm of the faeries and the dead. In the ancient Welsh poem *The Spoils of Annwn*, Arthur and his men sail to the faerie realm to steal a magical pearl-rimmed cauldron that is warmed by the breath of nine maidens. They sail into the west, to the land where the sun sets, to seek the cauldron. Geoffrey's Isle of Apples was Ynys Avallach in Welsh. It was ruled by a king named Avallach, the father of the goddess Modron. Her name means 'mother' and she is identified with Morgan le Fay.

Some say that Merlin keeps the mythical Thirteen Treasures of Britain on Bardsey Island off the Llyn Peninsula in North Wales. Bardsey was a Holy Island called Ynys Enlli ('the island in the tides' or 'the island of the great current') by the Welsh. Legend has it that twenty thousand saints are buried on the island and that three pilgrimages to Ynys Enlli were equal to one pilgrimage to Rome. In recent years, a gnarled apple tree growing up the side of one of the houses on Bardsey Island was recognised as the only survivor of an ancient orchard. Its fruit is thought to be the world's rarest apple. The tree is known as 'Merlin's Apple', and in the hillside above the house is a cave where Merlin is said to lie, buried in a glass coffin.

The Somerset town of Glastonbury has long claimed to be the legendary Avalon. The ancient Britons called it Ynys yr Afalon – 'Afal' was the Welsh word for 'apple', as 'Aval' was the Breton and Cornish word. Gerald of Wales called the Island of Avalon the Island of Glass. He noted that Glastonbury was also known as Ynys Vitrin, the Island of Glass, as *vitrum* was the Roman word for glass. Before the marshlands around Glastonbury Tor were drained, the hills of Glastonbury were an island surrounded by still lakes that reflected the light like glass. In 1191, the monks of Glastonbury claimed to have found the grave of Arthur and Guinevere. In the sixteenth century, the English antiquary John Leland recorded the inscription on the lead cross discovered in Arthur's grave: 'Hic Iacet Sepultus Inclitus Rex Arturius In Insula Avalonia' ('Here lies buried the renowned King Arthur in the Isle of Avalon').

Today Glastonbury is widely known as King Arthur's Avalon, but there are many other places that may be the legendary Isle of Apples. Off the coast of Brittany are the Île d'Aval, the Isle of Apples, and the Île de Sein, where nine druidic priestesses once lived. The earliest Roman geographer, Pomponius Mela, wrote in the first century AD of the Île de Sein that it was:

> in the British sea . . . remarkable for an oracle of the Gallic God. Its priestesses, holy in perpetual virginity, are said to be nine in number. They are called Gallicenae, and are thought to be endowed with singular powers, so as to raise by their charms the winds and seas, to turn themselves into what animals they will, to cure wounds and diseases incurable by others, to know and predict the future; but this they do only to navigators who go thither purposely to consult them.

There is also a small town called Avallon in Burgundy. Another candidate is Burgh by Sands in Cumbria. In Roman times, it was the fort of Aballava on Hadrian's Wall. The fort appears in the Ravenna Cosmology as Avalana. The Cosmology is a list of all the towns, forts, rivers and islands throughout the Roman Empire, compiled by a monk in the monastery at Ravenna, Italy, in the seventh century.

The storyteller and folklorist Stuart McHardy has suggested that Avalon is the Isle of May, north-east of Edinburgh, in the Firth of Forth, and that it could also have been the island off the east coast where, according to Celtic mythology, the warrior woman Scáthach trained Cú Chulainn. McHardy believes that the Isle of May was once an Isle of Maidens, a sacred place where a sisterhood of nine pagan priestesses lived. The Isle of Eigg in the Inner Hebrides was once known as Eilean nam Ban Mora, 'the Island of the Big Women'. It is said to have been ruled by a queen who ordered the massacre of St Donnan and his companions in the seventh century. There was another Isle of Women off Iona, the holy island of St Columba.

Inchcailloch in Loch Lomond may be named for a nunnery, but the name likely means 'the Island of the Cailleach', or Cailleach Bheur, the ancient hag goddess. The Cailleach Bheur could magically change her shape, appearing as an old woman with blue skin and one eye or as a fair young maiden. She brought the snow and ice with her eight storm hags. The highest point of the island is Tom na Nigheanan, the hillock of the girls or daughters. In his *Historia*, Geoffrey tells us that Arthur and his army fought three battles against the Scots and Picts. The Scots and Picts sought refuge on the islands of 'lake Lumond' – Loch Lomond. Geoffrey says that the lake contains

> sixty islands, and receives sixty rivers into it, which empty themselves into the sea by no more than one mouth. There is also an equal number of rocks in these islands, as also of eagles' nests in those rocks, which flocked together there every year, and, by the loud and general noise which they now made, foreboded some remarkable event that should happen to the kingdom.

In recent years, a white deer has been spotted on the island.

The real Isle of Avalon may lie in Wales, Scotland, England or France. It may recall the ancient islands of women, where sisterhoods of pagan priestesses gathered to worship their gods and goddesses. Avalon may be an enchanted island of the faerie realm where Morgan le Fay or Argante the elf-queen made potions to heal the wounds of Arthur. In the end, though, perhaps Avalon is simply the Isle of Apples, a grove of trees rich in fruit, where a wounded king or an old wizard could find peace.

In 1833, Alfred, Lord Tennyson's childhood friend Arthur Henry Hallam, who was engaged to the poet's sister Emily, died suddenly following a cerebral haemorrhage at the age of 22. A grief-stricken Tennyson wrote a draft of 'Morte d'Arthur'. He depicted King Arthur's final resting place, 'the island-valley of Avilion':

Where falls not hail, or rain, or any snow,
Nor ever wind blows loudly; but it lies
Deep-meadowed, happy, fair with orchard-lawns
And bowery hollows crown'd with summer sea

SEE ALSO: Arthur, King of the Britons; Glastonbury; Merlin; Morgan le Fay; Scotland; Tennyson, Alfred, Lord; Wales

BATTLES OF ARTHUR

King Arthur and his knights are often imagined riding into battle in suits of shining silver armour with brightly painted shields, colourful banners and glinting swords. In reality, Arthur and his men would have been battle-hardened warriors, fighting a bloody war against the Saxons, Angles, Jutes, Picts and Scots in the late fifth and early sixth century. We find the earliest surviving mention of Arthur in the Welsh poem *Y Gododdin*. This Arthur is not a king and he has no Camelot or Guinevere. This Arthur is a greater warrior than Gwawrddur, who leaves the bodies of his fallen enemies as food for the ravens. The Arthur who is spoken of in early histories of Britain was a military commander who led the Britons in twelve decisive battles against the invading Saxons.

It is thought that the Saxons were named after the *seax*, a vicious weapon that doubled as a working knife. The seax was single-edged with a sharp, stabbing point and could be used like a dagger or a short sword. The weapons of Arthur's battles were double-edged swords, spears, axes, short bows and arrows, and the seax. No quarter would have been given, so the fighting would have been brutal and ferocious, two opposing bands of warriors hacking each other to death.

Historia Brittonum, The History of the Britons, was written around AD 800. It is attributed to a Welsh cleric named Nennius. Nennius calls Arthur a 'dux bellorum', a 'leader of battles', saying:

> At that time, the Saxons grew strong by virtue of their large
> number and increased in power in Britain . . . Then Arthur

along with the kings of Britain fought against them in those days, but Arthur himself was the leader of battles.

So Arthur fought along with the kings of the Britons but was himself the equivalent of a military general. Nennius lists twelve battles in all:

His first battle was at the mouth of the river which is called Glein. His second, third, fourth and fifth battles were above another river which is called Dubglas and is in the region of Linnuis. The sixth battle was above the river which is called Bassas. The seventh battle was in the forest of Celidon, that is Cat Coit Celidon. The eighth battle was at the fortress of Guinnion, in which Arthur carried the image of holy Mary ever virgin on his shoulders; and the pagans were put to flight on that day. And through the power of our Lord Jesus Christ and through the power of the blessed Virgin Mary his mother there was great slaughter among them. The ninth battle was waged in the City of the Legion. The tenth battle was waged on the banks of a river which is called Tribruit. The eleventh battle was fought on the mountain which is called Agnet. The twelfth battle was on Mount Badon in which there fell in one day 960 men from one charge by Arthur; and no one struck them down except Arthur himself, and in all the wars he emerged as victor.

Scholars have argued over the possible locations of Arthur's battles for over a hundred years. It has been suggested that the first battle, at the mouth of the River Glein, may have taken place at the Glen Water in Ayrshire, at the Glen in Lincolnshire or at the Glen in Northumberland. The second, third, fourth and fifth battles above the River Dubglas in the region of Linnuis have been sited around Loch Lomond, at the source of the Douglas Water near Lanark, in Somerset, in Lincolnshire and at Devil's Water at Linnels near Hadrian's Wall. The River Bassas where Arthur fought his sixth battle might have been in Alnwick or Cramlington in Northumberland or near the Bass Rock, an island in the Firth of Forth. There is general agreement that the seventh battle, in the forest of Celidon 'that is Cat Coit Celidon', was fought somewhere in what is now southern Scotland.

Arthur's eighth battle, at the fortress of Guinnion – 'Castellum Guinnion', or 'White Castle' – has been identified as the Roman fort of Vinovium at Binchester, and the valley of the Gala Water a few miles from Melrose in the Borders of Scotland. The ninth battle was waged in the City of the Legion thought to have been the Roman legionary fortress at York or Chester, Caerleon, Dumbarton, Carlisle or Camelon. The tenth battle at the River Tribruit may have been fought near Edinburgh on the Forth, at Carlisle on the Eden, by the Ribble in Lancashire or by the Severn. The mountain called Agnet, where Arthur's eleventh battle was fought, is said variously to be Edinburgh or High Rochester.

Nennius tells that the twelfth battle was fought on Mount Badon, where 960 men fell in one day during one charge by Arthur. The siege of 'Badonici montis' was recorded by the British monk Gildas in the sixth century. The *Annales Cambriae* (*Annals of Wales*) records 'The Battle of Badon, in which Arthur carried the Cross of Our Lord Jesus Christ for three days and three nights on his shoulders and the Britons were the victors'. The location of the battle of Badon Hill has proved particularly controversial over the years. Bowdon Hill near Linlithgow, Bath in Somerset, Liddington Castle in Wiltshire and Buxton in Derbyshire have all been suggested as possible sites.

There is one curious fact that may throw some light on Nennius's battle list. Scholars have noticed that the names of several of the battle sites rhyme: Cat Coit Celidon, Guinnion, Legion, Badon. It is thought that Nennius may have based his list of Arthur's twelve battles on an earlier Welsh battle poem.

The *Annales Cambriae* also record Arthur's final battle, 'the Strife of Camlann in which Arthur and Medraut perished'. The battle of Camlann has been placed at the small Roman fort of Camboglanna at Castlesteads along Hadrian's Wall, at the River Cam near South Cadbury in Somerset, at Camelon near the Antonine Wall and at the River Camel in Cornwall. The Welsh Triads – fragments of legend and history scattered throughout Welsh manuscripts in groups of threes and thought to have been aide-memoires for poets as they composed their verses – list Camlann as one of the 'Three Futile Battles of the Island of Britain'. Rather cryptically, we are told that the first, the Battle of Goddau, was brought about because of a bitch, a roebuck and a lapwing; the second was the Battle of Arderydd, brought about because of a lark's nest; and the third, Camlann, was the worst, brought about by the quarrel between Gwenhwyfar (Guinevere) and her sister Gwenhwyfach. According to the Triads, one of the 'Three Harmful Blows of the Island of Britain' is the slap that Gwenhwyfach gave to her sister that caused the Strife of Camlann.

Geoffrey of Monmouth tells us that the battle of Camlann 'began with great fury'. King Arthur faced the treacherous Mordred across the battlefield, both men marshalling vast armies. 'It would be both grievous and tedious to relate the slaughter, the cruel havoc and the excess of fury that was to be seen on both sides.' The battle raged throughout the day until Arthur made a last push into Mordred's line 'and made a grievous slaughter'. In this final assault 'fell the wicked traitor himself, and many thousands with him'. The rest of Mordred's men would not flee the field and the fight 'grew more furious than ever, and proved fatal to almost all the commanders and their forces . . . and even the renowned King Arthur himself was mortally wounded'.

Sir Thomas Malory wrote that the battle began because of a tragic misadventure. King Arthur and Sir Mordred each took 14 knights and met between their armies. Arthur warned his men that if they should see any sword drawn, they should 'come on fiercely, and slay that traitor, Sir Mordred'. Mordred likewise warned his host that if they should see any sword drawn they should 'come on fiercely, and so slay all that ever before you standeth'. The two men met to negotiate a peace but an adder slithered out from the undergrowth and bit a knight on the foot. When the soldier felt the bite, he looked down and saw the snake. He drew his sword to 'slay the adder, and thought of none other harm'. But when the hosts saw the knight's drawn sword, 'they blew beams, trumpets, and horns, and shouted grimly. And so both hosts dressed them together . . . and never was there seen a more dolefuller battle in no Christian land . . . they fought all the long day, and never stinted till the noble knights were laid to the cold earth; and ever they fought still till it was near night, and by that time was there an hundred thousand laid dead upon the down.' King Arthur saw that all but two of his knights were slain and cried out, 'Jesu mercy . . . where are all my noble knights become?' The traitor Sir Mordred 'leaned upon his sword among a great heap of dead men'. Arthur took his spear in both his hands and 'ran toward Sir Mordred, crying: Traitor, now is thy death-day come'. Mordred ran at Arthur with his sword drawn in his hand. King Arthur attacked Mordred, running his spear through his son's body. Mordred dragged himself with all his strength along the shaft of the spear towards Arthur and struck him, his sword piercing Arthur's helmet. Mordred's sword slipped from his grasp and he fell down dead. Arthur collapsed unconscious on the ground.

SEE ALSO: Cornwall; Geoffrey of Monmouth; Knights of the Round Table; Malory, Sir Thomas; Mordred; Scotland; Wales

BLEEDING LANCE

The bleeding lance was first introduced into Arthurian legend in *Perceval, or the Story of the Grail* by Chrétien de Troyes. In Chrétien's story, Perceval witnesses an incredible procession in which first a young man carries the bleeding lance, then two boys enter carrying candles, after which a beautiful girl follows carrying the Grail itself. The lance is a long spear that bleeds continuously from its tip.

In the different versions of the Grail story, there are variations on this theme, but almost all follow a familiar pattern, with the lance accompanying the Grail. We see that the two are intrinsically linked and together are of great importance. Some versions of the Grail procession tell us that the Grail is accompanied by 'worthy relics' indicating that the lance, and not just the Grail itself, is worthy of reverence.

As the Grail romances evolved, the bleeding lance became associated with the Holy Lance, the lance or spear that the Roman soldier Longinus used to pierce the side of Christ while he was on the Cross. The bleeding lance, as the spear of Longinus, accompanies the Grail because it was Longinus's spear thrust that caused the wound from which the blood of Christ flowed into the Grail. The two objects were bound by this one act and it follows that the blood that runs down the bleeding lance is the blood of Christ. The fact that the lance usually precedes the Holy Grail in the procession lends support to this explanation, since the spear created the wound and so would occur first in the symbolism surrounding the two artefacts.

In the Middle Ages, the Holy Lance was a revered relic of the Passion. It was one of the relics of the Crucifixion kept in the Chapel of the Virgin of Pharos within the Imperial Palace in Byzantium (Constantinople). It rested alongside the Crown of Thorns, pieces of the True Cross and a phial containing the blood of Christ. The fame of this Holy Lance did not prevent the discovery of another spear of Longinus during the Siege of Antioch in 1097. A crusader named Peter Bartholomew claimed to have received a vision of St Andrew which guided him to the secret hiding place of the Lance. 'Miraculously' the Holy Lance was found, and for a time it raised morale among the crusaders. Unfortunately for Peter Bartholomew, his story was questioned and he died after undergoing a trial by fire.

Some authors suggest that the Grail is a symbol of the sacred feminine. It is possible to draw the parallel that if the Grail suggests female sexuality and the potential of the womb, then the bleeding lance represents the male aspect. Much has been written concerning the phallic nature of the bleeding lance and the damage that it was said to have caused. In Arthurian legend, the bleeding lance is found in the presence of the Fisher King, who is wounded and incapacitated. Often it is said that the Fisher King was wounded in a thigh, or in both thighs, an emasculating injury which may be a euphemism for a wound to the genitals. In the German epic *Parzival*, the Fisher King is described as having being pierced through the genitals by the lance.

In some versions of the Grail romance, the Fisher King's wound is struck by the lance itself and is termed 'the Dolorous Stroke' or 'the Dolorous Blow'. In these accounts, as a knight named Balin is attacked by the Fisher King, he desperately searches for a weapon and, grabbing the lance, drives it through the Fisher King's thighs. It is the Dolorous Blow that causes the surrounding kingdom to become the Wasteland. The wounded Fisher King may be seen as impotent; his kingdom is a barren Wasteland. The act of healing the Fisher King restores the Wasteland and returns the King to full health, making him potent and virile once again. Paradoxically, the bleeding lance, which causes the Fisher King's grievous wound, is also said to have the power to heal. In Thomas Malory's version of the story of the Grail, Galahad heals the Fisher King by anointing his wounds with the blood dripping from the bleeding lance.

It is possible that the bleeding lance motif has its roots in Celtic tradition. Some scholars have suggested a connection to the spear carried by the Celtic god Lug or have seen parallels with the thunderbolt of Zeus. Another precursor of the bleeding lance may be the weapon carried by Celtchar, a Celtic warrior featured in the Ulster Cycle of myths. Celtchar wields a spear that has a life of its own. If he fails to dip the spearhead into a cauldron of poisonous blood, the spear becomes too powerful, harming Celtchar. R.S. Loomis wrote in his book *The Grail: From Celtic Myth to Christian Symbol*:

> Lug's spear was one of the four chief treasures of the Tuatha dé Danaan, the Irish gods . . . Later Chrétien informs us that it will destroy the whole realm of Logres (England) — a prophecy which accords with the origin of the lance in the spear of Lug, noted for its destructiveness. We read that, when it passed into the possession of Celtchar, it would 'kill nine men at every cast, and one of the nine will be a king or crown prince or chieftain'.

It is interesting to note that in the Ulster Cycle Celtchar is castrated, just like the Fisher King. Celtchar is killed when, during a battle with his own hound, Dóelchú, a drop of blood drips down the shaft of the spear after Celtchar has cut out its heart, and this drop of blood slays the warrior. Bran, the Welsh giant king, was also traditionally wounded by a poisoned spear. So in these stories we may see the origin of the tale of the Fisher King and the bleeding lance. The spear of Celtic legend became identified with the spear of Longinus of Christian legend, neatly dovetailing into the Grail romances.

SEE ALSO: Chrétien de Troyes; Fisher King; Galahad; Malory, Sir Thomas; Percival; Sacred Feminine; Wolfram von Eschenbach

BROCÉLIANDE

The enchanted Forest of Brocéliande features in many Arthurian legends. Brocéliande is the legendary name of the Forest of Paimpont in Brittany, a remnant of the vast primeval forest that once covered much of north-west France. Beneath the oaks, beeches, alders, chestnuts and birches of Brocéliande, the wizard Merlin fell in love with Viviane, Lancelot du Lac grew into manhood and Morgan le Fay trapped wayward lovers. The French Symbolist poet Albert Samain called Brocéliande 'the forest of dreams and enchantment', and C.S. Lewis wrote that: 'Saint, sorcerer, lunatic and romantic lover, all alike are drawn to Brocéliande.'

In the Arthurian romances of Chrétien de Troyes, the Forest of Brocéliande was a magical place where knights encountered faeries. In his *Yvain, or the Knight with the Lion*, we learn that the knight Yvain finds the Fountain of Barenton within the forest. Beside the fountain is a tree with a golden cup and a *perron*, a stone slab. When Yvain fills the cup from the fountain and pours some water on the stone he sets off a fearsome thunderstorm that tears the leaves from the trees. When the thunderstorm suddenly dies down, Yvain is attacked by the Knight of the Fountain. He defeats the Knight, mortally wounding him, and pursues him back to his castle. As Yvain rides beneath the castle gates, the portcullis falls, slicing Yvain's horse in half. Yvain is trapped in the castle but is hidden by Lunete, the lady-in-waiting of Laudine, the mistress of the castle. Laudine is grief-stricken by the death of her husband, the Knight of the Fountain. Yvain falls in love with Laudine and, with the help of Lunete, wins her hand to become the new Knight of the Fountain.

BROCÉLIANDE

Brocéliande was the mythic enchanted forest where anything could happen. The forest was a doorway into the faerie realm, where supernatural creatures lurked behind the trees, druids collected mistletoe and knights could meet giants, wizards or treacherous faeries. Today, if you make the journey to Brocéliande, you will find numerous Arthurian locations within and around the Forest of Paimpont, and if you are lucky you may find yourself in Brocéliande with Merlin, Viviane and Morgan le Fay.

The Fountain of Barenton is a stone-lined pool whose waters 'boil whilst remaining cold'. Beside it is 'Merlin's perron', the stone slab that can summon thunderstorms. *The Charter of Usage and Customs of the forest of Brocéliande*, written in 1467, states that Guy de Laval, Lord of Comper, was the owner of the fountain and that only he had the right to conjure storms. In 1835, when the crops began to wither in the fields during a heatwave, the local priests turned to the magical fountain to bring much-needed rain. The belief that thunderstorms can be raised at the Fountain of Barenton is still very much alive. In the 1980s, a local Arthurian group wandered through the forest to the fountain and found themselves caught in a torrential downpour when they called up a storm. A few years ago, the author, Mark Oxbrow, found himself lost in the forest searching for the Fountain of Barenton when he was drenched by a sudden rainstorm.

According to legend, Merlin the Enchanter would walk amid the trees of Brocéliande. He met Viviane, the Lady of the Lake, deep in the forest. The old wizard and the young maiden talked about magic and love. Merlin spent the years that followed travelling between King Arthur's court at Camelot and Viviane in the Forest of Brocéliande. When Arthur married Guinevere, Merlin's thoughts turned to Viviane. He realised that he had fallen in love. Merlin used his magic to create a crystal castle for Viviane within a mirror lake in Brocéliande. He told her about his magic, teaching her spells, enchantments and incantations. Eventually, after she had learned almost all of Merlin's magic, Viviane asked if there was a spell that could keep a man captive. Merlin knew that she would use the spell to keep him forever in Brocéliande, but with a smile he nodded and taught Viviane the spell.

It is said that Merlin still lives in the Forest of Brocéliande with the faerie Viviane. Her crystal castle is hidden beneath the surface of the Lake of Comper. Near by are the remains of a megalithic monument known as the Tombeau de Merlin, the Tomb of Merlin. It was once a neolithic gallery grave consisting of at least a dozen stone slabs. In the 1890s, it was largely destroyed by a local farmer who is thought to have been looking for buried treasure under the stones. People who visit the tomb often leave presents and messages for Merlin. They ask him to grant wishes and push notes scribbled on tiny scraps of paper into cracks in the boulders. Other neolithic stone monuments around Brocéliande include the Monks' Garden, the Giant's Tomb, the Three Rocks of Tréban, which fell from a faerie's apron, and a burial cist called the Hôtie de Viviane, the House of Viviane.

Brocéliande also appears in Arthurian myth as the boyhood home of Sir Lancelot. When he was a child, his mother fled to Brocéliande. When she was deep within the forest, Viviane appeared and took Lancelot down beneath the waters of her lake. For years, he was raised by the Lady of the Lake. When Lancelot had grown into a young man, he left Viviane and the forest and travelled to Arthur's court at Camelot to join the renowned Knights of the Round Table. He was known as Lancelot du Lac, Lancelot of the Lake.

Near the village of Tréhorenteuc is the Val sans Retour, a maze of rocky crags and rough slate valleys. This is the Valley of No Return, where Morgan le Fay still spellbinds faithless lovers. The enchantress Morgan was once betrayed by a mortal, and she used her magic to turn the unfortunate man to stone, forever to stand as the Rocher des Faux-Amants, the Rock of False Lovers. Near the entrance to the Valley of No Return lies a still and silent pool known as the Miroir-aux-Fées, the Mirror of the Faeries. If you are gazing into the pool, you are already within Morgan's valley. If you are faithful, you will be able to leave, but the unfaithful can find themselves lost forever.

Between 1942 and 1954, Abbé Henri Gillard transformed the church at Tréhorenteuc into a chapel of the Holy Grail. Abbé Gillard restored the church and filled it with mosaics, stained-glass windows and paintings that brought the legends of Brocéliande and King Arthur into a Christian place of worship. The stained-glass windows of the nave include depictions of Lancelot and Morgan le Fay in the Valley of No Return, Yvain and the Knight at the Fountain of Barenton, Viviane enchanting Merlin and the Holy Grail appearing to the Knights of the Round Table. Jesus is depicted falling at the feet of Morgan le Fay, the incarnation of lust.

The Château de Comper-en-Brocéliande, in the north of the forest of Paimpont, is home to the fabulous Centre de l'Imaginaire Arthurien. The Château overlooks the Lake of Comper, where Vivian raised Lancelot and Merlin conjured a crystal castle. The Centre de l'Imaginaire Arthurien hosts exhibitions, storytelling and pageants featuring valiant knights in shining armour, wizards wearing pointy hats, fair maidens in flowing velvet dresses and even the Lady of the Lake bearing Excalibur from beneath the water.

SEE ALSO: Chrétien de Troyes; Faeries; Lady of the Lake; Lancelot; Merlin; Morgan le Fay

CAMELOT

For hundreds of years, the whereabouts of Camelot, Arthur's fabled capital and stronghold, has attracted much interest and speculation. Camelot is not in fact mentioned in the early Arthurian literature, and its eventual appearance in the legends is clouded with mystery over its location and appearance.

Appearing only fleetingly for the first time in *Lancelot, or the Knight of the Cart* by Chrétien de Troyes in the 1170s, Camelot is mentioned there in association with the Welsh stronghold of Caerleon, once a Roman fortification. Indeed, it is Caerleon that is the chief stronghold of Arthur not only in Chrétien's poem but also in Geoffrey of Monmouth's *History of the Kings of Britain*, eventually being superseded by Camelot in importance by the thirteenth century, when some French Arthurian prose elevates Camelot to the status of Arthur's main capital. However, it is clear from these romances that many of the descriptions of Camelot actually derive from the earlier accounts of Caerleon.

It would seem that the modern, romantic notion of Camelot – a major city beside a river, surrounded by lush forests and dominated by the magnificent cathedral of St Stephen's – stems mainly from the fifteenth-century *Le Morte d'Arthur* by Thomas Malory, which today is probably the most read of the Arthurian romances. Malory very definitely bases his Camelot on the English town of Winchester, which even today maintains its Arthurian heritage by ownership of what the town claims is the original Round Table. *Le Morte d'Arthur* was published in 1485, coinciding with a change in the ruling dynasty in England. King Henry VII, the new monarch, had Welsh ancestry and was keen to establish as many factors as possible to legitimise his somewhat shaky claim to the throne. Genealogists looked into his distant forbears and obligingly 'discovered' that Henry could trace his family back to the legendary King Arthur. When Henry's wife, Elizabeth of York, was expecting their first child, she was sent to Winchester, where in September 1486 she gave birth to their son, who was, perhaps not surprisingly, christened Arthur. The baby was baptised in Winchester Cathedral with all due pomp and majesty, with the location specifically chosen because Malory had identified Winchester with Camelot.

The power that the myths of Arthur exerted at this time was clearly sufficient to make the royal family keen to associate themselves with them. Winchester continued to be popularly thought of as the inspiration for Camelot over the centuries, but it was by no means the only candidate. Others have included: Carlisle in Cumbria, Caerwent in Wales, Cadbury Castle in Somerset, Camelon in Scotland, Colchester in Essex, Maiden Castle in Dorset, and Camelford and Tintagel in Cornwall.

By far the most reasonable assumption is that the original writers were right in naming Caerleon as the capital of Arthur's kingdom, this then being supplanted by the romantic vision of Malory's Camelot/ Winchester in the fifteenth century. It is interesting to note that even Malory's publisher, William Caxton, rejected the identification of Winchester with Camelot, preferring the Roman ruins of Caerwent in Wales as the location of Arthur's court.

The notion of Camelot as an idealised society of chivalric heroes and great deeds performed selflessly in the interests of a greater good has become an enduring myth. Even today, the name evokes a lost ideal and the echo of a place and time where life was simpler and more romantic than it is now.

SEE ALSO: Malory, Sir Thomas; Round Table

CHIVALRY

Many of the tales of the Knights of the Round Table involve the knights taking risks and exposing themselves to danger. They overcome fearsome enemies, right injustices and uphold the honour of ladies in peril. In addition to undertaking the quest or journey described in the tale, the knight himself often personifies the ideals of chivalry and emerges as a noble character as well as a victorious champion.

The concept of chivalry is associated with members of the equestrian order, or knights, in the Middle Ages. The word 'chivalry' comes from the Old French *'chevalerie'* (horsemanship), the modern French word for horse being *'cheval'*. We look to Latin for the original source word, *'caballarius'* ('horseman'), as we do for the root of 'equestrian'. *Equites* were the horsemen of Ancient Rome, originally prosperous citizens of the class just below senatorial rank. During the early days of the Roman Empire, these 'knights' had certain privileges: they were entitled to a horse provided at public expense, to distinctive clothing and to reserved seating when shows were put on. Long before the time of the first emperor, Augustus, the Romans regarded equites as members of the upper classes, not simply as warriors.

By the Middle Ages, mounted warriors were seen in a very similar light to the Roman equestrians in terms of rank and distinction. Their status was far above the common man but below the hereditary nobleman, although a duke, earl or baron would still have felt honoured to be knighted, and in England, for instance, to become a Knight of the Garter or of the Bath was a great privilege. A man might be knighted in recognition of his service as a warrior of distinction following a battle or simply as a mark of the monarch's favour. The knight, for his part, might aspire, through service to the king, to rise to become a member of the higher nobility.

John of Salisbury (c.1115–80), a respected scholar and Bishop of Chartres, believed that the functions of a knight were to protect the Church, fight against treachery, revere the priesthood, protect the poor from injustice, promote peace within his own territory, shed blood for his brothers and, if necessary, lay down his life for the cause of right. The French historian Jean Froissart, born c.1337, stated that knights were born to fight and that they were ennobled if they showed no fear or cowardice. Men who held land in return for service or who would be expected to make their way in the world as chevaliers (horse-owners) were trained to fight and learned to face hardship from an early age.

The traditional preparation for knighthood involved taking a bath (a pretty rare event at the time, at least in Western Europe) so that the body was cleansed. Fresh, clean clothes were donned and the night was spent in silent vigil before an altar to cleanse the spirit. Knightly accoutrements were laid on the altar to symbolise that they were, with their owner, being dedicated to God's work. This was followed by Mass at dawn. The new knight was struck a blow by one who had experience and seniority – this tradition is preserved to this day in the ceremony of laying a sword on the shoulder of a newly created knight. The knight was never to receive a blow again without returning it. Solemn vows were made and spurs were attached to his heels. On the rare occasions when a knight disgraced himself by some totally reprehensible act, such as committing treason, he might be deprived of his status by having his spurs struck off as part of his punishment.

The knight of the High Middle Ages would, in 'weak piping time of peace', take part in mock combat, sometimes singly, sometimes as part of a group. They were often grand affairs with brightly coloured tents and banners, tilting grounds for jousting, and lavish feasts and entertainments. These tournaments could become very violent. Jousting involved charging towards a similarly mounted opponent with a lance, attempting to break it on the opposing knight's shield. As late as 1559, King Henri II of France was jousting with the captain of his Scottish Guard when he was mortally wounded; a splinter from his opponent's lance broke off and embedded itself in his head.

In classical times, books were written on the art of warfare and some of these were still popular in the Middle Ages. In this period, new works were written, including Christine de Pisan's *Livre des fais d'armes et de chevalerie*, a faithful English translation of which was published by William Caxton in 1489. He had already issued *The Book of the Ordre of Chyvalry* five years before.

At Rosslyn Castle, Sir Gilbert Hay translated Continental books of knighthood and chivalry into Scots. In *The Buke of the Ordre of Knychthede*, Sir Gilbert writes that a chivalrous knight defends the weak, the poor, widows, maidens and motherless bairns. The knight's duty is to fight wickedness, cruelty and tyranny, and to maintain faith in Jesus Christ, his lord and the rights of the people, as 'God him self ordanyt knychthese'. He continues: 'And thus a knight has in his heart a noble dwelling place for the virtues and nobleness of courage that should govern and maintain knighthood.'

Hay's translations were made in the second half of the fifteenth century as Rosslyn Chapel was being built and Sir Thomas Malory was writing his *Le Morte d'Arthur*. Cavalry charges by heavily armoured knights were still seen as splendid, valiant affairs, but were nevertheless believed to be foolhardy and generally unsuccessful. An example of this is described in *Bosworth 1485* by Michael K. Jones. Jones suggests that it was an immensely brave but reckless cavalry charge that cost King Richard III his life, and that Richard's love of chivalry and desire for glory and honour led to this fatal charge. Jones suggests that it was not just the winning of a battle that mattered; the manner of achieving victory was also highly important to the chivalric leader. If this approach was to be successful, though, both sides needed to play by the same rules.

Philip IV of France contributed to the debasement of the knightly class in his realm when, around 1300, he began selling knighthoods to wealthy townsmen. The honour was an obvious attraction, but, even more tempting perhaps, tax exemptions were also part of this social elevation. It was just one element in the decay of the chivalric ideal. It was also Philip IV who in 1307 engineered the downfall of the Knights Templar and the confiscation of their property, a further example of his opportunistic behaviour. This was in marked contrast to one of his successors, King John II, who was captured by the English at the Battle of Poitiers in 1356 and held to ransom. John's son Louis was accepted as a substitute when the French king returned to try to raise the ransom, but the young man escaped and refused to surrender himself. Such was the loss of honour felt by John that he voluntarily returned to England himself.

It has been argued with some justification that the decline of the age of chivalry began at the Battle of Crécy in 1346. King Edward III of England had invaded France to pursue his claim, through his mother, to the French throne. His army was largely composed of infantry and archers, supplemented with some rudimentary cannon. The brave, chivalric French knights opposing him were furious that their own Genoese mercenary crossbowmen, shooting uphill, were unable to make much impression on the enemy. The French knights made repeated charges against an enemy who were, for the most part, not gentlemen and were therefore considered unworthy opponents who should have been easily swept aside. Many members of the noblest French houses fell that day, killed mainly by these 'inferiors'.

The nearly blind King of Bohemia, steeped in the concept of chivalry, insisted on being led onto the battlefield to assist his French allies – and duly fell. His heraldic device, which knights displayed to advertise their identity, was three plumes. After the battle this hero was recognised as a true knight and the Prince of Wales, son of the English king, took this heraldic emblem as his own. To this day, the eldest son of the British monarch has what became known as the Prince of Wales feathers on his coat of arms. The Battle of Crécy proved the usefulness of gunpowder to European armies, but even more importantly it demonstrated the principle that properly deployed infantry and accurate use of missile weapons will generally defeat cavalry. War was increasingly fought with the aid of mercenaries and experts in more specialised aspects of warfare. The romantic vision of the knight survived in pageants and jousts, but knights were losing their practical role on the battlefield.

Perhaps, nonetheless, something of the spirit of chivalry remains to this day. Charles Kingsley, 1819–75, best known as the author of *The Water Babies*, was a proponent of social reform, and these words are attributed to him: 'Some say that the age of chivalry is past, that the spirit of romance is dead. The age of chivalry is never past, so long as there is a wrong left unredressed on earth.'

SEE ALSO: Knights of the Round Table; Knights Templar; Malory, Sir Thomas

CHRÉTIEN DE TROYES

In the late twelfth century, the French poet Chrétien de Troyes composed five romances including *Perceval, ou le conte du graal* (*Perceval, or the Story of the Grail*). Chrétien's *Story of the Grail* was the first-ever Grail romance, introducing the mysterious vessel carried in a mystical procession that would capture the imagination of medieval poets and inspire thousands of works of art and literature.

In his earliest work, *Érec and Énide*, Chrétien calls himself 'de Troyes', telling us he was from the town of Troyes, to the east of Paris on the River Seine. This is confirmed by the fact that Chrétien composed his romances in the provincial dialect of western Champagne. From the ninth century, Troyes had been the capital of the counts of Champagne. Chrétien lived in Troyes as a clerk in the vibrant court of Henry I, Count of Champagne. His early works were composed under the patronage of Henry's wife, the Countess Marie de Champagne, daughter of Eleanor of Aquitaine and Louis VII, King of France. Between 1160 and 1190, Chrétien composed *Érec and Énide*; *Cligès*; *Yvain, or the Knight with the Lion*; *Lancelot, or the Knight of the Cart*; and *Perceval, or the Story of the Grail*.

Érec and Énide was the first French Arthurian romance. It tells the story of Érec, the youngest of Arthur's knights, son of the rich and mighty King Lac. It begins in the springtime, on Easter day, when Arthur holds court in Cardigan Castle and tells his knights that he wants to hunt the white stag 'to revive the tradition'. Whoever can kill the white stag must choose the most beautiful of the maidens of the court to kiss. During the hunt, Érec and Guinevere chance upon

an armoured knight on a charger, a maiden of noble bearing and an
'ill-begotten dwarf'. The dwarf hits Guinevere's own maiden and Érec
with a scourge. Érec sees that the knight is grim and armed so decides
to leave without a fight. He promises the Queen that he will avenge his
disgrace. Érec follows the knight and the villainous dwarf and meets
the lovely and wise Énide, who wears a white shift and a threadbare
gown with holes at the elbows. Chrétien tells us that 'Nature, who
had created her, had put all her care into the work' and that 'the hair
of the blonde Iseut did not shine so fair'. Érec goes on to defeat the
knight and avenge his dishonour. He marries Énide but becomes so
devoted to his young bride that rumours begin to circulate that he is
shamefully neglecting his duties as a knight. There follow a series of
misunderstandings and adventures until, in the end, Érec and Énide
are crowned King and Queen. At the feast that followed, a thousand
knights served the bread, a thousand served the wine and a thousand
served the dishes.

In the introduction to his next romance, *Cligès*, Chrétien tells
us that he 'wrote of Érec and Énide, and translated into French the
commands of Ovid and the *Art of Love*, and wrote the *Shoulder Bite*,
and about King Mark and the fair Iseut, and about the metamorphosis
of the Lapwing, the Swallow, and the Nightingale'. One French poem
based on Ovid is attributed to Chrétien; the other poems and his
version of the story of Tristan and Iseult are lost.

In *Yvain, ou le chevalier au lion* (*Yvain, or the Knight with the
Lion*), the knight Yvain first widows then marries the lady Laudine
and becomes the Knight of the Fountain of Barenton in Brocéliande.
As Yvain walks through a dense forest, deep in thought, he hears a
terrible cry. In a clearing, he finds a lion whose tail is being held by
a fire-breathing serpent, which scorches the lion's hindquarters with
searing flames. Yvain decides to help the lion as the serpent is an evil
creature. He cuts the serpent in two then hacks it to pieces. Yvain
now expects to be attacked by the lion, but instead it bows down
before him and acts nobly. From then on, the lion becomes Yvain's
close companion.

Lancelot, ou le chevalier de la charrette (*Lancelot, or the Knight of
the Cart*) was composed for the Countess Marie between 1164 and
1173. *The Knight of the Cart* includes the first-ever mention of 'the
magnificent court of Camelot', and it is also the earliest surviving
work to tell the story of Lancelot and Guinevere's love affair. Chrétien
intimately describes the passion of Lancelot and Guinevere's first
trysting. Lancelot aches for the day to end so he can be with Guinevere.

Chrétien tells us that the lovers felt 'a joy and wonder the equal of which had never yet been heard or known. But I shall ever keep it secret, since it should not be written of.' It is thought that Chrétien did not complete *The Knight of the Cart*. It is not known why he stopped work on the poem, but the last thousand lines are attributed to a Godefroi de Lagny, following a plan outlined by Chrétien. There has been speculation that the poet abandoned the work because he disapproved of the adulterous love affair it depicted. It has also been suggested that Chrétien did in fact complete *The Knight of the Cart* and that Godefroi de Lagny is an invention, as much a character in the story as Guinevere, Arthur or Lancelot.

At some time after 1174, Chrétien may have left Troyes and entered the service of Philip of Alsace, the Count of Flanders. Chrétien's *Story of the Grail* is dedicated to his patron, Count Philip of Flanders, 'whose merit exceeds that of Alexander'. In all of Chrétien's early romances there is a knight and his lady. The focus of Chrétien's art is the study of love; he skilfully portrays the flowering of love at first sight and the overwhelming need of forbidden love. In *The Story of the Grail*, however, Chrétien follows the story of Perceval as he is transformed from a naive boy into a worldly knight and finally embodies a new ideal – that of the spiritual knight. After 9,000 lines, *The Story of the Grail* simply stops. It is thought that Chrétien died before he completed it. French 'continuators' took up the Grail story, continuing the adventures of Perceval and Gawain and adding their own endings to Chrétien's story.

SEE ALSO: Brocéliande; Holy Grail; Knights of the Round Table; Lancelot du Lac; Patène de Serpentine; Percival; Philip, Count of Flanders

CINEMA AND THEATRE

The legends of King Arthur, the Knights of the Round Table and the quest for the Holy Grail have been spectacularly staged in the theatre for hundreds of years. Arthurian movies have tended to be something of a mixed bag. Over the years, great actors of stage and screen including Henry Irving, John Gielgud, Sean Connery, Helen Mirren, Gary Oldman, Isabella Rossellini and Richard Harris have appeared in Arthurian plays and films.

In 1882, Richard Wagner's three-act opera *Parsifal*, based on Wolfram von Eschenbach's epic poem, debuted at the Bayreuth Festspielhaus (Bayreuth Festival Theatre). *Parsifal* would be Wagner's final opera. Bayreuth was to be the spiritual home of Wagner's works and *Parsifal* was intended to 'consecrate' the theatre. Wagner was gravely ill when *Parsifal* debuted but still took the baton during the last performance of the first run and conducted the final bars of his opera. He died the following year and was buried in the garden of the Villa Wahnfried in Bayreuth, the place where he had composed *Parsifal*. For the next 20 years, staged public performances of *Parsifal* were held only in the Bayreuth Festspielhaus.

King Arthur brought the romances of Arthur and the Holy Grail to the London stage at the Lyceum Theatre in 1895. The play was originally to have been written by Alfred, Lord Tennyson. When Tennyson pulled out, J. Comyns Carr, the director of the Grosvenor Gallery, who was a great supporter and exhibitor of the Pre-Raphaelites, stepped in. The music was composed by Arthur Sullivan, of the famed Gilbert and Sullivan, and the sets were designed by

Edward Burne-Jones. Victorian England's foremost actor, Sir Henry Irving, took the role of King Arthur; Ellen Terry, the leading lady of the London stage, played Queen Guinevere.

The first major Hollywood production to deal with the story of King Arthur and the Holy Grail was the 1953 movie *Knights of the Round Table*, featuring Hollywood star Robert Taylor as a brooding Lancelot and Ava Gardner as Queen Guinevere. The film brought together many of the elements of Malory's *Le Morte d'Arthur* that would appear in later movies. *Knights of the Round Table* focuses on the love triangle between Arthur, Guinevere and Lancelot. Some of the battle scenes were shot near Tintagel in Cornwall, a legendary Arthurian location.

Lerner and Loewe turned to the tales of King Arthur to follow up their Broadway hit *My Fair Lady*. Julie Andrews went from Eliza Doolittle to Queen Guinevere. Alan Jay Lerner and Frederick Loewe's *Camelot* will be forever associated with the tragically short presidency of John F. Kennedy. The musical debuted a month after Kennedy's election and contributed to the idealised popular image of the Kennedy administration as a modern Camelot. Richard Burton won the 1961 Tony Award for Best Actor in a Musical for his performance as King Arthur, but turned down the chance to play the role when *Camelot* was filmed in 1967. Julie Andrews was also unavailable, so Richard Harris starred as King Arthur with Vanessa Redgrave as Guinevere. The set for the Great Hall of Camelot was one of the largest indoor sets ever constructed, filling almost an entire Hollywood sound stage. *Camelot* would win three Oscars and three Golden Globes, and see King Arthur sing 'How to Handle A Woman'.

In the age of disco, platform shoes and spacehoppers, two movies marked the high and low points of Arthurian cinema. *Monty Python and the Holy Grail* and Stephen Weeks' *Gawain and the Green Knight* appeared in the 1970s. The Pythons' take on the adventures of King Arthur was conceived as a cunning way to piece together a whole movie out of what was basically a series of short sketches. They took the enchanted fairytale musical world of Lerner and Loewe's *Camelot* and dropped it into the muck and gore of the Middle Ages, a time when life was nasty, brutish and short. A host of established Arthurian knights such as Sir Lancelot the Brave, Sir Bors, Sir Galahad the Pure and Sir Bedivere were joined by new characters including the Knights who say Ni, Tim the Enchanter, the Killer Rabbit and Sir Robin the Not-Quite-So-Brave-as-Sir-Lancelot. Graham Chapman, John Cleese, Terry Gilliam, Eric Idle, Terry Jones and Michael Palin played almost all of the main parts. *Monty Python and the Holy Grail* was made on a minuscule budget of just £229,000, partially made up of donations from rock bands including Led Zeppelin and Pink Floyd, who invested some of the money they made from their album *The Dark Side of the Moon*. Real horses were a bit too expensive and none of the Pythons could actually ride a horse, so the cast galloped along clicking half coconut shells. The quest to find the Holy Grail took the knights to Castle Anthrax, Swamp Castle, the Bridge of Death and Castle Arrrgghhh, but in reality most of the film was shot in Scotland at locations including Doune Castle near Stirling, Glen Coe and Rannoch Moor.

A little more than forty years after Richard Burton won a Tony as King Arthur in Camelot, another Arthurian Broadway hit won the Tony Award for Best Musical. *Monty Python's Spamalot* was billed as 'lovingly ripped off from *Monty Python and the Holy Grail*'. Python Eric Idle decided to risk public humiliation and financial disaster, as he put it, by taking an adaptation of *Holy Grail* to Broadway. *Variety* was soon to report advance ticket sales of $20 million. Tim Curry led the cast as King Arthur on Broadway and flew over the pond when *Spamalot* was brought to London's West End in 2006. Eric Idle co-wrote new songs with John Du Prez and incorporated Python favourites including 'Always Look on the Bright Side of Life'. Inventive merchandise includes Killer Rabbit glove puppets, toy cow catapults and 'I'm not dead yet' T-shirts.

Monty Python's Terry Gilliam told a very different story of the Holy Grail in the Oscar-winning *The Fisher King*. The film was billed as 'a modern day tale about the search for love, sanity, Ethel Merman and the Holy Grail'. It starred Jeff Bridges as the talk radio shock-jock Jack Lucas and Robin Williams as Parry, a homeless medieval scholar on a quest to find the Holy Grail. Mercedes Ruehl won the Best Supporting Actress Oscar for her role as Anne Napolitano. The film also included the best Arthurian one-liner in movie history:

Jack Lucas: Where would King Arthur be without Guinevere?
Parry: Happily married, probably.

Gilliam's *The Fisher King* is spellbinding – funny and tragic, gritty and magical. A fire-breathing Red Knight gallops down a Manhattan Street; hundreds of New Yorkers begin to waltz in the packed lobby of Grand Central Station; a Fifth Avenue townhouse becomes the Grail castle. Gilliam conjures a world where a suicidal cynic and a damaged fool can find love, redemption and a happy ending, a world where even the idea of the Holy Grail has the power to heal.

Meanwhile, *Sir Gawain and the Green Knight*, a magical Middle English romance once described by J.R.R. Tolkien as 'a fairytale for adults', has had the misfortune to be turned into not one but two of the worst Arthurian movies ever. Not content with his first attempt in 1973, writer-director Stephen Weeks was also responsible for *Sword of the Valiant: The Legend of Sir Gawain and the Green Knight* in 1984. *Sword of the Valiant* was a misguided attempt to reach the same market as the sword-and-sorcery movie *Conan the Barbarian*. Miles O'Keeffe, fresh from his debut starring in *Tarzan the Ape Man*, played Gawain while Sean Connery chewed the scenery as the outlandish Green Knight. Trevor Howard appeared as King Arthur, and the unfortunate cast included Peter Cushing and John Rhys-Davies.

Sean Connery and John Rhys-Davies would later find the Holy Grail in the Oscar-winning *Indiana Jones and the Last Crusade*. For the third Indiana Jones movie Steven Spielberg and George Lucas called on Connery to play the eccentric Professor Henry Jones, a renowned Grail scholar and father of archaeologist and adventurer Indiana Jones. In *Raiders of the Lost Ark*, Indiana, played by Harrison Ford, battled the Nazis in a race to uncover the Ark of the Covenant. *Indiana Jones and the Last Crusade* sees the Jones boys face the Nazis on a quest to find the Holy Grail, the cup of Christ. When 'Indy' first appears, he explains to a lecture theatre full of students that: 'Archeology is the search for fact, not truth . . . We do not follow maps to buried treasure and X never, ever marks the spot.' He is soon up to his neck in an adventure to find a mythical treasure, following a map on which X does indeed mark the spot. Ford and Connery are a wonderful double act and their adventure to recover the Grail parallels a personal quest in which father and son are reunited. The Grail is portrayed not as a fabulous treasure, a golden chalice encrusted with precious jewels, but as the simple cup of a carpenter. As museum curator Dr Marcus Brody (Denholm Elliott) says, 'The search for the Grail is the search for the divine in all of us.'

Connery went on to portray King Arthur in the 1995 Hollywood movie *First Knight*, in which Jerry Zucker, director of *Airplane!* and *Ghost*, made an Arthurian love story, sidestepping the tragedy of the fall of Camelot. Richard Gere as Lancelot retreads his familiar role of romantic lead, opposite Julia Ormond as an especially tearful Guinevere. Ben Cross isn't given much to play with as the cardboard cut-out villain Prince Malagant, while Connery does his best to lend the material some gravitas. Mark Ryan (Nasir in the cult '80s TV series *Robin of Sherwood*) helped to train Connery, Gere and Cross to sword fight. Ryan would later be the sword master and fight director on Jerry Bruckheimer's *King Arthur* and work on the stage fights for *Monty Python's Spamalot*. *First Knight* is a strange creature, featuring a bizarre deadly obstacle course called the Gauntlet that appears to have crept in from an entirely different film.

Three years later, Arthur returned to the big screen in the animated adventure *The Magic Sword: Quest for Camelot*, in which a brave young girl named Kayley sets out to recover Excalibur when it is stolen from Camelot. She is joined by the gruff Garrett and a madcap two-headed dragon called Devon and Cornwall. *The Magic Sword* is voiced by a host of famous actors with the starry cast including Pierce Brosnan as King Arthur, John Gielgud as Merlin and Gary Oldman as the villain, Baron Ruber. The show is stolen by Devon and Cornwall's double act, with Eric Idle of Monty Python fame voicing Devon.

King Arthur was first animated in 1963 in Disney's *The Sword in the Stone*. Director Wolfgang Reitherman had previously worked on *Snow White and the Seven Dwarfs*, *Pinocchio*, *Fantasia*, *Dumbo* and *One Hundred and One Dalmatians*. *The Sword in the Stone* was the first Disney animated feature with a single director. The movie was based on T.H. White's novel and tells the story of Wart, a young squire who is schooled by the eccentric Merlin the Magician and the curmudgeonly Sir Ector. Merlin is a wonderfully exotic figure who time-travels and shape-shifts and has a talking owl named Archimedes. In one outstanding scene, Merlin battles the mad witch Madam Mim. They turn themselves into a menagerie of real and fabulous animals including a crocodile, a mouse, a caterpillar, a rhinoceros, an elephant, a crab and a dragon. After many adventures, Wart pulls the sword from the stone and becomes King Arthur.

At the other end of the spectrum, the recent big-budget *King Arthur*, produced by Jerry Bruckheimer, was sold as 'the untold true story that inspired the legend'. Bruckheimer, producer of *Armageddon*, *Con Air*, *The Rock* and *Pirates of the Caribbean*, pulled out all the stops to turn the story of King Arthur into a massive Hollywood blockbuster. No expense was spared: a huge replica of part of Hadrian's Wall became the largest movie set ever built in Ireland and epic battle sequences were meticulously choreographed. Director Antoine Fuqua had helmed the Oscar-winning *Training Day* and Chow Yun-Fat action movie *The Replacement Killers*. *Gladiator* scribe David Franzoni banged out the screenplay, Keira Knightley was painted blue and strapped into leather as Guinevere and Clive Owen led a rugged cast of Dark Age warriors as Arthur.

King Arthur and his men are veteran soldiers of Rome sent on one last mission beyond Hadrian's Wall to rescue a Roman family, one of whom is the Pope's beloved godson. They face the mysterious 'Woads' (Picts), abandonment by Rome and a rampaging horde of Saxon invaders. Bruckheimer's *King Arthur* is an ambitious movie that ultimately fails to impress. The set-piece battle on a frozen loch is visually stunning but the movie falls apart whenever the fighting stops. Ioan Gruffudd as Lancelot, Mads Mikkelsen as Tristan, and Stellan Skarsgård as Cerdic manage to make an impression in their supporting roles, but Joel Edgerton as Gawain and the rest of Arthur's men are barely given any material to work with. Clive Owen and Keira Knightley are let down by awful dialogue and don't get the chance to build a credible love affair. Knightley's Guinevere is probably the only Pictish warrior woman in history with a cut-glass English accent.

The movie's claim to reveal the 'untold true story' of Arthur is based on its use of the theory that the historical Arthur had Sarmatian origins. Owen's Arthur is named Artorius Castus, a fictional descendant of the real Lucius Artorius Castus. Lucius Artorius was a second-century Roman military commander who scholars including Kemp Malone and Linda Malcor have suggested may be the historical Arthur. In the film, Arthur's 'knights' are Sarmatians. In reality, Sarmatian cavalry troops were stationed in northern Britain hundreds of years before the battles of Arthur. It is debatable whether their culture would have survived among their descendants for a thousand years to influence medieval Arthurian romances. Ultimately, *King Arthur* abandons any pretence of historical accuracy to become a big fireball-hurling, crossbow-wielding battle movie that simply namechecks Arthur, Lancelot, Guinevere et al. but ignores the stories that make an Arthurian movie actually Arthurian.

Excalibur, the greatest of all Arthurian movies, never pretended to be historically accurate. Director John Boorman said during shooting, 'I think of the story, the history, as a myth. The film has to do with *mythical* truth, not historical truth.' *Excalibur* is an epic fantasy jammed full of valiant knights in armour, bloody battles and willowy maidens. It seeks to distil the magical essence of Malory's immense *Le Morte d'Arthur* into a single film. Boorman depicts the world of the imagination, the coming of Christianity and the disappearance of the old pagan religions. Nicol Williamson is the wildly eccentric Merlin, forever laughing and talking in riddles under his breath. Helen Mirren is the seductive enchantress Morgana, Arthur's vengeful half-sister. Nigel Terry's Arthur grounds the film as he grows from a bewildered boy into a world-weary king.

Boorman was fascinated by the figure of Merlin. 'He's a mixture of real awesome power and foolishness,' said Boorman. 'He's both less human and more human than ordinary people.' Williamson's Merlin wears a metal skullcap throughout the movie, like the Borders wizard Michael Scott, who prophesied he would be killed by a stone that fell from the sky.

Boorman shot *Excalibur* in Ireland, where he lived with his family, many of whom were given parts in the film. His daughters Katrine and Telsche played Igrayne and the Lady of the Lake respectively, and Charley Boorman was the young Mordred. An excellent cast includes Liam Neeson, Gabriel Byrne, Patrick Stewart and Cherie Lunghi. Among the unsung heroes of *Excalibur* is armourer Terry English, who also provided armour for *King Arthur*. *Excalibur* was nominated for the Palme d'Or at the 1981 Cannes Film Festival.

SEE ALSO: Arthur, King of the Britons; Camelot; Gawain; Guinevere; Holy Grail; Lancelot; Malory, Sir Thomas; Percival; Wagner, Richard

CORNWALL

In Cornwall, belief in Arthur has always been strong. In 1113, a group of nine clergymen from Laon in northern France travelled across England collecting money to rebuild their cathedral. Their journey is recorded in *De Miraculis Sanctae Mariae Laudunensis* (*The Miracles of St Mary of Laon*). On their travels between Exeter and Cornwall, they saw megalithic monuments known as Arthur's Oven and Arthur's Seat. When the nine canons arrived at Bodmin in Cornwall carrying the Shrine of Our Lady of Laon, a man with a withered hand came to keep vigil. *De Miraculis* records that 'in just the same way as the Bretons are accustomed to arguing with the French about King Arthur', the man began to quarrel with one of the canons, insisting that Arthur still lived. A group of armed local men burst into the church, and it was only the timely intervention of the cleric Algardus that prevented bloodshed.

Cornwall is widely acknowledged as the birthplace of Arthur. Geoffrey of Monmouth tells us that Arthur was conceived in Tintagel Castle when Uther Pendragon lay with Igraine, the beautiful young wife of Duke Gorlois. It is usually assumed that Arthur was born at Tintagel, but Geoffrey says only that he was conceived in the castle. It wasn't until 1478, over three hundred years after Geoffrey completed his *History of the Kings of Britain*, that the chronicler William of Worcester first wrote that Tintagel was King Arthur's birthplace.

Tintagel is a wild, rocky promontory that juts out into the sea. The windswept ruins of a medieval castle cling to its rocks. It is thought that Reginald, Earl of Cornwall, built a castle at Tintagel around 1141, although the majority of the surviving ruins date to the 1230s, when Prince Richard, the younger son of King John, was Earl of Cornwall. Reginald was the brother of Robert, Earl of Gloucester, the patron of Geoffrey of Monmouth. It has been suggested that Reginald built a castle at Tintagel to capitalise on the popularity of Geoffrey's *History*.

In the nineteenth century, Tintagel became a world-famous Arthurian destination when Alfred, Lord Tennyson published *Idylls of the King*. Tennyson visited Tintagel in 1848, and ten years later, in the winter of 1858, he told an American publisher:

> I wish that you would disabuse your own minds and those of others, as far as you can, of the fancy that I am about an Epic of King Arthur. I should be crazed to attempt such a thing in the nineteenth century.

Seven months later, the first books of Tennyson's famed Arthurian poems appeared in print.

> They found a naked child upon the sands
> Of dark Tintagil by the Cornish sea;
> And that was Arthur; and they fostered him
> Till he by miracle was approven King:
> 'Guinevere', *Idylls of the King*, Tennyson

At the end of the nineteenth century, a railway station opened at nearby Camelford and visitors flocked to Tintagel. The King Arthur's Castle Hotel (renamed the Camelot Castle Hotel in recent years) was built to accommodate them. Tintagel village was actually named Trevena until the late nineteenth century. Tintagel – 'Din Tagell', meaning 'fort of the constriction' or 'fortress of the narrow entrance' – was strictly the castle's name until *Idylls of the King* brought hordes of Victorian tourists to the Cornish town.

King Arthur's Great Halls can be found in the heart of Tintagel village. In the 1920s, Frederick Thomas Glasscock, an eccentric entrepreneur, made a fortune as a partner in the Monk & Glass custard company. Glasscock sold his business in London and retired to Tintagel. Captivated by the legends of Arthur, he bought Trevena House and set about transforming it into King Arthur's Great Halls. Glasscock commissioned over 70 stained-glass windows from a pupil of William Morris, a series of Arthurian paintings, a round table and 125 granite shields representing 50 Cornish quarries. In 1929, Cornish craftsmen began work on King Arthur's Great Halls and the Hall of Chivalry was opened at Pentecost in 1933. Glasscock founded the Fellowship of the Knights of the Round Table to 'make known the ideals of chivalry' and keep the name of King Arthur alive. By the end of the 1930s, there were tens of thousands of members from America to Australia. Frederick Thomas Glasscock died in 1934, and his Fellowship was wound up two years later. In 1993, the diamond jubilee year of its foundation, the Fellowship was revived. Today, King Arthur's Great Halls are open to the public, attracting visitors from around the world.

Another Arthurian legend about Tintagel Castle is that it belonged to King Mark, the cruel uncle of Sir Tristan, one of the Knights of the Round Table. As Tristan escorted King Mark's intended bride, the fair Iseult, to Cornwall, they mistakenly drank a love potion and fell desperately in love. King Mark and Iseult were married, and Tristan and the queen became lovers. Tristan and Iseult began a secret affair, trysting under cover of darkness and evading the jealous king. When King Mark learned of his wife's infidelity, Tristan and Iseult were forced to flee Cornwall, helped by the hermit Ogrin. Tristan escaped from King Mark's men by leaping from the window of Ogrin's chapel. Tristan and Iseult's story ends tragically when Tristan is slain and Iseult dies of a broken heart. Some say that a hazel tree and a honeysuckle grew from their graves, their branches intertwining so the lovers would never be parted.

Another Cornish legendary stronghold of King Mark is Castle Dore, an Iron Age hill fort. Near by is Tristan's Stone, a stone pillar said to mark the knight's grave. An inscription on the stone reads 'Drustanus hic iacit Cunomori filius' ('Drustan lies here, the son of Cunomorus'). Drustan is thought to be the historic Tristan. The remote hermitage of Roche Rock may be Ogrin's church. It is a dramatic place, near the village of Bugle, where the remains of a small fifteenth-century chapel cling precariously to a massive rock outcrop.

Tristan was the king of the legendary Lyonesse. The lost lands of Lyonesse stretched from Land's End to the Isles of Scilly. In Cornish legend, it was a mystical land that disappeared beneath the waves. The sunken kingdom of Lyonesse is a looking-glass reflection of the legendary drowned Breton city of Ys. When Lyonesse vanished under the sea, a man named Trevelyan escaped the waves on a white horse, just as the King of Ys rode to land when his city was flooded. The shield of the Trevelyan family still shows a horse rising from the waves. The tidal islands of Mont-Saint-Michel in Normandy and St Michael's Mount in Cornwall seem to be mirror images of one another.

The Cornish name for St Michael's Mount is Carrack Looz en Cooz, which means 'the grey rock in the wood'. It is said that the Mount was once surrounded by a vast forest, and indeed fossilised tree trunks have been found on a beach near Penzance. Cornish fishermen are said to have found stones from the City of Lions, the capital of Lyonesse, in their fishing nets. Some even say that the church bells of Lyonesse may still be heard, tolling away beneath the waves, in the dead of night.

The legend of Lyonesse may have its origins in Cornish tales of the sunken kingdom of Lethowstow. Lethowstow was said to stretch from Land's End to form one vast land that joined up the Scilly Isles. Two of the Isles of Scilly are named Great Arthur and Little Arthur. The name Lyonesse is thought to have come from Leonais, the French name for Lothian in Scotland.

Along the coast from St Michael's Mount is the tiny village of Mousehole. In the harbour near Mousehole Quay is Merlin's Rock. According to local folklore, one of Merlin's prophecies stated that: 'There shall land on the Rock of Merlin those who shall burn Paul, Penzance and Newlyn.' When four Spanish galleys dropped anchor at Mousehole in 1595, Spanish troops armed with muskets and pikes put the villages to the torch, and Merlin's prophecy was fulfilled.

Cornwall also lays claim to the battle of Camlann. Just north of Camelford is Slaughter Bridge, which for centuries has been suggested as the site of Arthur's last battle. Near by, on the banks of the River Camel, lies the Arthur Stone, once thought to be the gravestone of the king. Richard Carew's *Survey of Cornwall*, published in 1602, tells us that upon the River Camel the 'last dismal battel' took place between the noble King Arthur and his treacherous nephew Mordred. Carew was shown the Arthur Stone: 'the olde folke thereabouts will shew you a stone, bearing Arthur's name'. On Bodmin Moor is Dozmary Pool. In Carew's time, the country people said the pool would ebb and flow and that a whirlpool spun in the midst of it. Local tradition declares that, as Arthur lay dying by the River Camel, Sir Bedivere took Excalibur from the field of battle and threw the sword into the bottomless waters of Dozmary Pool.

Arthur has given his name to natural features and megalithic sites across Cornwall. A small hollow worn in the rock of Tintagel headland has been called King Arthur's Footprint or King Arthur's

Footstep. Local tradition holds that Arthur could take a single giant stride from this spot across the sea to Tintagel Church. Tintagel is also home to Arthur's Bed, Arthur's Chair and Arthur's Cups and Saucers, while nearby is King Arthur's Quoit. Merlin's Cave lies below Tintagel Castle, lashed by the waves at high tide.

SEE ALSO: Battles of Arthur; Geoffrey of Monmouth; Merlin; Tennyson, Alfred, Lord

EGYPTIAN ARTHUR

Could it be that the true origin and meaning of the quest for the Holy Grail could be revealed by a clue in accounts of the Last Supper? Is there a link between the rituals introduced by Jesus and the religion of the Ancient Egyptians and their belief in the afterlife?

It has been suggested that what Jesus told his followers at the Last Supper broke many rules of conventional Judaism. Christ was instructing his followers to consume his body through eating and drinking the bread and wine, in effect commanding them to devour the god itself. In *The Templar Revelation*, Lynn Picknett and Clive Prince theorise that:

> Christians see the sacred meal of wine and bread – the climax of the Protestant communion and the Catholic Mass – as being unique to Jesus. In fact it was already a common practice of all the major Dying God mystery schools, including those of Dionysus, Tammuz and Osiris. In every case it was understood to be a way of becoming one with the god concerned and of achieving spiritual elevation (although the Romans expressed horror at the implicit cannibalism involved). All of the other cults were well represented in Palestine at the time of the Last Supper, so their influence is understandable.

This leads us to a very interesting and controversial possibility. It is not the first time that Osiris has been linked to the character of

Jesus, and the two share similar characteristics, such as returning from the dead. Furthermore, they just happen to share the same birthday. Tradition holds that both Jesus and Osiris were born on 25 December. Then there is the curious fact that Jesus was known as the 'Good Shepherd', while Osiris carried the shepherd's crook. Even the appearance of a new star in the sky at the time of the birth of Jesus is significant. The Pyramid Texts of the Egyptians tell how the dead king's soul would strive to become one with Osiris as an imperishable star; in the mythology of Ancient Egypt, stars held great significance. Furthermore, it is tantalising to consider that the star associated with the birth of Jesus was seen in the East, which is exactly where Sirius rises, the star linked with Isis, the wife of Osiris, who brought about his resurrection. The list of similarities between the old god of Egypt and the new god of Christianity goes on and on.

The Arthurian Grail quest also has a parallel in Ancient Egyptian culture. It is well understood that the quest for the Holy Grail is not simply the search for a holy relic. The achievement of the Grail is much more than merely locating a sacred artefact. The Grail romances show that the quest involved a great deal of soul searching and that it asked hard and testing questions of the seeker. It was said that because Sir Galahad was pure of heart, chaste and sinless, only he could achieve the Grail. The quest for the Holy Grail sounds suspiciously like the rituals that the dead soul had to undergo in Egyptian religion before reaching the blissful afterlife. There were trials and tests that the deceased's soul had to undertake in the Duat, or underworld, questions to answer, supernatural creatures to battle and words of power to be spoken at the right time. Finally, the dead soul, if successful in all of these quests, found himself in the presence of Osiris and a ceremony known as the weighing of the heart took place. The deceased would have his life's deeds judged and weighed and only if – like Galahad – he was deemed to have lived a good life, free from sin, could he hope to attain a place in the afterlife. Perhaps this was exactly what the quest for the Holy Grail truly was – a journey to reach spiritual perfection and a cherished place in the afterlife.

According to John Grigsby, author of *Warriors of the Wasteland*, there is even a passage in the Egyptian Coffin texts that mentions Osiris being wounded in the thigh, a euphemism for being impotent, in the same way as the Fisher King of Grail legend. Here is how Grigsby describes it:

Perhaps the biggest link between the two schemes [Egyptian

and Grail Myth] is the revelation in Coffin Text 228 that states
that Osiris is wounded in the thigh! Horus says:

> Tell him I have come thither to save myself . . .
> And to dispel the sickness of the suffering god, so that I
>   can appear an Osiris in strength,
> That I may be reborn with him in his renewed vigour,
> That I may reveal to you the matter of Osiris' thigh and
>   read to you from that sealed roll which lies beneath his
>   side,
> Whereby the mouths of the gods are opened.

The healing of this thigh wound, Egyptologist R.T. Rundle
Clark stated, restored fertility to the land.

So here we see how complex the story becomes. If all of this speculation
is true, then it means that Osiris, Jesus and the Fisher King are in
actual fact the same character − a single archetype − and all three
perform the same role in their respective mythologies.

Therefore the ceremonies introduced by Jesus at the Last Supper
may be a confirmation that he was heavily influenced by the Egyptian
death cults. Like Osiris, with whom the dead Egyptians would be
merged when they died (if they passed the many trials of the
underworld itself), Jesus was instructing his followers to become one
with him. The Last Supper could indeed mark the very point when
the quest for the Holy Grail truly began, or, at least, was reintroduced
to the world.

SEE ALSO: Fisher King; Galahad; Holy Grail; Last Supper

EXCALIBUR

There drew he forth the brand Excalibur,
And o'er him, drawing it, the winter moon,
Brightening the skirts of a long cloud, ran forth
And sparkled keen with frost against the hilt:
For all the haft twinkled with diamond sparks,
Myriads of topaz-lights, and jacinth-work
Of subtlest jewellery.

'Morte d'Arthur', Tennyson

According to the legends of the Welsh, the sword of Arthur was
called Caledvwlch. Geoffrey of Monmouth Latinised the name to
Caliburn or Caliburnus, and this version of the original Welsh was
then changed further when later, Continental Arthurian writers
called Arthur's sword Escalibor. This eventually became Excalibur,
which is how we know the weapon today. Historians and Arthurian
scholars argue about the origins of the name, with some pointing to
an Irish origin through the many Irish stories of heroes and their
magically named swords. One such claim is that the Welsh sword
Caledvwlch was derived from the Irish sword Caladbolg, meaning
'hard lightning', or Caladcholg, 'hard blade'. Caladbolg was the sword
of Fergus mac Róich. In Irish myth and legend swords are magical
weapons. It was said, for example, that Caladbolg could cut the tops
from hills. Cú Chulainn's sword was Claidheamh Solius, the Sword of
Light, while Freagarthach, the Answerer, was wielded by Manannán
mac Lir and by Lugh.

EXCALIBUR

In an exchange which speaks of the value of his sword to the king, when, in the early Welsh tale *Culhwch and Olwen*, Culhwch requests a boon from Arthur, he is told that he may have anything he asks for, 'as far as the sun rises, as far as the sea stretches, as far as the earth extends, excepting only my ship, my mantle, my sword Caledvwlch, my spear Rhongomynyad, my shield Wynebgwrthucher, my knife Carnwennan and my wife Gwenhwyvar'.

Excalibur, said to have been forged on the Isle of Avalon, seems to act as a form of royal sceptre for Arthur, bestowing upon him an otherworldly blessing and legitimacy as king. It arrives right at the start of his reign and is handed back at the end, having helped him overcome foes and claimants to the throne along the way. Thus Excalibur plays an enormously important role in the life of the king. Without it, his power and abilities are weakened. Excalibur remains throughout the tales a powerful and iconic symbol of Arthur's supreme power and his anointment from on high.

Excalibur was said to emit a blinding light, like that of 30 torches. The Welsh tale *The Dream of Rhonabwy* claims that Arthur's sword bore 'a design of two serpents on the golden hilt; when the sword was unsheathed what was seen from the mouths of the two serpents was like two flames of fire, so dreadful that it was not easy for anyone to look'. One of the Thirteen Treasures of Britain was the sword of Rhydderch the Generous, Dyrnwyn (White Hilt), which would burst into flame if anyone but Rhydderch drew it from its scabbard.

Two of the most enduring scenes in the Arthurian legends are those of Arthur receiving the sword Excalibur from the waters of the lake and the drawing of the sword from the stone. In Malory's *Le Morte d'Arthur*, the Lady of the Lake gives the sword its name, Excalibur, which is said to mean 'cut steel'. Malory tells us that he receives Excalibur after breaking his original sword in a fight with a king called Pellinore. Merlin takes Arthur to a lake where the mystical Lady of the Lake lives. The Lady of the Lake is not the otherworldly woman who raises the sword from beneath the water; she is the guardian of the lake, who lives in a castle on its shores. Arthur is then given the sword and is asked by Merlin whether he prefers to take the sword or the scabbard. Arthur replies that he prefers the sword, only to be told by Merlin that this is a bad choice because it is the scabbard that would have protected the king from harm.

The role of the Lady of the Lake is parodied in *Monty Python and the Holy Grail*: 'Listen, strange women lyin' in ponds distributin' swords is no basis for a system of government. Supreme executive power derives from a mandate from the masses, not from some farcical aquatic ceremony.'

In some of the Arthurian romances, Excalibur is wielded by Sir Gawain, Arthur's nephew and a Knight of the Round Table. For example, in Chrétien de Troyes' *Perceval, or the Story of the Grail*, Gawain carries Escalibor, 'the best sword ever, that cuts through iron like wood'. In the *Alliterative Morte Arthure*, written around 1400, Arthur has two named swords: Excalibur and a sword named Clarent. Clarent, which is used for knighting, is stolen by Mordred, who uses it against Arthur, dealing the king a fatal blow.

Excalibur is ultimately returned to the Lady of the Lake as Arthur lies mortally wounded after the Battle of Camlann. Arthur instructs Sir Bedivere to throw the weapon back into the waters. Bedivere fails to carry out these instructions on two occasions, believing that the sword should be saved. His failings are found out when Arthur asks him what he sees as he hurls the sword in the water. When the knight answers that he sees nothing, Arthur is furious and instructs him to do as he asked. On the third attempt, Sir Bedivere throws Excalibur into the waters of the lake, but before its shining steel can penetrate the depths, an arm, traditionally said to be clad in white samite, reaches up to catch the sword, brandish it and pull it beneath the surface of the water. This magical scene is a fitting end to the legend of this powerful emblem of Arthur's reign.

Just as Excalibur was returned to the lake, so the Celts gave swords to the water. In the Iron Age, swords were thrown or placed into rivers and lakes as sacred votive offerings. These swords were often deliberately damaged, put beyond use, as sacrifices. It was believed that they passed from our mortal world to the otherworld beneath the surface of the waters, the world of the Celtic water goddesses. Excalibur is said to lie in lakes, lochs and rivers in Wales, Scotland and England, incuding Llyn Llydaw in Snowdonia, the River Brue in Somerset and the Dozmary Pool in Cornwall.

SEE ALSO: Arthur; Gawain; Lady of the Lake; Merlin; Sword in the Stone

FAERIES

The legends of King Arthur are full of faeries who conjure spells to charm the Knights of the Round Table and who interfere in the lives and loves of mortals. The enchanted faerie realm is never far away. It lies beneath the surface of a mirror lake, amid the trees of the dark forest or within the walls of a magical castle.

Today, we tend to think of fairies as tiny creatures with fluttering gossamer wings. They live at the bottom of the garden, collecting dew from spring flowers and sitting on toadstools. These are the fairies of the nursery and the picture book – Tinkerbell in J.M. Barrie's *Peter Pan* and the flower fairies of Cicely Mary Barker. Fairy tales have lost their teeth and claws. Little girls dress up as fairies in pink floaty dresses with wings tied to their backs. In centuries past, however, people feared faeries.

The faeries of legend and folk tale were as tall as, or taller than, mortal men. They could disguise their form, taking the shape of a white deer, a seal or a wolf. They used 'faerie glamour', or enchantment, to transform themselves by illusion, appearing as radiant, beautiful creatures that bewitched any mortal man who gazed upon them. Faeries might appear as white or green ladies or dressed in red, grey or black. The colour green became so closely associated with the faerie folk that the Scots thought it unlucky to wear green at a wedding.

The faeries made mischief and played tricks on unwary travellers. They stole cattle and sheep from the fields and babies from their cradles. Superstitious men and women encircled their homes and their farmlands with fiery torches and left gifts of milk and food for the faeries. Horseshoes were nailed above doorways as the faeries were thought to have an aversion to iron, and crosses made of rowan twigs bound with red thread were tied to cows' tails to protect them from attack. The berries of the rowan and the red yarn were symbols of the blood of Christ.

Arthurian faeries include Morgan le Fay and Viviane, the Lady of the Lake. Morgan le Fay could transform herself into a hideous aged hag or a beautiful maiden at will. She was as capricious and wanton as any faerie lover. In the Forest of Brocéliande, she flew into a jealous rage when her mortal lover betrayed her, but thought nothing of being faithless herself. Viviane, the Lady of the Lake, lived in a magical faerie otherworld under the surface of the water. In Brocéliande, she raised Lancelot du Lac and enchanted the wizard Merlin, learning his magic so that she could hold him captive. Water faeries were renowned for their treachery. They lay in wait for any mortal foolish enough to come close to the water's edge then dragged them beneath the surface.

Merlin himself was half faerie. His mother is said to have been either a maiden or a nun who loved a mysterious stranger for one night and fell pregnant. Merlin's father was said to have been a faerie, an incubus or even the Devil himself. Christian writers smelled brimstone in the tales of Merlin's magical powers, but ancient Gods and faerie men had long been believed to father sons who inherited supernatural gifts.

While Queen Guinevere is depicted in myths of Arthur as a mortal woman, the daughter of King Leodegrance, she acts like a faithless faerie lover. The Welsh name for Guinevere is Gwenhwyfar, which translates as 'white phantom' or 'white faerie'. Tales of white ladies are found across France and the British Isles. In Brittany, they are said to wait in rocky passes to dance with passing men or throw them into thorny briar bushes. Supernatural white ladies haunt ruined castles, dolmens, ancient trees, dark caves, fountains, springs, still ponds and lakes, graveyards and abandoned chateaux. The faerie white ladies are clad in flowing dresses that shine as though made of moonlight. Their radiance echoes the illumination of the halls of the Fisher King's castle as the Grail maiden bears the Grail and all is bright as if lit by the sun and moon. At Rosslyn Castle, a few miles south of Edinburgh in Scotland, legend has it that an enchanted White Lady lies sleeping in a secret underground chamber. Beneath the ruins of the castle she waits for a knight to free her from a wicked spell. It is said that she guards a wondrous treasure worth many millions of pounds.

FAERIES

Arthur's kingdom of Logres and the realm of faerie are woven together. The faerie otherworld of Celtic legend is not a faraway land but a magical place that is revealed, like the Grail castle, when you are least expecting it. The mystical Isle of Avalon, the lake where Arthur was given Excalibur and the Forest of Brocéliande are among the Arthurian places that belong to the faerie realm. The enchantresses that King Arthur and his knights met in these locations were supernatural beings like the elf queens of the faerie world.

The Isle of Avalon was an Arthurian paradise that mirrored the Celtic Fortunate Isles and the wonders of the faerie otherworld. The apple trees of Avalon's orchards were full of fruit and blossom. The island was a fertile land of never-ending spring where grain and grapes grew and Morgan le Fay tended Arthur's battle wounds. Avalon was a magical realm without war or hurt, where winter winds never blew.

The hierarchy of the faerie realm closely matched the feudal system of medieval Europe. The faerie realm was ruled by the King and Queen of Elfland. There were two opposing faerie courts; the Seelie Court was made up of 'good' or at least generally benevolent faeries while the Unseelie Court was filled with vicious and malevolent faeries that attacked, abducted and ate unfortunate mortals.

The Kings and Queens of Faerie were attended by lords and ladies, elfin knights and faerie ladies. The Queens of Faerie entertained mortals and faerie folk alike in huge subterranean halls full of colour, light and music. Their feasts were lavish; every mouthful of food tasted more wonderful than the last, great golden goblets were filled to overflowing with the richest wine, and gold coins lay upon the tables. Faerie musicians played fabulous music as faerie dancers, in silk and satin, spun and whirled.

But when the midnight revels ended mortal visitors to Elfland found themselves alone on desolate hillsides. The faerie food in their mouths was half-eaten worms and dead leaves, the wine was dirty bogwater, and the faeries' gold coins had turned to stones in their pockets. Like the faeries who hold court underground, Arthur and his knights are said to sleep in caves and hollow hills. The fabulous court of Camelot has much in common with the wondrous courts of faerie, while Arthur and Guinevere rule like a King and Queen of Elfland.

In *The Spoils of Annwn*, a Welsh poem from the fourteenth-century *Book of Taliesin*, Arthur and his warriors journey to the faerie otherworld to steal a wondrous cauldron warmed by the breath of nine maidens. The legendary Welsh bard Taliesin tells how Arthur and his men sailed in his ship *Prydwen* bound for Annwn, the Welsh realm of faerie. Annwn is given a host of names including Caer Sidi (faerie fort), Caer Colur (the gloomy fort) and Caer Vedidwid (the fort of the perfect ones). Three boatloads of Arthur's men, 'thrice the fullness of *Prydwen*', sailed to Annwn, but none returned save seven.

In Celtic legends and folk tales, the veil between the world of mortals and the faerie realm is said to be 'thin' at certain times of the year. Beltane (the eve of May) and Samhuinn (Hallowe'en) were seen as particularly perilous times, when the faeries would 'flit', travelling between their summer and winter homes. The light half of the year fell between Beltane and Samhuinn, while the dark half fell between Samhuinn and Beltane. The seasons themselves were not seen as particularly hazardous, but the boundaries that separated them, the actual time of change, was unsafe as it was neither one thing nor the other. Dawn and dusk are neither night nor day. A doorway is neither inside nor outside. The surface of the water is neither dry land nor beneath the waves. It was in these magical 'in-between' places that mortals and faeries were thought to meet.

In the Arthurian romances, enchanted beings enter Arthur's court at special feasts and festivals. The supernatural Green Knight came to offer his challenge to the court at Christmastide, while Galahad arrived to complete the circle of the Round Table, thereby working miracles, at Pentecost. It should also be noted that Mordred, the child conceived in an incestuous union between Arthur and his half-sister Morgause, was born on the first of May. The birth of Mordred at the ancient festival of Beltane may point to some echo of the faerie threat that led villagers to light huge bonfires at Beltane and to make pilgrimages to holy wells and springs to wash in their magical waters on the first of May. It was customary for people to 'bring in the May' at Beltane, to take branches of spring blossom from the woods to decorate their homes. Queen Guinevere is said to have first met Sir Lancelot as she was gathering May blossom with her ladies-in-waiting. 'Bringing in the May' was often a cover for wanton behaviour as young couples met and trysted in the woods at night. The illicit nature of these 'greenwood marriages' appears to hint at the secret love affair that would develop between Lancelot and Guinevere.

In 1570, Janet Boyman of Edinburgh was accused of witchcraft. She was said to have taken the shirt of a smith who lived in the Canongate, Alan Lauderstone, to a local well in an attempt to cure him of an illness. The 'elreth well' was at Arthur's Seat, the huge hill near Holyrood Palace at the foot of the High Street. There, Janet called on 'evil spirits' and there was 'a great blast like a whirlwind'. A man appeared on the other side of the well. Janet addressed the man in the name of the Father and the Son and of King Arthur and the Faerie Queen Elspeth, asking him to either give Alan Lauderstone back his health or take him and relieve him of his pain. She then washed Alan's shirt in the well and sent it back to the smith and his wife. It was said that Alan made a full recovery.

It was also recorded that Janet had seen the faeries ride out of Arthur's Seat at Hallowe'en. As she watched the faeries with a friend, they were hit by a 'wind with a thing like a hat in it whirling about the sky'. Her companion, Janet Henderson, was so terrified that she died of fright eight days later. Janet Boyman was executed for witchcraft on 29 December 1572. In Edinburgh, every May morning, hundreds of people still rise at first light and wash their faces in the dew at Arthur's Seat.

Some say that King Arthur and his knights lie sleeping within Arthur's Seat, in a cave at Alderley Edge, deep within a green mound in Caerleon, or beneath Cadbury Castle. Legends of Arthur and the sleeping knights appear across Britain. It is even said that Arthur sleeps under Mount Etna. In the hollow Eildon Hills, the thirteenth-century Border poet and prophet Thomas the Rhymer is said to gather horses for King Arthur and his knights. Thomas spent seven years in the enchanted court of the Queen of Elfland and was gifted a tongue that could not lie. It is said that one day Arthur and his knights will return, when they are woken by the blast of a hunting horn:

> Mysterious Rhymer, doomed by fate's decree
> Still to revisit Eildon's fated tree . . .
> Say, who is he, with summons long and high,
> Shall bid the charmed sleep of ages fly,
> Roll the long sound through Eildon's caverns vast,
> While each dark warrior kindles at the blast,
> The horn, the falchion, grasp with mighty hand,
> And peal proud Arthur's march from Fairy-land?
>
> *Scenes of Infancy*, Dr John Leyden

SEE ALSO: Avalon; Brocéliande; Gawain; Knights of the Round Table; Lady of the Lake; Merlin; Morgan le Fay; Scotland; Wales

FISHER KING

The Fisher King is the guardian and keeper of the Holy Grail and the bleeding lance. He was wounded by the Dolorous Stroke, when a spear or lance was thrust through his thighs or groin. He is tormented by the wound, which can only be healed when a knight asks the right question when he sees the Grail procession. He is commonly known as the '*roi pêscheur*', the 'Fisher King' but is sometimes called the '*riche pêscheur*', the 'Rich Fisher'. '*Pêscheur*' is the Old French word for a fisher but it is pronounced the same as the Old French for 'sinner'. It has been suggested that this double meaning shows that the Fisher King was wounded because he had sinned and could only be healed once his sins were redeemed.

In Chrétien de Troyes' Arthurian romance, *Perceval, or the Story of the Grail*, the young knight Perceval meets the Fisher King. Perceval is trying to find a way to cross a river when he sees two men in a small boat and calls out to them. One of the men is fishing with a rod and line, and he tells Perceval that there is no way to cross the river but that the knight is welcome to stay the night in his castle. Perceval thanks the fisherman and climbs to where the castle should be. At first, he cannot see the castle and curses the fisherman. Suddenly, he sees a wondrous castle, within which he witnesses the Grail procession but fails to ask who is served from the Grail. Only once he has left the castle will Perceval learn that he was the guest of the Fisher King, that the Fisher King is Perceval's cousin and that the Fisher King's father is sustained by a single Mass wafer carried in the Grail. The Fisher King is unable to stand because of his wound. He is described as a handsome man with greying hair.

In Robert de Boron's *Joseph of Arimathea*, the Fisher King is Bron, the brother-in-law of Joseph of Arimathea. Bron earns his name because he catches a fish when he, his wife and their 12 children are starving. The fish is placed beside the Grail on a table that Joseph has built in remembrance of the Last Supper. In the Grail castle, Bron tries to prompt Perceval to ask the question. Perceval remains silent and Bron becomes most distressed, as he can only be healed when the finest knight in the world asks the question. Perceval wanders for seven years before he returns to the Fisher King's castle. This time, when the lance with the bleeding head and the Grail are brought out, Perceval asks Bron to tell him the purpose of the things he sees. In that moment, the Fisher King is finally healed. Bron teaches Perceval the sacred words that Joseph of Arimathea had taught him, and Perceval becomes the new guardian of the Grail.

The Grail king in Wolfram von Eschenbach's *Parzival* is named Anfortas. Anfortas was riding alone one day in search of adventure 'compelled to it by Love's desire', when he jousted with a heathen, born 'where the Tigris River flows forth from Paradise'. Anfortas was grievously wounded by a poisoned spear that was thrust into his groin, piercing his genitals. The wound will only be healed when Parzival asks the question. The bleeding spear that wounded Anfortas is carried in the Grail procession and Anfortas's suffering can be relieved for a short time by placing the spear in his wound. When Parzival comes to Munsalvaesche, the Grail castle, for the second time, Anfortas is healed and Parzival becomes the new Grail king.

Arthurian scholars including R.S. Loomis and Richard Cavendish have connected Bron, the Fisher King, with the giant Welsh king, Bran. Bran's full name was Bendigeid Vran ab Llyr, Blessed Bran, son of Llyr, which means 'blessed raven, son of the sea god Llyr'. The wondrous cauldron of Bran could bring the dead back to life, and Bran was wounded when his foot was pierced by a poisoned spear.

The Arthurian scholar and folklorist Jesse Weston suggested that the figure of the Fisher King was derived from ancient pagan fertility rites. When the Fisher King is wounded, the land becomes a barren wasteland; only when he is healed will it become fertile once more. Weston argued that the Fisher King had his origins in the pagan mystery cults and the Irish tale of Finn Mac Cumhail and the Salmon of Knowledge. Finn caught the salmon for the old man he served. He was told to watch the salmon as it roasted but not to eat any of the fish. Finn reached for the fish but burned his thumb in the fire. As he put his thumb in his mouth, he gained the magical knowledge of the salmon. It should be noted that Weston's theories are no longer highly regarded and whether the romances of Arthur have their roots in Celtic mythology is disputed. Much ink has been spilt in the ongoing debate over the origins of the Fisher King and the Grail story.

The fish is, of course, an ancient symbol of Christ. When Jesus was walking by the Sea of Galilee, he saw the fishermen Simon Peter and his brother Andrew casting a net into the sea. Jesus said to them, 'Come ye after me, and I will make you to be fishers of men.' Early Christians drew a simple fish with two curved lines to symbolise Jesus, and *ichthus*, the Greek word for fish, was used as an acronym for Christ: Iesous CHristos Theou HUios Soter (Jesus Christ, Son of God and Saviour).

SEE ALSO: Chrétien de Troyes; Grail Maiden; Holy Grail; Percival; Robert de Boron; Wales; Wolfram von Eschenbach

GALAHAD

Galahad was the son of Sir Lancelot, one of King Arthur's most trusted knights. He was conceived due to the mischief of the Fisher King, guardian of the Holy Grail, who conspired to have his daughter Elaine enchanted so that she appeared as Lancelot's love, Guinevere. She tricked Sir Lancelot, who desired Arthur's wife above all women, into believing that she was the queen, and he slept with her. This union led to the birth of a son, Galahad, who had the strength of ten men and was pure of heart.

In several Grail romances, Galahad is the perfect knight destined to sit at the Siege Perilous, the seat reserved at the Round Table for the Grail knight. Both Sir Thomas Malory and later Lord Tennyson cast Galahad as the special Grail knight in their versions of the story. However, neither Galahad nor his father is mentioned in Geoffrey of Monmouth's *History of the Kings of Britain*, one of the earliest British accounts of the legend. Galahad's first appearance is in the Vulgate Cycle, a series of French prose works of the early thirteenth century, where he replaces Percival as the Grail hero.

On the eve of the feast of Pentecost, a woman arrives at Camelot with a youth who she asks should be knighted. Lancelot's cousins Bors and Lionel notice that the lad bears a striking resemblance to Lancelot, and it is later revealed that he is none other than Galahad, son of Lancelot by Elaine, the Fisher King's daughter. The next day, they find that a large stone has floated downstream and sits just outside Camelot. It contains a sword set into the stone with an inscription that reads: 'Never shall man take me hence, but only he by whose side I ought to hang, and he shall be the best knight of the world.' Lancelot himself says he is not worthy of the attempt and so the knights Percival and Gawain try, but fail. Eventually, it is the newly knighted Galahad who comes forward and, grasping the hilt of the sword, pulls it free. It is realised that Galahad must have been sent for a very special purpose and that his gaining this sword, and so the title of the best knight in the world, signifies something of extreme importance.

That evening, as King Arthur and his knights dine in the great hall, the Holy Grail appears, shrouded in white fabric. The Grail magically passes around the hall, and wherever it moves it bestows a great feast upon the plates of the knights. Gawain rises to his feet and swears an oath:

> 'My lord king, indeed we have been honoured, to be served and graced by the Grail itself. But yet we were so blinded by our sins that we could not see it plainly, but only veiled and hidden. I now make this vow: to leave in the morning in quest of the Holy Grail, and pursue it as long as I may until I have looked openly upon this mystery, if I am worthy to do so; if not, I will return.'
>
> *Chronicles of King Arthur*, Andrea Hopkins

The timing of Lancelot's appearance at Camelot was significant. The feast of Pentecost, seven Sundays after Easter, was also known as Whitsunday, and it commemorated the descent of the Holy Spirit upon the Apostles, when they were filled with knowledge. Galahad completed the circle of the Round Table, and the Grail miraculously appeared in King Arthur's hall. So it was that the quest for the Holy Grail began, and all the knights present made the same vow as Gawain and left on their long search.

Lancelot began his quest with Percival, and on their journey they encountered Galahad; for some reason, however, they did not recognise him and attacked him. Galahad gained the upper hand and unseated Lancelot before doing the same to Percival. Galahad would have certainly killed them both, but an angel warned him to leave or he would be responsible for the death of his father.

Malory writes that at the Castle of Carbonek Sir Galahad, with his companions Percival and Bors, witnessed a mysterious Mass being celebrated using a holy vessel containing the Host. Then they saw a man emerge from the vessel:

[He] had all the signs of the passion of Jesu Christ, bleeding all openly, and said: 'My knights, and my servants, and my true children, which be come out of deadly life into spiritual life, I will now no longer hide me from you, but ye shall see now a part of my secrets and of my hidden things: now hold and receive the high meat which ye have so much desired.'

This apparition then gives Communion to Galahad and his companions. Galahad is asked if he knows what the figure holds in his hands; he says he does not and asks to be enlightened. The mystical figure says, 'This is . . . the holy dish wherein I ate the lamb on Sher Thursday [at the Last Supper].' The apparition also tells Galahad that the holy vessel must be taken from the realm of Logres and that only he, Sir Percival and Sir Bors must travel across the sea. The figure then disappears.

The following chapter sees them aboard ship in search of the city of the Grail, Sarras, with the Grail set upon a silver table covered with a rich red cloth. After further mystical adventures during which Galahad cures a man who has been lame for ten years, echoing one of Christ's own miracles, the companions are imprisoned by the tyrant king of Sarras, one Estorause, who was a pagan. Estorause falls ill and repents of his injustice, and the knights forgive him before he dies. The citizens then insist that Galahad become their new king. A princely chest is made to hold the Grail. A year later, Galahad sees the Grail again, held by a man surrounded by angels. The man performs Mass, and after the sacrament Galahad is called by the celebrant, who confides that he is none other than Joseph of Arimathea, who had taken charge of Christ's body after the Crucifixion. The young man is told that he himself resembles Joseph in that he has seen the Grail and that he is also pure and totally without sin, which is why he has been singled out for the special honour of Joseph's presence. Galahad says farewell to both of his companions, prays and then:

suddenly his soul departed to Jesu Christ, and a great multitude of angels bare his soul up to heaven, that the two fellows might well behold it. Also the two fellows saw come from heaven an hand, but they saw not the body. And then it came right to the Vessel and took it and the spear, and so bare it up to heaven.

No man has dared since then, we are told by Malory, to claim to have seen the Holy Grail.

Other versions of the Grail quest story up to the present day offer countless variations on the theme. 'Sir Galahad', written by Alfred, Lord Tennyson, in 1834, begins with the lines:

> My good blade carves the casques of men,
> My tough lance thrusteth sure,

This Galahad revels in wreaking havoc on other humans, who, we are to assume, deserve their fate. Tennyson's Galahad also declares:

> I never felt the kiss of love,
> Nor maiden's hand in mine.

So, unlike his father, Lancelot, he is chaste and pure in the way that a celibate priest is expected to be. He is in this respect a figure worthy of the privilege of seeing the Grail. Having successfully achieved the holy quest, Sir Galahad reached the absolute peak of joy and, in that moment of perfect bliss, he died:

> A gentle sound, an awful light!
> Three angels bear the holy Grail:
> With folded feet, in stoles of white,
> On sleeping wings they sail.
> Ah, blessed vision! blood of God!
> My spirit beats her mortal bars,
> As down dark tides the glory slides,
> And star-like mingles with the stars.

SEE ALSO: Gawain; Geoffrey of Monmouth; Joseph of Arimathea; Lancelot; Last Supper; Malory, Sir Thomas; Percival; Round Table; Tennyson, Alfred, Lord

GAWAIN

Sir Gawain of Lothian and Orkney was, in many Arthurian tales, the foremost Knight of the Round Table. Gawain was the nephew of King Arthur, a knight noted for his courtesy, his chivalry and his valour. From the earliest Grail romances, Sir Gawain was named as one of the knights who quests for the Grail. In some versions of the story of the Holy Grail, it is Sir Gawain rather than Sir Percival or Sir Galahad who finally achieves the Grail.

Gawain was the son of King Loth, the legendary king of the Lothians and Orkney. His mother was Morgause (sometimes known as Anna), sister of Morgan le Fay and King Arthur. In the thirteenth-century Old French poem *L'Âtre périlleux* (*The Perilous Cemetery*), it is said that Gawain's mother was a faerie, suggesting that Morgan's sisters shared her supernatural nature.

Gawain's brothers were Gareth, Gaheris, Agravaine and Mordred. His sisters are variously named as Thanew, Soredamors, Clarissant, Elaine, Curdrie and Itonje. Loth was one of the British kings who rebelled against Arthur. He was slain by King Pellinore, igniting a murderous feud between the sons of Loth, known as the Orkney clan, and the sons of Pellinore. Morgause was killed by her own son, Gaheris, when he discovered her in bed with Lamorack de Galles, one of King Pellinore's sons.

Sir Gawain was said to have been 'famous seven years before he was born'. After he was born and baptised, Gawain was set adrift in a wooden casket, rescued by a poor fisherman and sent to Rome to be educated. There he was knighted by Pope Sulpicius, after which he returned to Britain, sought out King Arthur's court and became a Knight of the Round Table. Sir Gawain became the perfect knight; he was without equal in the court, and became known as 'the father of adventures', the living embodiment of all the knightly virtues.

Sir Gawain and the Green Knight is arguably the finest version of any of the adventures of Gawain. The Middle English alliterative poem, composed around the year 1400, survived in a single manuscript but was almost lost forever when a fire broke out in the house of the royal librarian at Westminster in 1731. The unknown writer is generally referred to simply as 'the Gawain poet'. The story begins in King Arthur's court as they celebrate New Year's Day. The giant Green Knight bursts into the feast and challenges Arthur and his knights to a test of their courage. The otherworldly visitor offers to trade blows from his axe. He will take an axe blow from any man brave enough to receive a strike in return one year later. Gawain accepts the Green Knight's challenge. He takes up the axe and with a single blow cuts off the Green Knight's head.

As the court looks on in disbelief, the body of the Green Knight picks up its decapitated head and turns to face Sir Gawain. The head reminds Gawain of his promise and tells him to seek out the Green Chapel in a year and a day. The seasons pass, and eventually Gawain prepares to leave and search for the Green Knight's Chapel. Gawain rides through North Wales, past Anglesey and 'the wilderness of the Wirral'. Gawain's sense of dread grows as his encounter with the Green Knight draws nearer. On Christmas Day, Gawain finds a castle and is met by its lord, his lady and a mysterious old woman. The lord of the castle tells Gawain that each day he will ride out to hunt and each night he will trade his quarry for whatever Gawain has won that day in the castle.

On the first day, the lord hunts a herd of deer as Gawain sleeps in his bed. That morning, his wife enters Gawain's bedchamber. She tries to seduce him, but he courteously fends her off. She gives Gawain a single kiss. That night, the lord exchanges his winnings with Gawain, receiving a kiss. On the second day, as the lord hunts a savage wild boar, his lady again pursues Gawain. She kisses him twice, and that night he is given the boar's head in exchange for the two kisses he has won. The third morning dawns, and the lord hunts a wily fox. The lady gives Gawain three kisses and persuades him to take a magical green silk girdle that will protect him from death. That night, Gawain gives his host three kisses in exchange for the fox's skin but fails to mention the green girdle.

The next morning is New Year's Day, and Gawain rides out to

meet his fate at the hands of the Green Knight. Sir Gawain finds the mysterious Green Chapel, and the Green Knight appears bearing his axe. Twice, Gawain prepares to take the blow but flinches when the Green Knight is about to strike. At the third stroke, the Green Knight draws blood, making a small cut in Gawain's neck. Gawain leaps up, angrily insisting that the challenge is now met. The Green Knight laughs at the indignant Gawain and reveals that he is actually Bertilak de Hautdesert, the lord of the castle where Gawain had stayed. Bertilak was transformed into the Green Knight by an enchantment conjured by Morgan le Fay. He had drawn blood with his third blow because Gawain had failed to reveal the green silk girdle that the lady of the castle had given to him. Morgan had appeared in the castle disguised as the old woman. Lord Bertilak calls her 'Morgan the Goddess'.

Sir Gawain takes his leave and rides back to Camelot relieved to have survived but overwhelmed by guilt. Gawain tells the court of his adventures in the castle of Lord Bertilak and his encounter with the Green Knight. He decides to wear the green girdle as a mark of his cowardice. Arthur comforts Gawain, the court laughs in wonder at the tale and the Knights of the Round Table agree that they will all wear a girdle of bright green from that day forth.

In one passage of *Sir Gawain and the Green Knight*, the poet tells us that Gawain's shield is emblazoned with a pentangle, a five-pointed star. The poet explains that the pentangle reminded Gawain of the perfection of his five faultless senses, his five unfailing fingers, the five wounds of Christ, the five joys of Mary in her child and the five courtly virtues of frankness, fellowship, cleanness, courtesy and compassion. The Gawain poet's masterpiece ends at exactly 2525 lines long, with an additional five lines and the words 'Hony soyt qui mal pence', 'Shame to him who thinks ill of it', the motto of the Most Noble Order of the Garter.

The chronicler Jean Froissart (c.1337–1410) tells us that King Edward III of England 'took pleasure to new re-edify the Castle of Windsor, the which was begun by King Arthur, and there first began the Table Round, whereby sprang the fame of so many noble knights . . . King Edward determined to make an Order . . . to be called Knights of the Blue Garter'.

One of the most popular medieval tales of Sir Gawain concerned his marriage to the 'loathly lady'. In *The Weddynge of Sir Gawen and Dame Ragnell* and the ballad 'The Marriage of Sir Gawaine', the knight makes a promise to marry a hideously ugly hag.

The story begins as King Arthur is out hunting in Inglewood Forest.

A knight named Gromer Somer Joure threatens to behead Arthur if he cannot find out 'what women love best in field and town'. Sir Gawain asks every man and woman what women desire most, filling a great book with the answers. In the woods, King Arthur is met by a lady, 'as ungoodly a creature as ever man saw'. Her face is red and her nose full of snot, her hair matted and her mouth wide and crammed with yellow teeth. She has a hump on her back and giant, bleary eyes. She warns Arthur that the answer he seeks is not in Gawain's book, saying, 'If I help thee not, thou art but dead.' She asks for one thing in return: Arthur must grant her a knight to wed – Sir Gawain. The hag's name is Dame Ragnelle.

Arthur tells Gawain he has met the foulest lady he ever saw and that she will save his life if Gawain will marry her. 'Is that all?' says Sir Gawain. 'I shall wed her and wed her again, though she were a fiend.' Dame Ragnelle then tells Arthur that above all things women desire to have sovereignty – the right to rule their own lives. Arthur's life is saved, but Gawain must wed the loathly lady. On their wedding night, in their bedchamber, Gawain acts with the utmost courtesy. His bride asks for a kiss and when Gawain turns to her he is faced with the fairest creature he ever saw. 'A, Jhesu!' he says, 'Whate ar ye?' The fair Dame Ragnelle tells Gawain that her beauty will not last. He must choose if she will be fair each night and foul each day, or else fair during the day and foul at night. Sir Gawain gives the choice to Dame Ragnelle.

'Garamercy, courteous Knyght,' says the lady. 'Of all earthly knights blessed may thou be. For now am I worshipped thou shall have me fair both day and night.' Dame Ragnelle explains that she was shaped by necromancy and that because Gawain has given her the sovereignty that women most desire, the enchantment is broken.

A loathly lady famously appears in Geoffrey Chaucer's *The Wife of Bath's Tale,* and the character also appears in the Grail romances of Chrétien de Troyes and Wolfram von Eschenbach. Goddesses and supernatural faerie women often have the magical ability to shape-shift; take, for example, Morgan le Fay in *Sir Gawain and the Green Knight* and the Queen of Elfland who seduced Thomas the Rhymer under the Eildon Tree. In the Irish tale 'The Adventures of the Sons of Eochaid Mugmedon', a loathsome hag is the Sovereignty of Erin, and when Niall of the Nine Hostages kisses her she gives him the kingship of all Ireland.

In Heinrich von dem Türlin's thirteenth-century Grail romance *Diu Krône* (The Crown), Gawain meets a goddess who tells him how to achieve the Grail, warning him not to eat or drink in the castle of the Grail. The courteous lord of the castle offers wine to Gawain and his companions Lanzelet and Kalocreant. Gawain does not drink, but Lanzelet and Kalocreant take the wine and fall into a deep sleep. A procession enters the hall, with two fair and graceful maidens bearing candlesticks and two youths carrying a sharp spear. Then two maidens bring a salver of gold and precious stones upon a silken cloth. Behind them, treading softly, is the fairest woman all in the world, wearing a crown of gold. She carries a reliquary of gold and gems on a rich cloth of samite, and at the reliquary's base is a jewel wrought of red gold.

As Gawain watches, the spear sheds three drops of blood. He recognises the maiden with the crown as the goddess. He can no longer contain himself, saying, 'I pray for the sake of God, and by His Majesty, that you tell me what is the meaning of this great company, and of these marvels I behold?' As Gawain speaks, all the knights and ladies of the castle leap from their seats with a great cry and rejoice. The reliquary is the Grail, and Gawain has freed the company and healed the land by asking the question.

In the *Alliterative Morte Arthure*, it is said that Sir Gawain was unmatched on earth:

> He was Gawain the good, most gracious of men,
> And the greatest of knights who lived under God,
> The man boldest of hand, most blessed in battle,
> And the humblest in hall under all the wide heavens;
> In leadership the lordliest as long as he lived,
> And lauded as a lion in lands far and wide;
> Had you known him, sir king, in the country he came from,
> His wisdom, his valour, his virtuous works,
> His conduct, his courage, his exploits in arms,
> You would weep for his death all the days of your life.

Sir Thomas Malory tells us that when Gawain lay dying Arthur was overcome with sorrow, saying: 'Alas, Sir Gawaine, my sister's son, here now thou liest; the man in the world that I loved most; and now is my joy gone.' William of Malmesbury writes that the sepulchre of Walwin (Gawain) was found in Wales, on the coast, in the province of Ros. His grave was 14 ft long. A fifteenth-century manuscript simply known as *Arthur* states that Arthur sent the body of Gawain to Scotland, where it was buried. According to Malory, in his time Gawain's skull was still kept in Dover Castle.

Gawain appears in a Gaelic song collected in the Western Isles of Scotland by Alexander Carmichael. Two versions of 'The Sweet Sorrow' are included in *Carmina Gadelica*. In one version, collected in 1865 from a South Uist crofter named John MacLeod, Sir Gawain is lured to his death by a fair maiden. King Arthur dreams of a beautiful young maiden and Gawain offers to search for her:

> Then spoke Sir Gawain right generously,
> 'I shall go myself to seek her for thee,
> Myself, my lad and my hound,
> The three of us the woman to seek.'
>
> Seven weeks and three months
> I was weary traversing the sea
> Ere harbour or land was won
> Or a place where the ship might lie.
>
> Nearing the edge of the rough sea
> A smooth azure castle was seen;
> It had windows of glass facing the waves,
> And plenteous there were cups and horns . . .
>
> The young white-coiffed lady was seen
> On a chair of gold within,
> A carpet of silk beneath her soles;
> I greeted her fair face . . .
>
> A harp there was in the lap of the fair young damsel,
> Of bluest eye and whitest teeth,
> And sweetly though she played the harp,
> Sweeter than that the song from her lips.
>
> He fell into a deep sleep
> After voyaging on the rough sea . . .
>
> She took the sharp sword from his baldric,
> And she swept off his head by stealth;
> That is the end of my tale
> And how the Sweet Sorrow is sung.

SEE ALSO: Cinema and Theatre; Faeries; Grail Maiden; Holy Grail; Mordred; Morgan le Fay; Scotland

GEOFFREY OF MONMOUTH

Geoffrey of Monmouth was a monk, probably Welsh or possibly Breton, said to have been born in Monmouthshire, Wales. Geoffrey sited the legendary court of King Arthur in the old Roman town of Caerleon, quite near to his birthplace, and he often refers to local places such as Llandaff. It is likely that for over 20 years he lived in or near Oxford, which was at that time a magnet for men of ideas and letters, and during the last four years of his life he probably lived in London. Geoffrey rose in the Church hierarchy. From Archdeacon in 1140, he became Bishop-Elect of St Asaph (now in Flintshire, Wales) in 1151, despite not actually having been ordained as a priest. His ordination took place in 1152, and he was consecrated Bishop in London the following week. This was the period of the wars between King Stephen and the Empress Matilda over the succession to the English throne. It was a lawless time when no one in England, or much of Wales, was safe. The Welsh leader, Owain Gwynedd, had raised his banner and taken up arms, so Geoffrey may never have been able to visit his diocese. Geoffrey's name appears among the witnesses to the Treaty of Westminster, agreed in 1153 between Henry, son of the Empress, and King Stephen.

Geoffrey's work inspired later writers such as Wace and, more indirectly, Layamon. His great work, *Historia Regum Britanniae*, the *History of the Kings of Britain* (completed around 1135–7), survives in more than two hundred manuscripts, a tribute to its popularity in view of the time each copy took to create. Before the year 1200,

Geoffrey's *History* was being read across Europe and as far afield as the Byzantine Empire.

While Geoffrey called his book a history, he incorporated numerous legends and inventions. This was not, however, atypical of writers in the Middle Ages or in the ancient world. What Geoffrey appears to have done, with great success, is to have made a compilation of tales and legends already in existence that purports to be an account of people and events of earlier times in Britain. He claimed that his writing, in Latin, the lingua franca of literary Europe at that time, was at least in part derived from an old book in 'the British language', which can be assumed to be early Welsh. There has been much controversy over what this book might have been or if it ever existed. Most of the *History* delves into the legends of the origins of Britain, from Brut, after whom the land was named, who was supposed to have been descended from the Trojan Aeneas, to King Lear, the fight against the Romans, Julius Caesar and the coming of the Saxons. Geoffrey's magic ingredients, however, were King Arthur and Merlin, and the Arthurian material comprises about 20 per cent of the *History*.

Geoffrey's Merlin is a combination of two seers, the Myrddin of Welsh poems and Merlin Ambrosius, or Myrddin Emrys, who featured in the ninth-century chronicler Nennius's *Historia Brittonum*. Geoffrey wrote, in verse, his *Vita Merlini*, or *Life of Merlin*, around 1150. The portion of the *History of the Kings of Britain* devoted to the Arthurian legends includes Arthur's heroic deeds as a giant-killer, a warrior and a ruler.

Around 1190, William of Newburgh wrote waspishly about Geoffrey's *History*:

> It is quite clear that everything this man wrote about Arthur and his successors, or indeed about his predecessors from Vortigern onwards, was made up, partly by himself and partly by others, either from an inordinate love of lying, or for the sake of pleasing the Britons.

This seems a rather unsympathetic view, particularly as Geoffrey is believed to have died in around 1155 and so was no longer able to defend himself. Yet what can we make of his work? Geoffrey tells us about Brutus, descended from the survivors of Troy, coming to Britain, for which we have no evidence, and he includes an account of Britons sacking the city of Rome, which certainly never happened; the Roman Lucius Tiberius is not a genuine historical figure. Geoffrey's

King Arthur is an idealised monarch of the writer's own period rather than the warrior Arthur, the leader of battles, described by Nennius. William of Newburgh is justified in being highly sceptical since the *History* is a romantic piece, at best semi-fictional, and by no means history as we know it, or as he knew it ought to be.

The chronicler and churchman Gerald of Wales (*c*.1146–*c*.1223) was also highly critical of Geoffrey's *History*. In his *Journey through Wales*, Gerald tells us of a Welshman who was plagued by unclean spirits. When St John's Gospel was placed on his lap, the demonic spirits immediately vanished, 'flying away like so many birds'; however, if the Gospel was removed and Geoffrey of Monmouth's *History of the Kings of Britain* put in its place, the demons would alight all over his body, and on Geoffrey's book, too, staying longer than usual and being even more demanding.

Geoffrey is clever enough to give his stories a veneer of credibility by asserting that they happened at the same time as events in other lands. For instance, he would refer to contemporaneous happenings in the Old Testament or the Ancient Roman world. Since the well-worn tales from antiquity were accepted as fact, the chronicler's dubious stories acquired a false authenticity by association. Geoffrey was undoubtedly well read, and this enabled him to mention other historians and their themes from time to time. In his preface to *Wace and Layamon: Arthurian Chronicles*, Gwyn Jones wrote: 'The literary history of the Arthurian legend in the twelfth century is distinguished by Geoffrey's flair for exploiting an opportunity and Chrétien's ability to enrich and enhance it.'

Geoffrey's greatest gift to literature, despite whatever reservations we might have about his honesty and veracity, was the ability to inspire later generations of writers to follow him in telling and retelling the story of Arthur. Without Geoffrey's *History*, Wace, Layamon, Chrétien de Troyes, Wolfram von Eschenbach and Sir Thomas Malory might have turned to other subjects and the stories of King Arthur might never have been told.

SEE ALSO: Chrétien de Troyes; Layamon; Merlin; Wace; Wales

GLASTONBURY

Amid the patchwork fields and gentle green hills of Somerset lies Glastonbury, a small English market town believed by many to be the legendary Isle of Avalon. Glastonbury is said to be the final resting place of King Arthur, Guinevere and the Holy Grail.

Glastonbury has been associated with King Arthur since Caradog of Llancarfan wrote his *Life of Gildas*, between 1130 and 1150. Caradog tells us that King Melwas, who reigned in the 'Summer Country' (Somerset), had violated and carried off Arthur's wife Gwenhwyfar. Melwas took the queen to his stronghold at Glastonia, 'the glassy city', amid thickets of reed, river and marsh. Arthur brought an army from Cornwall and besieged Glastonia. The abbot of Glastonia and Gildas the Wise negotiated a peace between the two kings. Gwenhwyfar was returned, and Arthur and Melwas visited the temple of St Mary to pray. From this small acorn the Glastonbury legends have grown and flourished.

Every year, thousands of believers, pagans and pilgrims travel across England to Glastonbury in search of the mystical Vale of Avalon, the Grail, the Goddess and the magic of the Arthurian legends. Glastonbury seems to be a place caught between two worlds: a twenty-first-century town where the locals live and work as in any rural community; and a spiritual haven where new-age practitioners and seekers rub shoulders with tourists in vegan cafés and alternative bookshops. The shops will sell you amethyst crystals, Gregorian wind chimes and aromatherapy oils, Tibetan singing bowls, dream catchers and environmentally friendly candles. You will find books on goddess spirituality, organic gardening, Froudian faeries, chakra healing and ancient earth mysteries.

In the midst of the town lie the ruins of Glastonbury Abbey, like giant broken gravestones. The Glastonbury legends say that Joseph of Arimathea built the first-ever Christian church in all of Britain on the site of the abbey's Lady Chapel. It is said that Joseph left the Holy Land and travelled to France with a group of companions that included Mary Magdalene, Lazarus, Mary and Martha of Bethany and their maid, Marcella. Joseph then sailed on to Britain. In those days, Glastonbury Tor was not just a hill but an island set amid lakes and marshes. Joseph's boat made land at nearby Wearyall Hill. There he rested and planted his staff in the ground. Miraculously, it took root, and twigs, leaves and flowers appeared as it grew into a thorntree. This was the origin of the Glastonbury Holy Thorn.

The Glastonbury Thorn blooms twice a year, at Easter and Christmas. For over a thousand years the plant flourished, until Cromwell's troops cut it down and burned it during the English Civil War. A new thorn was grown from a cutting, and today the descendants of the original Holy Thorn can be found on Wearyall Hill and in the grounds of Glastonbury Abbey. There are two more Holy Thorns in the grounds of St John's Parish Church in the village, and cuttings have been sent around the world, from the United States to Australia. Every Christmas, a sprig of the Glastonbury Thorn is cut and sent to the reigning British monarch. Queen Elizabeth II returned the favour in 1965 when she had a wooden cross erected in Glastonbury bearing the inscription: 'The cross. The symbol of our faith. The gift of Queen Elizabeth II marks a Christian sanctuary so ancient that only legend can record its origin.'

Joseph, it is said, built a simple wattle-and-daub church in the shadow of the Tor. Some versions of the legend tell that Jesus himself, the son of a carpenter, helped to build 'the Old Church', as it became known. John of Glastonbury's fourteenth-century *Chronicle* states that Joseph brought two cruets, or vessels, to Glastonbury from the Holy Land. These cruets were sacred relics of the Passion: one held the blood of Christ, the other his sweat. When Joseph finally died, it is said, he was buried in secret with the two cruets. Included in the *Chronicle* is a prophecy attributed to a fifth-century seer named Melkin, thought to point to the burial place of Joseph. In the sixteenth century, it was claimed that the original manuscript of Melkin's prophecy was still in the library of Glastonbury Abbey. The prophecy stated that Joseph of Arimathea lay in perpetual sleep in a marble tomb, on a forked line by the south corner of the wattle oratory. In Joseph's sarcophagus, according to Melkin, were the two cruets, white and silver, 'filled with blood and sweat of the Prophet Jesus'. The two vessels buried with Joseph may be an echo of the body, blood and sweat of Christ wrapped in linen and buried in the tomb of Joseph in the Holy Land.

Alternatively, they may be an origin legend for the two natural springs at the foot of Glastonbury Tor: the sweat of Christ during the Passion would be the clear waters of the White Spring and the blood of Christ would be the red waters of the Chalice Well. Another version of the legend tells that Joseph hid the Holy Grail at the Chalice Well. The natural spring waters taste like blood, turn anything they touch a bright orange and are reputed to have healing powers. The Chalice Well is also called 'the Red Spring' and 'the Blood Spring'. The red waters of the spring are said to symbolise the blood of Christ that was miraculously preserved in the Grail or on the iron nails of the Crucifixion. The well cover is made of English oak, decorated with the sacred geometric symbol of the vesica piscis and the legendary bleeding lance in wrought iron.

In the tenth century, Dunstan, the Abbot of Glastonbury and later Archbishop of Canterbury, had the church at Glastonbury enlarged. The Domesday Book records that the Abbey's lands stretched across five counties. But in 1184, Glastonbury Abbey was devastated by a fire that gutted the Old Church and destroyed many precious relics. Holy relics attracted pilgrims from near and far, bringing money and prestige to the abbey, so their loss was a terrible blow. Luckily for the Glastonbury monks, King Henry II sent a message telling them that the remains of the famed King Arthur and Queen Guinevere were buried in the abbey grounds. It was claimed that Henry had been told by a Welsh bard that the royal couple would be found buried deep in the churchyard between two stone pyramids.

Dutifully, the monks erected a pavilion between the two pyramids and began to dig. They unearthed a tomb that held the bones of Arthur and Guinevere and a tress of golden hair, plaited and coiled with consummate skill. The bones were found within a hollow oak, with an inscribed lead cross as a grave marker, which read: 'Hic Iacet Sepultus Inclitus Rex Arturius In Insula Avalonia' ('Here lies buried the renowned King Arthur in the Isle of Avalon').

The monks' discovery, in early winter 1191, ensured the survival and restoration of Glastonbury Abbey. Miraculously, a host of precious relics were found at this time, turning Glastonbury into a centre of medieval pilgrimage, a 'second Rome'. At Easter 1278, King Edward I and Queen Eleanor made a pilgrimage to Glastonbury. With all the ritual and reverence normally reserved for a saint's relics, Arthur's bones were wrapped in a precious cloth and placed by King Edward in a chest marked with the royal seal. Eleanor did the same with Guinevere's remains. The skulls and knee joints were kept out for the devotion of the people. King Edward had a vast black-marble tomb carved for Arthur and Guinevere, sculpted with lions and an image of King Arthur, which was set before the high altar in Glastonbury Abbey.

Medieval monks, however, were accomplished fraudsters. The discovery of Arthur's grave was massively profitable for Glastonbury Abbey at a time when it needed to make up the revenue it had lost as a result of the fire. It was also an act of propaganda. King Henry II and King Edward I were both troubled by Welsh rebels. The Welsh believed that Arthur was still alive and that he would return to lead them against their enemies. Henry II was said to have provided proof that Arthur was dead and buried. Edward I reinforced this message with the royal ceremony and the immense black marble tomb.

The grave marker was supposed to 'prove' that the bones were those of King Arthur and Guinevere. In fact, the real Arthur would never have been known as 'Rex Arturius', 'King Arthur', as he was not a king. The lead cross was a medieval forgery. The discovery of King Arthur and Guinevere's grave at Glastonbury was an ingenious and highly successful fraud. Henry II had in fact died two years before the monks dug Arthur's bones. Richard the Lionheart was King of England at the time of the discovery, and he was far too interested in crusading to worry about the troubles of Glastonbury's monks. In the centuries that followed, the abbey displayed a crystal cross given to King Arthur by none other than the Virgin Mary. It was also claimed that Arthur's sword Excalibur was thrown to the Lady of the Lake from Glastonbury's Pomparles Bridge, the 'Perilous Bridge' of Arthurian legend.

The story of Arthur and Guinevere's grave at Glastonbury began with one King Henry and ended with another. The tomb was destroyed when the abbey was attacked during the dissolution of the monasteries under Henry VIII. The bones of Arthur and Guinevere were lost, but the lead cross survived and was last seen in the eighteenth century.

Once King Arthur was brought to Glastonbury Abbey, the Holy Grail and Joseph of Arimathea soon followed. In 1130, the cleric

William of Malmesbury wrote *De Antiquitate Glastontensis Ecclesiae, On the Antiquities of the Church of Glastonbury*. He made no mention of Joseph or Avalon. By the middle of the next century, the monks of Glastonbury had rewritten William's *Antiquitate*, adding Joseph of Arimathea, the early church built at Glastonbury and the Isle of Avalon.

In 1906, the Glastonbury Cup, thought by some to be the Holy Grail, was discovered at the Well of St Bride by Bride's Mound. The site is said to have been named for St Bridget, who had visited Glastonbury in the fifth century and prayed there in an oratory dedicated to Mary Magdalene. The Glastonbury Cup was found by two sisters, Christine and Janet Allen, and later retrieved by Catherine 'Kitty' Tudor Pole. It was a mysterious blue-glass bowl hidden in the waters under a thorntree, full of ribbons and rags. The blue bowl was carefully cleaned and taken to Clifton, Bristol, where an oratory was created for the cup, with candles, white drapes and an altar. Christine, Janet and Kitty became a triad of Grail maidens who officiated at sacred ceremonies, including baptisms and marriages. Kitty's brother, Wellesley Tudor Pole, would write in 1907: 'All three have been preparing the Way for the Coming of the Holy Graal . . . Their efforts resulted in the bringing of the Holy Cup, encrusted with mud, to the surface of a certain Holy Well.'

According to Wellesley, his sister had been sent to Glastonbury 'to bring back the Holy Grail for a shrine prepared for It'. He claimed that the cup was not found by accident but revealed to him after years of pilgrimages and psychic visions. As the sisters went to Bride's Well, Christine had a vision of an old pilgrim with a staff walking before them. Janet wrote of her 'awed feeling of responsibility' when she realised the vessel was the Holy Grail. In the Oratory, visions of a white dove and a beautiful angel appeared about the cup.

Scholars, clerics, occultists and clairvoyants examined the blue bowl. Experts were at a loss to explain its origins, saying simply that it was 'ancient'. Wellesley took the cup to the home of Archdeacon Basil Wilberforce, Canon of Westminster, where the American author Mark Twain saw it while visiting London. Wellesley and Wilberforce were convinced that the cup was the Holy Grail. Twain was moved to write:

> I am glad I have lived to see that half-hour – that astonishing half-hour. In its way it stands alone in my life's experience. In the belief of two persons present this was the very vessel

which was brought by night and secretly delivered to
Nicodemus . . . the very cup which the stainless Sir Galahad
had sought with knightly devotion in far fields of peril and
adventure in Arthur's time.

The cup became a sensation when Archdeacon Wilberforce revealed
its existence to a gathering of dignitaries on 20 July 1907. Newspaper
articles trumpeted the appearance of the mysterious relic believed to
be the Holy Grail. The cup returned to the Oratory and in time the
media circus died down. The 'Grail maiden' Christine Allen would
marry the Scottish Celtic-Revival artist John Duncan. Janet Allen
became a Benedictine nun, a Bride of Christ named Sister Brigid.
Kitty Tudor Pole kept the cup in a wooden box under her bed.

All, however, was not quite as it seemed. The Glastonbury Cup
was bought from a tailor's shop in the town of Bordighera in Italy
in the 1890s by a Dr John Arthur Goodchild. It is a mosaic of silver
leaf and blue, green and reddish-brown glass with flower designs.
It has never been dated conclusively. In 1897, Dr Goodchild was
staying in the Hotel St Petersbourg in Paris when he had a powerful
psychic experience; a voice told him that the bowl was the Holy
Grail, the vessel that Christ had once carried. He was to take the
cup to Glastonbury and hide it at Bride's Well. The following year,
Goodchild hid the blue-glass bowl under a stone in the muddy pool,
into which rainwater ran from the fields. For eight years, the bowl lay
in the pool until, in 1906, Christine and Janet Allen found it. It later
emerged that Dr Goodchild knew Wellesley Tudor Pole and that the
Allen sisters were friends of Wellesley and Kitty. Wellesley had told
the Allen sisters of a psychic vision he had had of the cup, and had
told them to search the murky pool at Bride's Well.

In 1959, Wellesley Tudor Pole founded the Chalice Well Trust.
He died in 1968, while Kitty died at the great age of 104. Her ashes
were scattered in the Chalice Well garden, and the Glastonbury Cup
is now in the care of the Trust. Today, the Chalice Well gardens are a
sanctuary, a holy place for quiet contemplation, healing and harmony.
The gardens are full of flowers, sacred symbols and sculptures; there
are wizened yew trees, one of Glastonbury's Holy Thorns and an old
apple tree. Visitors can drink the waters of the Chalice Well.

The remains of a 2000-year-old yew tree have been uncovered by
archaeologists near the Chalice Well. Two ancient trees, the Oaks of
Avalon, named Gog and Magog, lie in the shadow of Glastonbury
Tor. Excavations near Bride's Well have revealed neolithic stone tools,
Iron Age pottery, Roman coins, post holes from early wattle-and-

daub buildings and a Saxon chapel. No matter what the truth of the legends surrounding the town is, it is beyond doubt that the magical landscape of Glastonbury has been a sacred site for thousands of years, during which its legends have inspired poets, pilgrims and artists.

SEE ALSO: Arthur, King of the Britons; Guinevere; Holy Grail; Joseph of Arimathea

GRAIL MAIDEN

In Chrétien de Troyes' *Perceval, or the Story of the Grail*, as Perceval sits in the Fisher King's castle he sees the mysterious procession of the Grail. Three handsome young men walk by bearing two golden candlesticks and a lance that drips blood. The youths are followed by a maiden who bears a Grail and a damsel who carries a silver carving-dish. When the Grail maiden enters the hall, the whole room is brightly illuminated, as though lit by the sun and the moon. Chrétien does not tell us the name of the maiden who bears the holy vessel. It is possible that the radiance that illuminates the Fisher King's castle as the Grail is carried into the hall comes not from the Grail itself but from the maiden who carries it. In *Cligès*, one of Chrétien's earlier Arthurian romances, a maiden who hurries into a great hall with her head and face uncovered lights the room with 'the radiance of her beauty'.

Just as the nature of the Grail differs in the various medieval Grail romances, so the name and the story of the Grail maiden changes. In Wolfram von Eschenbach's *Parzifal*, only a virgin maiden can bear the Grail. Parzival's mother, Herzeloyde, is the sister of the Grail King Anfortas, and it is Parzifal's aunt, Repanse de Schoye, who bears the Grail. At the end of the poem, Repanse de Schoye (whose name translates as 'spreading of joy') is married to Parzifal's Muslim brother Feirefîz, who converts to Christianity. Feirefîz and Repanse then have a son, Prester John.

In some of the romances, the Grail maiden is Elaine of Corbenic, daughter of the Fisher King Pelles. Elaine of Corbenic, the Grail maiden, is often confused with Elaine of Astolat, the Lady of Shalott. The story of the Lady of Shalott's tragic love for Sir Lancelot was immortalised by Alfred, Lord Tennyson and the Pre-Raphaelite artists. Both Elaine of Astolat and Elaine of Corbenic fell in love with Sir Lancelot, but he failed to return their affections. The Lady of Shalott died of a broken heart and was placed in a boat to drift downriver to Camelot. Elaine of Corbenic lived, so her story lacked the tragic element that appealed to the Pre-Raphaelites.

When Elaine of Corbenic fell in love with Sir Lancelot, her father took the practical step of having a sorceress disguise her in the likeness of Lancelot's beloved Queen Guinevere so that Elaine could spend a night in the arms of the knight. The next morning, when Lancelot learned of her trickery, he grew enraged and drew his sword. Elaine pleaded with Lancelot, telling him that she now bore their child. Lancelot refused to return Elaine's love, abandoned her and rode away. Elaine and Lancelot's son, Sir Galahad, was destined to become the pure, perfect knight who would achieve the Holy Grail.

Malory tells us that after Galahad's birth Sir Bors meets King Pelles and his daughter Elaine at Corbin, the Grail castle which Bors names 'the Castle Adventurous'. Bors tells Elaine that Sir Lancelot has been held in prison for half a year by Queen Morgan le Fay. He sees the child in her arms, Sir Lancelot's son, and, as Bors weeps for joy, a white dove bearing a little censer of gold appears. The Grail maiden bears the Sangreal and says, 'This child is Galahad, that shall sit in the Siege Perilous, and achieve the Sangreal, and he shall be much better than ever was Sir Lancelot du Lake, that is his own father.'

Dante Gabriel Rossetti was commissioned by William Morris to paint a watercolour *The Damsel of the Sanct Grael* in 1856. Rossetti's Grail maiden, who has bright auburn hair and an emerald green gown, holds a gold chalice brimming with dark red blood. She carries a basket full of bread and raises her hand in blessing. A white dove appears above her head, illuminated by a golden halo and carrying a little censer in its beak, as in *Le Morte d'Arthur*.

It has been suggested that the Holy Grail is in fact a symbol of the sacred feminine, that the Grail is feminine as the lance, spear or sword blade is masculine. In the late twentieth century, a theory arose that the Holy Grail itself was in reality a woman – Mary Magdalene. In their book *The Holy Blood and the Holy Grail*, published in 1982, three writers and researchers, Michael Baigent, Richard Leigh and Henry Lincoln, suggested that Mary Magdalene had married Jesus and was the real Holy Grail, as she bore the child of Christ in her womb. This bloodline theory was taken up by a series of writers and in 2003 found its way into Dan Brown's novel *The Da Vinci Code*. The incredible popular success of Brown's novel brought the Magdalene Grail theory to tens of millions of readers and led to an unprecedented backlash from theologians, academic historians and even the Vatican. Although there is virtually no evidence to support the theory that Mary Magdalene was secretly the Holy Grail of medieval romance, the idea now seems firmly embedded in the popular imagination.

The Holy Grail has more usually been depicted as a platter, a dish, a chalice or a stone, but notions of the sacred feminine have never been far away. In the Welsh poem *The Spoils of Annwn*, a magical cauldron is warmed by the breath of nine virgins. According to legend, nine enchantresses, renowned for their knowledge of the healing arts, live on the magical Isle of Avalon. It may be significant that in the pagan religions of the British Isles there were priestesses as well as priests. The historian Tacitus records in his *Annals* that when the Romans invaded Britain, they met resistance led by the druids and marched on the druid stronghold at Mona (the ancient name of the Isle of Anglesey, Wales). As the Romans watched from the far shore, they saw dark druid priestesses running amongst the pagan warriors. The priestesses were dressed in black; their hair was wild, and they ran screeching, bearing fiery torches. Their appearance terrified the Roman soldiers, who thought they were the legendary Furies. When the Romans landed on the Isle of Mona, they slaughtered everyone, man and woman alike, and burned the sacred groves of the druids. There are stone circles, islands and sacred wells associated with a cult of nine maidens across Europe.

The figures of Ecclesia and Synagoga were symbolic figures in medieval Christian art. They appear carved in stone on the western façade of Notre Dame de Paris. Synagoga represented Judaism: blindfolded, her staff broken and her crown fallen to the ground by her feet, she bears witness to medieval anti-Semitism. Ecclesia represented the Church, a fair maiden with a crown, a halo, a banner and a chalice. The Church is feminine, Mater Ecclesia, the bride of Christ. She appears in medieval art as a maiden at the Cross catching the blood of Christ in a chalice. Depictions of the Crucifixion from the Carolingian period (seventh to ninth centuries) onwards show a variety of figures at the foot of the Cross: Longinus pierces the side of Christ with a lance; a Roman soldier holds a branch with a sponge soaked in vinegar; St John, the Virgin and Mary Magdalene bear witness; and Ecclesia collects Christ's blood in a chalice as it flows from the wound in his side. 'The chalice at the Cross' also appears catching the blood of Christ unsupported or borne by angels. The images of Ecclesia bearing the chalice may have become a visual source for some of the Grail romances.

In *The Virgin and the Grail*, Professor Joseph Goering of the University of Toronto suggests that early-twelfth-century church paintings in the Spanish Pyrenees may be the origin of the Grail and the Grail maiden. A painting from the church of Sant Climent de Taüll shows the Virgin Mary, 'Sancta Maria', holding a shallow, radiant vessel. The Catalan images of the Virgin with the radiant dish may have travelled north through France in poetry to influence, eventually, Chrétien de Troyes. The Sant Climent frescos are on display in the Museu Nacional d'Art de Catalunya in Barcelona.

In Chrétien's *Story of the Grail*, the Grail contains a sacred Mass wafer that miraculously sustains life. It is worth noting that in the Middle Ages, when the Grail romances were composed, only men were allowed to carry the consecrated Mass wafer. In the chapels, churches and cathedrals of medieval Europe, it was male clergy who bore the chalices of communion wine, carried the paten, touched the ciborium that held the mass wafers and led the Catholic mass. Women were entitled to carry such vessels only for sickbed communion services. Yet in the Arthurian romances, the Grail containing the sacred Host is borne by a pure maiden.

SEE ALSO: Fisher King; Galahad; Holy Grail; Lady of the Lake; Lancelot; Mary Magdalene; Percival; Pre-Raphaelites; Sacred Feminine; Tennyson, Alfred, Lord; Wolfram von Eschenbach

GUINEVERE

As the wife and queen of King Arthur, Guinevere is one of the most significant characters in the Arthurian myth cycle. Her dramatic and far-reaching love affair with the knight Sir Lancelot has become a central theme of Arthurian romances, poems, novels and films.

Guinevere appears in *Historia Regum Britanniae, The History of the Kings of Britain*, written around 1136 by Geoffrey of Monmouth. From this early mention, Guinevere's character and history develop and change, though not always consistently, with authors adopting and adapting various attributes and events from earlier tales whilst omitting others. In Geoffrey's *History*, for example, Guinevere is called Guenhumare. She is a noblewoman of Roman blood, renowned for her great beauty, whereas in Welsh tradition she is King Ogrfan Gawr's daughter. Gwenhwyfar, the Welsh rendering of Guinevere's name, can be translated as 'white ghost' or 'white faerie'. In the Welsh Triads, all three of Arthur's Great Queens are named Gwenhwyfar, and it is said that Gwenhwyfar is more faithless than the Three Faithless Wives of the Island of Britain.

By the thirteenth century, Guinevere is the daughter of King Leodegrance. This is first mentioned in the Vulgate *Estoire de Merlin* (*c*.1215–35), and again in later adaptations such as Malory's *Le Morte d'Arthur* (*c*.1470), where King Arthur first meets Guinevere at a banquet given by her father in gratitude to Arthur for helping to defeat King Royns. By the time of *Le Morte d'Arthur*, Guinevere had become the beautiful and glorious queen of the finest medieval court in Europe.

Guinevere's romance with Sir Lancelot also develops throughout Arthurian literature. Although Chrétien de Troyes' late-twelfth-century *Lancelot, or the Knight of the Cart* does not mention an affair, it does reveal that Lancelot was besotted with his queen and highlights a brief liaison: namely, one incident when the couple make love after Lancelot rescues Guinevere. However, it is from this point that the romance becomes central to the Arthurian tales, with the notable exception of Ulrich von Zatzikhoven's *Lanzelet* (*c*.1195), which has no account of Guinevere's love affair with Lancelot. The Vulgate Cycle and Malory's *Le Morte d'Arthur* relate the couple's love affair and its dramatic consequences for all concerned.

The medieval depictions of the Guinevere–Lancelot romance reflect contemporary literary concepts of love and loyalty between knights and ladies. The knight was portrayed as subservient to his lady, willing to do anything for her and putting her needs before his own. These concepts are highlighted and parodied in Chrétien de Troyes' *The Knight of the Cart*. In this, Guinevere snubs Lancelot even after he has rescued her from Meleagant (just one of a number of abductions the queen has to endure) because she discovers that he had briefly paused before stepping into a cart that was going to help him find her. For a knight to travel in a humble cart was considered to be very undignified, hence an act of hesitation on Lancelot's part had shown Guinevere that for a fleeting moment Lancelot had considered his own pride and honour first, something a true lover would never have done.

In the Vulgate *Lancelot propre* (*c*.1220s) the affair is considered acceptable, even being condoned by the Lady of the Lake, who tells Guinevere that it is right for her to love Lancelot. However, other Vulgate prose romances are not so tolerant, with the *Queste del Saint Graal* and *Morte Artu* making it clear that it is Guinevere's infidelity with Lancelot that causes the knight to fail in his quest for the Holy Grail. Indeed, *Morte Artu* directly blames the affair for the collapse of Arthur's kingdom. However, Malory's *Le Morte d'Arthur* indicates that there was no shame in the affair. In fact, Merlin comments to Arthur that Guinevere was destined to love Sir Lancelot, and he her, and that many disasters would result from their love. It is therefore assumed to be Guinevere's fate to be with Lancelot – the misfortunes that occur are not the result of the affair but happen because the couple are denied their true path. Malory describes their amour as 'true love' and writes with a sense of pity for a woman who falls in love with a man she is unable to marry, in stark contrast to other authors who have painted Guinevere as a seductress, placing all the world's ills at her feet.

It would appear from Malory's tale that Arthur was indulgent of his wife's affair due to his love for her and Lancelot and that love affairs were not unusual in the court of King Arthur. One story concerns a magic horn or cloak which reveals a person's infidelity. Both Arthur and Guinevere were shown by this device to have been unfaithful, as were all the other couples of the court – apart from an old knight and his young wife.

Guinevere's relationship with Mordred is interesting. In Monmouth's *History*, Guenhumare became the wife of Mordred (Arthur's nephew in Monmouth's account) after he took the throne from Arthur. Wace's poem *Roman de Brut*, Layamon's *Brut* and John Hardyng's *Chronicle* (c.1457) all state that Guinevere married Mordred after his usurpation of Arthur's throne. In Wace's and Layamon's accounts, Guinevere feels guilt at her treatment of Arthur and fear about his reaction, suggesting that she was a willing accessory to Mordred's disloyalty and betrayal. In contrast, in Hardyng's *Chronicle*, Guinevere is forced to marry Mordred, no doubt to legitimise his claim to the throne.

The abduction motif is a recurring theme in Arthurian literature and traditional tales. Caradog's *Life of Gildas* (early twelfth century) relates how Guinevere was abducted by King Melwas of Somerset and held captive for a year until Arthur eventually found her, her release being negotiated by St Gildas. In Chrétien de Troyes' *The Knight of the Cart* it is Meleagant who abducts her, whereas the antagonist in Ulrich von Zatzikhoven's *Lanzelet* is Valerin, who abducts Guinevere twice, the second time putting her into a magical sleep. The abduction of Guinevere also appears in the earliest Arthurian sculpture, the archivolt of the Porta della Pescheria of Modena Cathedral, Italy.

In Malory's account, as in the majority of Arthurian tales, there is no mention of Guinevere having children, suggesting that she was barren. However, the anonymous narrative poem *Morte Arthure*, written around 1400, states that Guinevere had two sons by Mordred, while Welsh tradition relates that she had sons with King Arthur. According to *Le Morte d'Arthur*, when Mordred and Agravain expose Guinevere's infidelity with Lancelot to Arthur and the court, the king is forced to sentence Guinevere to be burnt at the stake. Half naked and waiting to be taken to the flames, Guinevere is rescued by the faithful Lancelot who takes her to live with him at his castle before eventually returning her to Arthur so she can take her place again as his queen. Guinevere finally finds redemption by leaving the material world for a religious life, entering Amesbury Abbey and living a blameless life in repentance of her past sins.

SEE ALSO: Chrétien de Troyes; Lancelot; Layamon; Malory, Sir Thomas; Mordred; Wace

HOLY GRAIL

The Holy Grail is a golden platter set with precious gems and pearls; it is the dish that Jesus used at the Last Supper, the cup in which Joseph of Arimathea caught the blood of Christ. The Grail is a magical stone that sustains life and provides food; it is the fabled Ark of the Covenant, the Turin Shroud, an emerald that fell from Lucifer's Crown, the treasure of the Cathars or the Templars. The grail is the chalice of the Eucharist, a stone fallen from the heavens, the Holy City of Jerusalem. It is the womb of Mary Magdalene, a holy bloodline descended from Christ, a flying saucer. The list is seemingly endless.

The Grail first appears in Chrétien de Troyes' *Perceval, ou le conte du graal* (*Perceval, or the Story of the Grail*). A young knight named Perceval is directed to a mysterious castle by a man fishing from a boat with a rod and line. Perceval is given shelter for the night and sits down on a couch to dine with his courteous host. The hall is brightly lit with many candles, and a fire blazes in the hearth. As Perceval sits on the couch, he bears witness to the Grail procession as it passes between him and the bright fire.

First, a youth enters the hall bearing a white lance tipped with a shining head. A drop of blood runs from the tip of the lance head down to the youth's hand. He is followed by two handsome youths who bear candlesticks of pure gold inlaid with black enamel. At least ten candles burn in each candelabrum. With the handsome youths comes a maiden bearing the Grail. As she enters the hall, the candles appear to lose their brilliance as the stars do when the sun or moon rises. The hall is illuminated by a radiant light. The Grail maiden is fair and beautifully adorned. The Grail itself is of pure refined gold, set with the richest and most costly precious stones on earth or in the sea. Behind the Grail maiden comes a second damsel, who holds a silver carving dish. Throughout the procession, Perceval says nothing. He has been advised to beware of talking too much, and so fails to ask who is served by the Grail. If Perceval had asked the question, he would have healed the wounded Fisher King.

In Chrétien's *Story of the Grail*, the grail is a platter, a serving dish for a medieval feast. It is also described as a 'holy thing'. A contemporary of Chrétien, the poet and Cistercian monk Hélinand of Froidmont commented on the story of the Grail, saying that: 'gradalis or gradale in French means a broad dish, not very deep, in which precious meats in their juice are customarily served to the rich . . . it is called "graalz" because men are grateful for it'. Hélinand says that these serving dishes were usually made of silver or some other precious material. The word 'graal' may have its origin in the Latin *gradale*, a dish or cup. Alternately 'graal' may have developed from *garalis*, a Roman dish that held a fish sauce. Clearly, Chrétien expected his audience to know that a grail was a serving platter that carried fish, as he specifically tells us that the Grail does not contain pike, lamprey or salmon but a single sacred Mass wafer.

Chrétien died before he completed *The Story of the Grail*, and a series of continuators took up the poem and shaped their own endings. The anonymous First Continuation tells of the adventures of Gawain. It is Gawain who visits the Grail castle, is tasked with mending a broken sword and learns the story of the bleeding lance. The Holy Grail miraculously feeds the company in the hall and moves through the air. The poem also mentions grails laden with more than a hundred boars' heads. The Second Continuation was written by Wauchier de Denain. Here the Holy Grail is borne by a girl 'fairer than a flower in April upon a sapling's branch'. Perceval succeeds in mending the broken sword, but the story ends before the king tells him about the Grail. The Third and Fourth Continuations were written by Gerbert de Montreuil and Manessier respectively. Manessier ends the story with Perceval's succession to the throne of the Fisher King. Perceval rules for seven years, then wanders into the woods and becomes a hermit. When he dies, the Grail disappears from the world.

Robert de Boron sanctified the Grail in his Arthurian romances *Joseph of Arimathea* (also known as *The Romance of the History of the Grail*), *Merlin* and the *Didot Perceval*. Robert's Holy Grail was the vessel of the Last Supper into which Jesus broke bread. In his account, it was given to Pontius Pilate who then passed it to Joseph of Arimathea, who used the vessel to catch the blood of Christ when his body was taken from the Cross and washed. Joseph of Arimathea was imprisoned, and Christ appeared to him and gave him the Holy Grail. Christ explained to Joseph the symbolism of the objects used in the Eucharist, telling him that the chalice is a reminder of the tomb in which Joseph laid him to rest, the paten is the stone that was rolled from the tomb, and the cloth is the linen winding sheet that wrapped him. Bron, the brother-in-law of Joseph of Arimathea, becomes the Fisher King, the next keeper of the Holy Grail. When a knight asks what purpose the Grail serves, the Fisher King will be healed. The knight will have the blood of Christ in his keeping and the enchantments of the land of Britain will vanish.

The story of the Holy Grail gradually evolved. Each new poet brought his own ideas to the story; each writer brought his own beliefs and imagination. In the Old French *Perlesvaus*, also known as *The High History of the Holy Grail*, the Holy Grail appears in five forms, 'but they should not be revealed, for the secrets of the sacrament none should tell save he whom God has granted grace'. The fifth and final form of the Grail was the holy chalice.

In the Welsh Grail romance *Peredur, Son of Efrawg*, two youths enter the hall 'bearing a spear of mighty size, with three streams of blood flowing from the point to the ground'; then two maidens enter 'with a large salver between them, in which was a man's head, surrounded by a profusion of blood'. The bloody head in the Grail salver in *Peredur* has led scholars to cite the Celtic cult of the head as a possible origin for the scene. There is, however, a simpler explanation. In the *Perlesvaus*, two maidens enter the chapel of the Grail; one carries the Grail, the other 'held the lance with the bleeding head'. The bloody head of the lance in any of the Grail romances may have turned into a bloody head in the Grail platter by scribal error, a misheard tale or a deliberate change by the writer of *Peredur*.

In the German romance *Parzival* by Wolfram von Eschenbach, the Grail is not a dish, platter, cup or golden chalice but a stone. To Wolfram, the Grail was a mystical stone that had fallen from heaven. It was guarded in the Grail castle, Munsalvaesche, by an order of knights called the Templeisen. When Lucifer made war in heaven, some of the noble and worthy angels took neither side. God sent these angels to the earth to become the custodians of the Grail, 'which is forever pure'. Wolfram says that he does not know if the angels that guarded the Grail were forgiven or destroyed by God, but the Grail passed into the protection of mortals whom God had called.

Wolfram tells us that the story of the Grail that Chrétien de Troyes composed was wrong. He says that a heathen named Flegetanis, who was descended from Solomon and worshipped a calf 'as if it were his god', wrote of the marvels of the Grail. Flegetanis had read the name of the Grail in the stars and seen hidden secrets in the constellations with his own eyes. The story of the Grail that the heathen Flegetanis wrote lay neglected in Toledo, Spain, and was discovered by 'the wise master' Kyot. Meister Kyot learned the writing of the heathens so that he could read Flegetanis' Grail story and told Wolfram the real story of the Grail which a host of angels had left on earth.

The Grail stone provides an abundance of food and drink, like the mythical Horn of Plenty or the magical cauldrons of the Celts. Warm and cold food, old and new dishes, wild and tame meats are found before the Grail. Mulberry, white or red wine fills every cup by 'the power of the Grail'. The essence of the Grail is pure. It is 'by the virtue' of the Grail stone that the phoenix burns to ashes and is reborn. The phoenix moults and changes its plumage; its new feathers are dazzlingly bright and shining. Anyone, 'maid or man', who looks on the Grail will appear in the prime of life for two hundred years afterwards, as the flesh and bones of mortal men are made young by the powers of the Grail.

Wolfram calls the Grail '*lapsit exillis*'. These two small words have proven highly controversial among Arthurian scholars. The *lapsit exillis* of Wolfram's *Parzival* may simply mean 'a small or paltry stone' or it may mean 'the stone which came down from the stars'. It has been suggested that Wolfram's Grail was a meteorite, literally a stone fallen from heaven. Small black stones, believed by some to be fragments of meteorites, have been found in the Languedoc region of southern France. When these stones are wetted and ground together, they 'bleed' a bright red. This red 'blood from a stone' may even have healing properties.

Arthurian scholars have argued about the origins of the Grail story for over a hundred years. Many look to classical texts, as Chrétien tells us that he made translations of Ovid; others point to Eastern influences, as crusaders brought tales and relics from Byzantium and Palestine. Many look for ancient echoes of the Grail in Celtic tales of marvellous cauldrons and wondrous dishes, while some say that the symbolism of the Grail is purely Christian, that the Grail was the chalice of the Eucharist (the ciborium) or the paten on which the Host was placed.

Another possible source for the Grail legends is the Horn of Plenty, a mythological vessel that has the magical ability to fill with whatever food or drink its owner wishes. The name is derived from the Latin *cornucopia*: *cornu* (horn) and *copia* (plenty). In Greek mythology, the Horn of Plenty was the horn of the goat that had suckled the god Zeus. When the horn was broken off, it magically filled with fruit. In some myths, the horn is said to have been a horn of Achelous, the river god. The cornucopia appears in classical sculpture and art as a symbol of abundance, overflowing with fruit, corn and flowers. It was borne as a symbol of fertility and fruitfulness by the Greek goddess of luck, Tyche, and her Roman equivalent, Fortuna. The Horn of Bran the Niggard is one of the Thirteen Treasures of Britain that appears in Welsh poetry and the Triads.

In *The Grail: From Celtic Myth to Christian Symbol*, the Arthurian scholar R.S. Loomis theorised that there was a mistranslation in the Grail romances. He noted that the Old French for both 'horn' and 'body' was '*li cors*'. Loomis pointed out that while the Grail romances lack a miraculous horn, you do find the 'wonder-working mass-wafer, the Corpus Christi'. In the Catholic Mass, the consecrated wafer was literally the body (*cors*) of Jesus Christ.

Loomis also noted that among the Thirteen Treasures was the Dish of Rhydderch, which had the same magical virtue as the Grail: 'whatever food one wished thereon was instantly obtained'. Rhydderch was a sixth-century king of Strathclyde, the royal patron of the holy man Kentigern. Kentigern was the grandson of King Loth. Loth was married to Morgause (sometimes known as Anna), the sister of King Arthur. Sir Gawain was one of the sons of King Loth. Chrétien tells us that the Grail story was found in a book that Count Philip of Flanders gave to him. That book may simply be a figment of Chrétien's fertile imagination, but it is possible that the book was real and that it held an earlier version of the Grail story involving Gawain and Rhydderch's dish.

Welsh and Irish mythology are filled with magical cauldrons that can provide endless quantities of food and heal the fallen, even bringing the dead back to life. The giant king Bran the Blessed, Bendigeid Vran ab Llyr (literally 'blessed raven, son of the sea god'), had a cauldron that could resurrect the dead. Warriors who fell in battle were thrown into Bran's cauldron. They clambered out alive but without the power of speech. One of the names given to the Fisher King is Bron.

In Welsh legend, Ceridwen's cauldron of inspiration and science revealed the mysteries of the world, gave knowledge of the future and inspired poetic genius. The cauldron of the giant Dyrnwch Wyddel would not boil meat for a coward, but it would quickly boil meat for a brave man. In *The Spoils of Annwn*, the bard Taliesin tells us that the cauldron of the chief of Annwn, the Welsh underworld, has a dark ridge around its edge set with pearls. It is kindled from the breath of nine maidens and will not boil the food of a coward.

In Irish mythology, the Dagda's Cauldron was one of the treasures of the Tuatha dé Danaan. The Tuatha dé Danaan, the people of the goddess Danu, were the inhabitants of the Irish *sídhe* (faerie) mounds. They were learned in lore and magic, druidism, wizardry and cunning. No company ever went from the Dagda's Cauldron unthankful. The cauldron of the ancient hag goddess of Celtic legend, the Cailleach, was the awe-inspiring Corryvreckan whirlpool between the isles of Jura and Scarba. Corryvreckan is one of the world's seven major whirlpools. Here the Cailleach washed her plaid at the beginning of winter. She would ride out for winter from the mountain of Ben Nevis with eight storm hags to bring the frost and ice. At the winter's end, the ancient blue hag would journey to the Green Isle of the West. There she would drink the magical waters of the Well of Youth and grow young again.

Was Chrétien's Grail inspired by the Cailleach's cauldron or the Dish of Rhydderch, the Holy City of Jerusalem or the vessel of the Last Supper? Chrétien de Troyes was arguably the most gifted poet of his age. It may be that the Grail was conjured from Chrétien's imagination. He was a wonderful teller of tales, more than capable of inventing the mysterious story of the Grail, thereby inspiring thousands of works of art and literature.

In *The Story of the Grail*, Perceval has to ask the question: 'Who is served from the grail?' The question that we have asked for hundreds of years is: 'Is there a real Holy Grail?' There have been many purported Grails: the Holy Chalice of Valencia, the Cup of Antioch, the alabaster Marian Chalice, the Nanteos Cup, the Sacro Catino 'emerald' vessel in Genoa, the Antioch Chalice now on display within the Metropolitan Museum of Art in New York, the blue-glass Glastonbury Cup. One particular artefact, however, has been overlooked. It is a sacred vessel that precisely matches Chrétien de Troyes' descriptions of the Grail, a platter of pure refined gold set with precious gems and pearls: the Patène de Serpentine.

SEE ALSO: Chrétien de Troyes; Fisher King; Galahad; Gawain; Grail Maiden; Nanteos Cup; Patène de Serpentine; Percival; Philip, Count of Flanders; Robert de Boron; Valencia Holy Chalice; Wolfram von Eschenbach

JERUSALEM

To the popes, bishops, kings and knights of medieval Europe, the crusades to take Jerusalem and the Holy Land from the Saracens were acts of faith. To reach the Church of the Holy Sepulchre in Jerusalem became the ultimate goal of the crusaders, and it has been suggested that the quest for the Holy City gave rise to the romances of the quest for the Holy Grail.

Medieval maps show the known world in a circle. The islands, continents, seas, oceans and rivers of the world are depicted within that circle, outlined simply with a few curved lines, with drawings of castles and church steeples to represent cities. Europe is usually pushed to the edge of the map. At the very heart of the medieval worldview was the Holy City of Jerusalem. In 1095 Pope Urban II described Jerusalem as he called on the people of medieval Europe to become 'soldiers of St Peter'; his speech is recorded in Robert the Monk's *Historia Hierosolymitana*:

> Jerusalem is the navel of the world; the land is fruitful above others, like another paradise of delights. This the Redeemer of the human race has made illustrious by His advent, has beautified by residence, has consecrated by suffering, has redeemed by death, has glorified by burial. This royal city, therefore, situated at the centre of the world, is now held captive by His enemies, and is in subjection to those who do not know God, to the worship of the heathens. She seeks therefore and desires to be liberated . . . undertake this

journey for the remission of your sins, with the assurance of the imperishable glory of the kingdom of heaven.

In the years that followed, the crusaders cut a bloody swathe towards Jerusalem. In November 1098, they took the Syrian city of Ma'arra. There the crusaders slaughtered all the inhabitants. Radulph of Caen, who chronicled the First Crusade, wrote that in Ma'arra the crusaders 'boiled pagan adults in cooking-pots . . . impaled children on spits and devoured them grilled'. The crusaders later told the Pope that they had been racked by a terrible famine. When they left Ma'arra, they set fire to the city. In June 1099, the crusaders arrived at the city of Jerusalem, where after a siege that lasted a month and a half they took the city and massacred the people within, Muslims, Jews and Christians alike.

A History of Deeds Done Beyond the Sea, written by William, the Archbishop of Tyre, became the major source for later histories of the First Crusade. In 1481, William Caxton, who printed Sir Thomas Malory's *Le Morte d'Arthur*, translated and printed William of Tyre's *History* under the title *Godeffroy of Boloyne, or the Siege and Conqueste of Jerusalem*:

> The valiant duke Godfrey of Bouillon, the knights, and the other men of arms . . . went together through the streets with their swords and spears in hand. All them that they met they slew and smote right down, men, women, and children, sparing none. There might no prayers nor crying of mercy avail. They slew so many in the streets that there were heaps of dead bodies, and one might not go nor pass but upon them that so lay dead.

In *The Perfect History*, Ibn Al-Athir gave an account of the Muslim world from its beginnings to AD 1231. He tells us that the crusaders laid siege to Jerusalem for six weeks before the city fell and the population was put to the sword:

> In the Masjid al-Aqsa the Franks slaughtered more than 70,000 people, among them a large number of Imams and Muslim scholars, devout and ascetic men who had left their homelands to live lives of pious seclusion in the Holy Place. The Franks stripped the Dome of the Rock of more than forty silver candelabra . . . and a great silver lamp weighing 44 Syrian pounds, as well as 150 smaller silver candelabra

> and more than 20 gold ones, and a great deal more booty. Refugees from Syria reached Baghdad in Ramadan . . . They told the Caliph's ministers a story that wrung their hearts and brought tears to their eyes.

The crusaders who took Jerusalem believed that the Al-Aqsa Mosque was the site of the Temple of Solomon. It became a palace of the Latin kings of Jerusalem until it was given to the Knights Templar on their foundation *c*.1120. The Templars (The Order of Poor Knights of the Temple of Solomon) were a military religious order dedicated to protecting the pilgrim routes to Jerusalem.

On 8 June 1147, Louis VII, King of France, and his queen, Eleanor of Aquitaine, set off on crusade to Jerusalem. Their journey to the Holy Land began at the Abbey of St Denis, north of Paris. There the king prostrated himself before the high altar; Pope Eugenius III and Abbot Suger brought out a silver reliquary of the saint and Louis took up the oriflamme (the banner of St Denis) and received the blessing of the pope. The following year, King Louis would write to Suger from the city of Antioch, asking the abbot to collect money and send it as quickly as possible, 'for save by great expense and great effort, we cannot prosecute the business of Christ'.

When Louis and Eleanor set off to the Holy City, their daughter Marie de Champagne was two years old. When Marie had grown to womanhood, she became the patron of Chrétien de Troyes. Chrétien tells us he was devoted to her. She was a close ally of Count Philip of Flanders, the dedicatee of Chrétien's *Perceval, or the Story of the Grail*. In 1177, Philip journeyed to Jerusalem, where he was greeted by his cousin, the leper King Baldwin IV of Jerusalem. Baldwin's leprosy was crippling; he had to be carried in a litter from the city of Ascalon to Jerusalem as he was unable to ride. The king summoned the Patriarch of Jerusalem, his barons, the masters of the Knights Templar and the Hospitallers, and the priests. King Baldwin took counsel, then offered Philip the regency of the Crusader Kingdom, asking him to take command of the army to guard and protect the Kingdom of Jerusalem. Count Philip considered the offer but in the end refused, saying he had come to serve God as a humble pilgrim. Philip then suggested that Baldwin's widowed sister Sybil, the Princess of Jerusalem, should be married to one of his vassals. William of Tyre recorded that the barons 'were amazed at his malicious thinking'. Philip left the Holy Land two years later.

In 1943, the Arthurian scholar Helen Adolf set out to demonstrate that Chrétien de Troyes' *Story of the Grail* was inspired by real people, places and events. She posited that the Holy City of Jerusalem was the Grail castle where the maimed Fisher King lived. The Fisher King was Baldwin IV, King of Jerusalem, whose sufferings meant that he had to be carried in a litter. Baldwin's leprosy would have been seen as a sign that he had sinned. In the same way, the Fisher King's wound can be interpreted as a mark of sin. The Old French for 'sinner' was *'pecheor'* while 'fisher' was *'pêscheur'*. Count Philip of Flanders was Sir Percival, who travelled to the Grail castle but failed to ask 'Whom does the Grail serve?' when he saw the Grail procession. Count Philip's failure to accept the regency of the Crusader Kingdom represented a similar omission. Sybil, the sister of Baldwin, was Percival's cousin, the lady mourning a dead knight. Sybil's husband had died while she was pregnant, and her choice of a new husband was crucial to the Crusader Kingdom. According to this theory, then, Chrétien's *Story of the Grail* is a veiled plea for Count Philip, his patron, to return to Jerusalem, become regent and in effect achieve the Grail.

Professor Antonio L. Furtado notes in his recent article 'The Crusaders' Grail' that an earlier king of Jerusalem, Baldwin I, was grievously wounded by a javelin that struck him close to his heart, between his backbone and ribs. King Baldwin I survived but 'often felt a fresh pain in the wounded spot'. Baldwin later went to the mouth of the Nile, which was said to sprout from one of the four rivers of Paradise. He ordered his men to catch fish. While Baldwin was eating some of the fish they had caught, he felt a great pain as his wound 'started to ache anew, so that he was in utter fear of death'. Baldwin was too ill to ride and was carried in a litter to 'a very ancient city of the desert, called Lars', where 'he could go no further, and died'.

Furtado also recounts one of Count Philip's darker moments. Around 1166, in an attempt to raise the status of a new church in Aire, Flanders, Philip snatched the severed head of St Jacques from the Abbey of St Vaast in Arras. Abbot Hughes of St Amand arbitrated between Philip and the outraged Pope Alexander III, and it was agreed that the miraculous head would be divided in two; the larger part was returned to St Vaast, the smaller was given to the new church in Aire.

Chrétien recounts that he found the story of the Grail in a book given to him by Count Philip. Professor Furtado suggests that this source book was William of Tyre's chronicle of the crusades *A History of Deeds Done Beyond the Sea*, which includes accounts named 'How Count Philip of Flanders behaved badly in the land beyond the sea' and 'How the Count of Flanders went back without accomplishing anything'. Was Philip keen to present an idealised version of his deeds in Jerusalem? Did Philip give the book to Chrétien to have his deeds in Jerusalem rewritten in a more flattering light?

Chrétien's *Story of the Grail* may have been inspired by Count Philip's failure to accept the regency of Jerusalem. Philip returned to France in 1179 to find that King Louis VII was ailing, while the heir to the throne, Philip II Augustus, the half-brother of Chrétien's patron Marie de Champagne, was in his teens. Louis turned to Philip of Flanders, as the leper King Baldwin had, and offered him the regency of France. This time, the count accepted. Did Marie suggest that her court poet Chrétien de Troyes compose a romance based on Count Philip's refusal of the regency of the Crusader Kingdom and his acceptance of the regency of France? If so, did the Patène de Serpentine, a sacred vessel of the queens of France kept at the royal treasury at the Abbey of St Denis, serve as the inspiration for the Grail?

In 1187, the great Muslim warrior Saladin captured Jerusalem. When the crusaders took Jerusalem in 1099, they had massacred the inhabitants, building funeral pyres like pyramids. While the crusaders had bathed the city in blood, Saladin purified Jerusalem with rose water. It was said that Saladin brought hundreds of camels laden with rose water made from Damascus roses. He allowed the Latin crusaders to pay a ransom and leave the Holy City. In 1188, Count Philip of Flanders took up the cross and joined the Third Crusade. He died at Acre three years later. Chrétien would never complete *The Story of the Grail*.

SEE ALSO: Chrétien de Troyes; Holy Grail; Knights Templar; Patène de Serpentine; Philip, Count of Flanders

JOSEPH OF ARIMATHEA

Joseph of Arimathea first appears in the New Testament to ask Pontius Pilate for the body of Jesus. Medieval legend depicted him as the first guardian of the Holy Grail, which he was said to have taken from Jerusalem to Glastonbury in Somerset, where he founded the first Christian church in Britain. Joseph of Arimathea is a controversial figure. His legend has become linked to modern theories of a 'Grail bloodline', the idea that a holy family descended from the marriage of Jesus and Mary Magdalene exists to this day.

There is no mention of Joseph of Arimathea in the Gospels until he suddenly appears at the Crucifixion, 'a rich man of Arimathaea, named Joseph, who also himself was Jesus' disciple'. Joseph begs the body of Jesus from Pontius Pilate. Pilate is surprised that Jesus has already died, but agrees to Joseph's request. Jesus is brought down from the cross by Joseph and Nicodemus. The body of Christ is laid to rest in the rock-cut tomb of Joseph of Arimathea. The Bible tells us nothing more about him.

Joseph of Arimathea next appears in the apocryphal *Acta Pilati*, *The Acts of Pilate*, also known in the Middle Ages as the Gospel of Nicodemus. There are 14 apocryphal gospels, which were included in the medieval Vulgate Bibles but excluded from the Protestant Bibles. In *The Acts of Pilate*, Joseph is described as a member of the Sanhedrin, the Jewish high council and court of justice. It was the court of the Sanhedrin that tried and condemned Christ. The Gospel of Nicodemus tells us that Joseph was away when the trial of Jesus took place, absolving him of any blame. It is stated that Joseph took the body of Christ from the Cross, wrapped it in a clean linen cloth and 'laid it in a hewn sepulchre wherein was never man yet laid'. When the Jews learned that he had interceded with Pilate, they sought him out. Joseph told the Jews:

> Why is it that ye are vexed against me, for that I begged the body of Jesus? Behold I have laid it in my new tomb, having wrapped it in clean linen, and I rolled a stone over the door of the cave. And ye have not dealt well with the just one, for ye repented not when ye had crucified him, but ye also pierced him with a spear.

The Jews had Joseph imprisoned, saying: 'Know thou that the time alloweth us not to do anything against thee, because the sabbath dawneth: but know that thou shalt not obtain burial, but we will give thy flesh unto the fowls of the heaven.' They shut up Joseph in a house with no windows, sealing the door and placing a guard outside. On the day after the Sabbath, they discovered that he had miraculously disappeared, escaping his prison. He was found in Arimathea with no memory of how he got there. All that Joseph could remember was that Jesus had appeared to him in his prison on the Sabbath night and released him. He said:

> At midnight as I stood and prayed the house wherein ye shut me up was taken up by the four corners, and I saw as it were a flashing of light in mine eyes, and being filled with fear I fell to the earth. And one took me by the hand and removed me from the place whereon I had fallen; and moisture of water was shed on me from my head unto my feet, and an odour of ointment came about my nostrils. And he wiped my face and kissed me and said unto me: Fear not, Joseph: open thine eyes and see who it is that speaketh with thee. And I looked up and saw Jesus and I trembled.

At the end of the twelfth century, the story of Joseph of Arimathea was interwoven with the story of the Grail. For the first time, the Grail was said to be the Cup of Christ − the Holy Grail. The Burgundian poet Robert de Boron wrote the first life of Joseph of Arimathea, which was known as *Joseph d'Arimathie* or *Le Roman de l'Estoire dou Graal* (*The Romance of the History of the Grail*). Robert de Boron took Chrétien de Troyes' *Perceval, or the Story of the Grail*, the Gospel accounts of the Last Supper and the apocryphal Gospel of Nicodemus and connected Chrétien's mysterious grail platter with the vessel that Christ and his disciples used at the Last Supper.

According to Robert de Boron's account of his life, Joseph of Arimathea was actually a soldier under Pilate and a secret follower of Christ. After the Last Supper, the vessel in which Christ broke bread was passed to Pilate. Pilate gave it to Joseph, as the Roman consul feared that he would be suspected of following Christ if he was found to have anything that had belonged to him. After Christ had died upon the Cross, Pilate gave Joseph permission to bury him. When the body of Jesus was brought down from the cross and washed, his wounds began to bleed again and Joseph used the vessel to catch the blood of Christ.

Christ's body was entombed and, as in the Gospel of Nicodemus, the Jews arrested Joseph and imprisoned him. Jesus appeared in Joseph's prison cell and gave him the vessel of the Last Supper. Christ told Joseph that the vessel would be a reminder of the stone tomb in which he was laid, the paten which is placed on top would be a reminder of the lid that covered the tomb and the cloth called the corporeal would be a reminder of the linen winding sheet in which his body was wrapped, and so the work of Joseph would be remembered until the world's end. Christ then revealed the mystery of the Grail to Joseph.

Robert tells us that after 40 years the Emperor Vespasian visited the imprisoned Joseph. Vespasian had been cured of his leprosy by the Veil of Veronica and had then heard of Joseph. During this time, Joseph of Arimathea had been miraculously sustained by the vessel of the Last Supper. Vespasian freed Joseph, who left the Holy Land with his sister Enygeus, her husband, Bron, and a few close followers.

When the group were starving, Joseph, inspired by the Holy Ghost, set up a table in commemoration of the table of the Last Supper. Bron caught a fish, which was placed on the table by the vessel. As Joseph and the group experience a miraculous bliss, Robert finally calls the vessel of the Last Supper 'the Grail'. It is stated that those who stay in the presence of the Grail feel as elated as a fish that escapes from a man's hands into the wide water.

Robert de Boron's life of Joseph of Arimathea ends as Joseph returns home to die and the Grail passes to Bron, the husband of Joseph's sister, who is known as '*le Riche Pescheor*', the Rich Fisher. Perceval, a descendant of Bron, is destined to become the keeper of the Holy Grail.

Above: Tower of St Michael's Church, Glastonbury Tor

Below: Holy Thorn, Glastonbury Abbey, Somerset

Above: Winchester Round Table, Winchester Castle, Hampshire

Below: The legend of Sir Yvain, fifteenth-century misericord, Chester Cathedral

Opposite: Arthur pulls the sword from the anvil and stone,
King Arthur's Great Halls, Tintagel, Cornwall
(reproduced by kind permission of King Arthur's Great Halls)

Above: Castell Dinas Bran, Llangollen, Denbighshire, Wales

Below: Rosslyn Chapel, Midlothian, Scotland

Opposite above: Patène de Serpentine, Musée du Louvre, Paris

Opposite below: A scene from Chrétien de Troyes' *Perceval*, fourteenth-century ivory casket, Musée du Louvre

Opposite: 'And when they came to the sword that the hand held, King Arthur took it up' – N.C. Wyeth, *The Boy's King Arthur*, 1917

Above: Glastonbury Abbey, Somerset

Below: The Lion's Head, Chalice Well Gardens, Glastonbury

Above: Roche Rock, Cornwall

Below: Dinas Emrys, Gwynedd, Wales

The tale of Joseph of Arimathea and the story of the Holy Grail became incredibly popular throughout the Middle Ages. As new romances were written, the legend evolved. It was said that Joseph of Arimathea had travelled by ship from the Holy Land to escape persecution by the Jews. He was accompanied by Lazarus and his two sisters, Martha and Mary. They arrived in Marseilles, southern France, bearing the Grail, and converted France, Spain and England to Christianity.

The romances of Joseph and the Holy Grail were connected with medieval legends that told how Joseph founded the first Christian church in Britain, at Glastonbury. The fourteenth-century chronicler John of Glastonbury claimed that Joseph of Arimathea brought two cruets, or vessels, from the Holy Land. One held the sweat of Christ, the other the blood of Christ, washed from his body when he was taken down from the Cross. John also claimed that King Arthur was a descendant of Joseph of Arimathea, through a rather fanciful genealogy: 'Helaius, nepos Joseph, genuit Josus, Josue Genuit Aminadab, Aminadab Genuit Filium, qui Genuit Ygernam, de qua Rex Pen-Dragon, Genuit Nobilem et Famosum Regum Arthurum, per Quod Patet, Quod Rex Arthurus de Stirpe Joseph descendit [. . . thus King Arthur is descended from the line of Joseph]'. Meanwhile, in the medieval French romance *Perlesvaus*, also known as *The High History of the Holy Grail*, three richly ornamented damsels take the shield of Joseph of Arimathea, 'the good soldier knight that took down Our Lord of hanging on the rood [cross]', to King Arthur's castle at Cardoil.

Sir Thomas Malory also told the story of Joseph, his mission to Britain and the Holy Grail:

> And here followeth the noble tale of the Sangreal, that called
> is the holy vessel; and the signification of the blessed blood
> of our Lord Jesu Christ, blessed mote it be, the which was
> brought in to this land by Joseph of Aramathie.

Malory describes Joseph of Arimathea as the 'gentle knight' who took 'our Lord' down from the Cross. Joseph departed Jerusalem with 'a great party of his kindred with him' and came to 'this land to teach and preach the holy Christian faith', after which 'all the people were turned to the Christian faith'.

In the middle of the sixteenth century, Queen Elizabeth I of England noted that 'the records and chronicles of our realm' testified that 'Joseph of Arimathea be the first preacher of the word of God within our realms'. The story of Joseph and the Grail can be seen as a myth of the Christianisation of Britain. When Joseph came to Britain, he carried with him the Holy Grail – the Cup of Christ, the vessel of the Last Supper, the sacred chalice of the Christian Mass.

The Glastonbury legend is that Joseph of Arimathea was the uncle of the Virgin Mary, a rich merchant who traded Cornish tin. It is said that Jesus spent some of his 'missing years' with his great-uncle Joseph in England and that Joseph built a simple wattle-and-daub church in Glastonbury with the help of Jesus. When Joseph eventually died, he was laid to rest in secret, in a marble tomb near his church.

The legends of Glastonbury, Jesus and Joseph of Arimathea inspired William Blake to pen 'Jerusalem' in the early years of the nineteenth century:

> And did those feet in ancient time
> Walk upon England's mountains green?
> And was the holy Lamb of God
> On England's pleasant pastures seen?
>
> And did the Countenance Divine
> Shine forth upon our clouded hills?
> And was Jerusalem builded here
> Among these dark Satanic mills?
>
> Bring me my bow of burning gold!
> Bring me my arrows of desire!
> Bring me my spear! O clouds, unfold!
> Bring me my chariot of fire!
>
> I will not cease from Mental Fight,
> Nor shall my Sword sleep in my hand,
> Till we have built Jerusalem,
> In England's green and pleasant Land.

SEE ALSO: Glastonbury; Holy Grail; Robert de Boron; Round Table

KNIGHTS OF THE ROUND TABLE

The Knights of the Round Table were the noblest, most trusted, bravest and most chivalrous of all King Arthur's followers. They occupied a special place in his court and formed what could be described as his innermost circle of trusted allies and compatriots.

Different versions of the legend of King Arthur describe varying numbers of knights: some state that there were only 12, while others mention 25, 150 and even 366. It may be that these higher numbers actually include lesser knights and that they were not all Knights of the Round Table. It is true that King Arthur had so-called lesser orders of chivalry, and we find the following designations in the Arthurian cycle: the Queen's Knights, the Knights of the Watch, the Table of Errant Companions and even the Table of Less Valued Knights. So it is entirely possible that when the number of knights is stated as 366, this could in fact refer to all of these knights and not just the select inner circle of the Round Table.

A list of the most prominent Knights of the Round Table would include Bors, Ector, Galahad, Gawain, Lancelot, Lionel, Mordred, Pelleas, Percival and many others. These knights feature in the tales and legends of King Arthur, and they participate in many tasks and quests, particularly the search for the Holy Grail.

Chivalry was the essential quality of the Knights of the Round Table, at least according to the Arthurian romances. Here is Thomas Malory's summary of the code that each knight swore to uphold when he was ennobled and took his seat at the Round Table:

> [Arthur] charged them all never to do outrage nor murder,
> and always to flee treason; also, by no means to be cruel,
> but to give mercy unto him that asked mercy, upon pain of
> forfeiture of their worship and lordship; and always to do
> ladies, damosels, and gentlewomen service, upon pain of
> death. Also that no man take battle in a wrongful quarrel, for
> no law, nor for any world's goods.

Honour was paramount to each of the knights and to lose one's honour was often considered worse than death itself. In addition to the chivalric code we find in Malory, these other rules are also mentioned at various times in the Arthurian legends: to never lay down arms; to give one's life for one's country; and to defend the weak with all the strength that one is given.

As well as leading a chivalrous life, there was a tradition that all of the knights should gather at King Arthur's Camelot for the major feast days of the year. So it is that in the romances we see the Knights of the Round Table meeting at Easter, Pentecost and Christmas. It has been noted that many of the quests and adventures that befell the Knights of the Round Table began when they were all gathered at Camelot for one of these feasts. For example, when the Grail appears at Camelot, all of the knights are conveniently assembled together so that they all witness the spectacle.

Another way in which the knights bonded was through attending tournaments where they would joust against each other and take part in other organised fights as well as mock battles called mêlées. A tournament was an arena in which knights could hone their fighting and riding skills, pitting their accumulated expertise against their colleagues. In time, these events became grand social occasions, although they could also be very bloody and violent affairs. For a time, the Church even banned them, but so unpopular was this edict that it was eventually revoked.

Medieval knights were granted land and fiefdoms; in return, they agreed to fight for their lord or king, maintaining a number of fighting men and cavalry that could be called to battle. The knights collected an income from their lands which they used to maintain their own bodyguard and force of arms. In such a way, the burden of maintaining an army did not fall on the king himself. Medieval accounts of the court of King Arthur present an idealised version of this system: by creating an elite band of knights who gathered at the Round Table and were bonded to one another as if brothers, Arthur ensured the security of his kingdom.

Some authors have suggested that the Knights of the Round Table were more than just brothers in arms and that they were also a spiritual or religious group. Arthur's knights embark on the spiritual quest for the Holy Grail, and it has been theorised that the fact that they had to be pure of heart to achieve the Grail has a parallel in the Perfecti of the Cathars and that their fortress of Montségur was the Grail castle. The Cathars, a heretical sect persecuted by the Catholic Church, followed a very austere code that tried to emulate the poverty and simplicity of Christ. The Perfecti were the enlightened individuals who were at the heart of Cathar society and who led pious and pure lives. Similarly, the Knights of the Round Table were a group at the core of King Arthur's kingdom who strove for perfection on behalf of the whole realm.

The Round Table itself is said to have been built in memory of the table of the Last Supper and Joseph of Arimathea's Grail table. The Holy Grail that appeared to King Arthur and his knights was the vessel that Jesus used at the Last Supper. In some Arthurian tales, there are 12 Knights of the Round Table, so that King Arthur's knights appear as a fellowship echoing that of Christ's disciples.

SEE ALSO: Camelot; Chivalry; Holy Grail; Last Supper; Malory, Sir Thomas

KNIGHTS TEMPLAR

Early in the reign of Baldwin II, the King of Jerusalem (1118–31), a newly formed religious and military order was given possession of the Al-Aqsa Mosque atop Temple Mount, then believed to be the site of King Solomon's Temple. The knights were founded as 'Pauperes commilitones Christi Templique Salomonis' (the Poor Fellow-soldiers of Christ and the Temple of Solomon), and became known as the Knights Templar.

The Templars, founded in 1118, were 'poor knights' who dedicated their lives to protecting Christian pilgrims travelling to Jerusalem, the city at the centre of their religious beliefs. Each member of the order took vows of chastity, poverty and obedience. His conduct was expected to be exemplary; that of the perfect knight. Chrétien de Troyes, in his twelfth-century *Lancelot, or the Knight of the Cart*, tells us the virtues expected of the ideal, or 'parfait', knight: he should be merciful without wickedness, affable without treachery, compassionate towards the suffering, and generous and helpful towards those in need. He should prevent murder and robbery and judge those accused of crimes fairly. Death should be preferable to dishonour. He must defend the Holy Church against its enemies. These are clearly aims and expectations that only the most dedicated might be expected to fulfil.

It may be hard for us today to understand what attracted recruits to the Order until we remember the immensely strong attraction of the Church, the desire to do God's will and secure a place in heaven, and, more down to earth, the necessity for young, landless sons of noble families with little prospect of inheriting wealth to make a living. Joining holy orders or a military group were two possible career prospects; the Templars offered both at once. Perhaps even more attractive than the bed and board which went with the job was the Patriarch of Jerusalem's promise of remission of their sins in return for their policing role. Unlike their contemporaries the Knights Hospitaller, the Templars were primarily a fighting force. Their military capability quickly took them into the work of manning castles in the Holy Land. They began to take part in aggression against those they saw as enemies of Christianity and took to wearing the red cross of Christ on their white surplices.

Their work defending strongholds meant that those inhabitants with money or precious objects sometimes looked to the Templars to act as bankers to ensure the safety of their possessions. Naturally enough, having expenses to cover, the Templars began to accrue wealth of their own, which was not at all in accordance with their original brief. It became possible for Templars to issue notes of credit for a traveller to carry to cash in a distant place. They became international bankers.

By the time of King Philip IV of France (ruled 1285–1314), Jerusalem had been taken by the followers of Islam, and, while there were ambitions in some quarters, there was little realistic expectation that it could be recaptured in the foreseeable future. Rich Templar communities lived in Philip's realm and the king had insufficient funds to finance his kingdom. He had already banished the Jews and Lombard bankers from France, sequestrating their wealth; the ruthless monarch was not satisfied, however, and he looked around for a fresh victim. He did not have to search far.

The problem for Philip was that the Templars were answerable only to the Pope. In 1139, Pope Innocent II had issued the papal bull *Omne Datum Optimum*, which established the order under papal protection and gave it exemption from tithes and taxes. Strictly speaking, the Templars were not subject to the laws and justice of any king or country. Throughout his reign, Philip, good Catholic though he claimed to be, had been in conflict with the Papacy, principally over issues of taxation. In 1303, the power struggle came to a head when Pope Boniface VIII had Philip excommunicated and France placed under an interdict so that none of the usual sacraments could be administered. Souls had been put in peril, and Philip retaliated swiftly, demonstrating that the authority of the Pope, and even the sanctity of his person, did not overawe him. Boniface VIII was seized by men working under the king's orders and ill-treated. The Pope was released but was so ill as a result of this experience that he died soon afterwards.

By 1305, Clement V, a Frenchman who was virtually a client of Philip and not in a strong position to stand up to him, was Pope. In early autumn 1307, King Philip ordered that all the Templars within his dominions were to be arrested. He had tried unsuccessfully to unite the Templars and Hospitallers under his command to lead a new crusade and was well aware of the fact that the Templars did not enjoy much popularity in France. Philip knew that he was on fairly safe ground as they were considered too worldly on account of their wealth and excited the envy of their peers.

Pope Clement tried to save the Templars, acting against the French king's persecution. The Pope's emissaries questioned the Grand Master Jacques de Molay and other Templars in 1308 in the dungeons of Chinon Castle. Accusations of idolatry, blasphemy, heresy and sodomy were examined, and the Templars were ultimately exonerated by the Pope. Clement absolved them, decreeing that they could again receive Christian sacraments, but the Pope's intervention could not save the Templars.

Many Knights Templar in France were tortured to extract damning confessions, and the order was suppressed. Some were put to death, including Jacques de Molay, who was burned at the stake in Paris in March 1314. The treatment of de Molay by Philip has an added twist, since on Thursday, 12 October 1307, just one day before the arrest of the Templars, de Molay had been a pall-bearer at the funeral of King Philip's sister-in-law. Maybe Philip believed in keeping his friends close and his enemies closer still.

It is said that Jacques cursed the king and his successors and challenged both Philip and the Pope to appear before God's throne for judgement. They would have to answer, he claimed, for the injustice they were committing. Within the year, both the king and the Pope had joined de Molay in death.

Over the years, many legends have attached themselves to the Templars. Among these is one which suggests that their occupation of Temple Mount in Jerusalem may be linked to the enormous wealth and prestige they enjoyed prior to their annihilation. Those who believe this argue that the nine knights who were the first Templars had in fact succeeded in a mission to discover the lost treasures of the Temple of Jerusalem, including the Ark of the Covenant.

The Templars were reputed to be in possession of secrets which they would die for rather than reveal. Jacques de Molay intimated as much when facing his accusers shortly before his death. Raoul de Presle, a lawyer working at that time, spoke of the great secret known only to the Templars; it should be noted, however, that he was one of the legal team helping Philip IV to tighten his power over his kingdom. Some say that this alleged secret concerned the nature and whereabouts of the Holy Grail. Legend has it that a few loyal knights escaped France with the Templar treasure.

Some authors claim that these refugee Templars sought sanctuary in Scotland with the St Clair family of Rosslyn. It has even been suggested that their treasure was hidden beneath Rosslyn Chapel. In 1309, a trial was held in Edinburgh at which the Templar order was accused of refusing hospitality to the poor and being rapacious towards the property of others. Various local nobles, including Henry and William St Clair, testified that the Templars had been poor neighbours and bad Christians. It was alleged that they had lost Jerusalem and failed in their mission in the Holy Land because they were not good Christians. The two accused Templars were ultimately absolved and sent to Cistercian monasteries.

In Wolfram von Eschenbach's *Parzival*, the Grail is guarded by an order of knights called the Templeisen. Wolfram's Templeisen have been associated with the Knights Templar by some authors. The Templeisen are described as chaste, as were the Templars, who took a vow of chastity. Theirs was a religious and military order, like the Templars. Was Wolfram, a contemporary of the Knights Templar, writing a story of the Templars and the Holy Grail? Some Arthurian scholars have suggested that Wolfram's Grail castle, Munsalvaesche, the Mount of Salvation, symbolised Temple Mount in the Holy City. The Templeisen guarded the Grail castle as the Templars had guarded Jerusalem. It should be noted that in Germany the Templars were known as the *Templeherren* not the Templeisen, so Wolfram's Grail knights may simply be associated with the Temple rather than the Templar order.

The Knights Templar have become a favourite secret society of conspiracy theorists, alternative historians and thriller writers. They neatly connect ancient wisdom and the lost treasures of Jerusalem with the courtly intrigues of medieval France, and their end was dramatic – condemned as heretics and supposedly abandoned by the Catholic Church. Not only this, but the legends tell that the Templars hid a wondrous treasure and that the secrets of the order were passed to the Freemasons.

How guilty were the Templars and did they deserve their fate, at least by medieval standards? They certainly became extremely wealthy and were evidently in breach of their vows of poverty. They had, as the subjects of successive popes, been above the laws and taxes to which other inhabitants of the countries in which they lived were subject and had inevitably attracted the envy of others. Ultimately, the Templars failed to be faithful to the promises on which they were founded. In the end, they were destroyed because the Crusader Kingdom had fallen; the Templar order was founded to protect pilgrims in the Holy Land, and once Jerusalem was lost, it was only a matter of time until the Templars were brought down.

Although the Templars themselves did not always live up to their own chivalric principles, their ideals seem to have struck a chord with medieval writers. The Knights of the Round Table of Arthurian romances were expected to follow a chivalric code much like that of the Templars, to defend the weak and do good deeds without thought for their own safety.

SEE ALSO: Chrétien de Troyes; Holy Grail; Rosslyn Chapel; Wolfram von Eschenbach

LADY OF THE LAKE

One of the most iconic images of the Arthurian legends is that of an arm rising out of the waters of a lake clasping the sword Excalibur for King Arthur to take. As Arthur lies dying, the arm rises up once more to catch the sword as it is thrown back into the lake by Sir Bedivere. This arm is often assumed by many to belong to the Lady of the Lake, but in Malory's *Le Morte d'Arthur* at least, it does not. There, the arm which rises from the depths of the lake is that of a water nymph, while Malory makes it clear that the Lady of the Lake is a flesh-and-blood mortal who lives in a castle 'hewn in the rock' at the edge of the lake. Merlin states that Arthur must ask the Lady of the Lake, who is crossing the water in her boat, for permission to take the sword Excalibur, implying that her position was in fact that of guardian of the magic sword. In *Le Morte d'Arthur*, rather than referring to a particular individual, 'Lady of the Lake' was an honorific title encompassing the role of guardian and sorceress, and thus could pass from one woman to another.

Indeed, shortly after allowing Arthur to take Excalibur, the unfortunate Lady of the Lake is beheaded by Sir Balin, one of Arthur's knights, and after this incident it is another lady, whom Malory calls Nyneve, who is given the title Lady of the Lake, although the transition is not referred to specifically but rather implied. Given that Nyneve appears in the text after the death of the unnamed first Lady of the Lake, she is clearly a different lady from the one who gave Arthur the sword. Initially, Malory states that Nyneve had formerly served the Lady of the Lake, but it is not made clear how she then inherited the title. It may have been that she was a relation of and heir to the previous Lady of the Lake, or perhaps, given her tutelage under Merlin and her later role as 'the good sorceress Nyneve', she was an initiate in the magical arts.

Referred to mainly as Nyneve, sometimes as the Lady of the Lake or the Lady of Avalon, the character is a strange mix of good and bad, desire and contempt, saviour and murderer. After King Pellinore brings Nyneve to Arthur's court, Merlin falls hopelessly in love with her, following her everywhere. At first, Nyneve is happy with Merlin's attentiveness because she wants to learn the secrets of his magical crafts from him. However, during their time travelling together so that Merlin can teach her, Nyneve eventually tires of the wizard, who is so besotted with her that he uses all his magical skills to try to seduce her. Unable to take it any longer, a desperate Nyneve begins to search for ways in which she can rid herself of Merlin. Eventually, she traps him within a secret underground cave that he had shown her, magically sealing the entrance with a huge stone that even a hundred men could not move. Returning alone to King Arthur's court, Nyneve then takes on the role of Arthur's magician. She shows no remorse for her act, nor for the unfortunate death of the lady Ettarde, who dies of a broken heart as a direct result of one of Nyneve's spells.

Thus by the early part of *Le Morte d'Arthur*, Nyneve is a sorceress acting as Arthur's protector, in part taking on the position left vacant by Merlin and in part due to her love for the king. In this role, she discovers that Morgan le Fay has tricked an unknowing Arthur and her lover Accolon into a tournament against each other, giving Accolon Excalibur to fight with and Arthur a counterfeit Excalibur. At the point when an unsuspecting Accolon is about to kill his king, Nyneve casts a spell, causing Excalibur to fly out of Accolon's hand, thus saving Arthur. In another attempt to kill her brother, Morgan le Fay sends Arthur a magnificent cloak, but Nyneve prevents him from wearing it, insisting that Morgan's maid try it first. The unfortunate maid bursts into flames as soon as she puts it on.

In other versions of the Arthurian legend, the Lady of the Lake is called Viviane, Éviène or Nimuë, and, as in *Le Morte d'Arthur*, she takes on a number of different roles that act as the basis for, or expand upon, Malory's tale. In *Vita di Merlini con le sur Profetie* (*The Life of Merlin with his Prophecies*), the Italian translation of Robert de Boron's thirteenth-century *Merlin*, the Lady of the Lake is Merlin's scribe, who writes down his spells and prophecies. By learning his spells, she is able to deceive Merlin into lying down in a tomb within which she then encloses him. This theme is also taken up in the Vulgate cycle and in the prose romance of the Post-Vulgate cycle called *Suite du Merlin*. Merlin is again besotted by the Lady of the Lake, building her a fabulous castle in the lake, keeping it hidden from others by use of magic.

In Ulrich von Zatzikhoven's *Lanzelet* (*c*.1195), the Lady of the Lake takes the infant Lancelot and raises him after the death of his father, King Ban de Benoic. In this earlier tale, it is the Lady of the Lake, a fairy called Niniane, who takes Lancelot to King Arthur's court once he reaches the age of 18 so that he can be knighted. At this point, Niniane informs Lancelot that he is of royal blood, giving him a magic ring for protection. Later on in the tale, the Lady of the Lake helps Lancelot capture the castle of Dolorous Guard.

It has been suggested that a precedent for the Lady of the Lake can be found in Celtic mythology in the shape of a Celtic water goddess called Covianna, hence the name Viviane used for the Lady of the Lake in some of the Arthurian romances. It has also been suggested that the motif of Excalibur rising from the water and returning there is connected to the Celtic practice of throwing valuable items, including weapons, into the water as votive offerings to the goddesses beneath the waves.

SEE ALSO: Excalibur; Malory, Sir Thomas; Merlin; Morgan le Fay

LANCELOT

Sir Lancelot was arguably the greatest of all of the Knights of the Round Table. He is probably the most famous of all Arthur's knights, his name forever associated with that of Guinevere and with the search for the Holy Grail. Lancelot is a flawed character and his forbidden love for Guinevere brings about the fall of Camelot. The love triangle of Arthur, Guinevere and Lancelot was one of the major subjects of both the English and French Arthurian cycles.

Lancelot was a late addition to the court of King Arthur. It is thought that an Anglo-Norman *Lancelot*, now lost, was the source for Ulrich von Zatzikhoven's Middle High German *Lanzelet* and Chrétien de Troyes' *Lancelot, ou le chevalier de la charrette* (*Lancelot, or the Knight of the Cart*). It has been argued that the Arthurian romances of France emphasise Sir Lancelot over King Arthur.

Lancelot was the son of Queen Elaine and King Ban, the ruler of a kingdom called Benwick or Benoic. King Ban was driven from his kingdom by Claudas de la Deserte while Lancelot was a baby. Ban, Elaine and the infant Lancelot escaped to the enchanted forest of Brocéliande, but when King Ban looked back and saw his beloved castle in flames, he fell into a swoon. Queen Elaine placed Lancelot down as she tended to her dying husband. In that moment, Viviane, the Lady of the Lake, appeared and took Lancelot, sometimes referred to as Lancelot du Lac, to her magical home beneath the waters.

Viviane raised Lancelot and also took his cousins Lionel and Bors, sons of King Ban's brother, under her wing. Lancelot grew into a handsome youth who excelled in all he did. At the age of 18, he left the sanctuary of Brocéliande and rode out into the world seeking adventure, still not knowing his ancestry or his parentage. In the *Prose Lancelot*, Viviane takes Lancelot to King Arthur's court to be knighted. In some versions of the story he leaves her when he still has much to learn, and it is only after venturing forth into the world on his own that he finds himself at Arthur's court.

When Lancelot first caught sight of Guinevere, King Arthur's queen, he fell in love with her and vowed to be her champion and to honour her above all others. This fateful meeting was the beginning of a love affair that would tear apart the fellowship of the Round Table and destroy Arthur's kingdom.

In the course of Lancelot's adventures, he met a lamenting damsel and learnt that her knight had been slain at the castle of Dolorous Guard, where an evil custom had been established. The lord of Dolorous Guard was Brandin of the Isles, who made it his custom to challenge any knight who approached the castle walls. A knight had to battle a total of twenty deadly opponents before facing Brandin himself. Lancelot is given three miraculous shields by a damsel of the household of the Lady of the Lake. The first shield, with a single band, will double his strength; the second, with two bands, will triple his strength; and the third, with three bands, will quadruple his strength. Using these, Lancelot defeated Brandin and all of his knights to become the new lord of Dolorous Guard. He was given the keys to the castle and taken to a nearby graveyard, where he was shown a slab bearing a strange prophecy: 'This slab shall never be raised by the efforts of any man's hand but by him who shall conquer this Dolorous castle, and the name of that man is written here beneath.'

Lancelot was told that many knights had tried to lift it but all had failed. He was able to raise the slab and found these words etched on its underside: 'Here shall lie Lancelot du Lac, the son of King Ban Benwick.' So it was that the knight finally discovered the truth about his royal ancestry. He removed all enchantments from the castle and renamed his new home Joyous Guard.

In *The Knight of the Cart*, when the villain Meleagant abducts Guinevere, it is Lancelot who comes to the rescue. Meleagant, the son of King Bagdemagus, was once a Knight of the Round Table. Lancelot rides to Guinevere's rescue, but his horse is killed by Meleagant's men, so Lancelot is forced to ride in a cart (humiliating for a knight, as common criminals were carried in carts) to continue his pursuit. Lancelot has to cross the perilous Sword Bridge to reach Meleagant's castle, removing his gauntlets to better grip the giant sword, cutting his hands and bare feet as he crosses. King Bagdemagus is impressed by Lancelot's bravery and persuades his villainous son to allow Lancelot some time to recover before fighting him. Lancelot faces Meleagant and gains strength from seeing Guinevere looking down from a high window. Meleagant is defeated, his life spared on account of his father, and Guinevere is freed. Lancelot and Meleagant finally fight to the death at Arthur's court. When they joust, they pierce each other's shields and are both dismounted. They then fight on foot with swords, and Lancelot cuts off Meleagant's arm before pummelling the wicked knight's helmet into his face and beheading him. According to Malory's version of the story, Lancelot fought Mellyagaunce without his helmet and with his left hand tied behind his back. With a single blow, he hacked Mellyagaunce's head in two.

Lancelot was tricked by King Pelles, the guardian of the Holy Grail, into sleeping with his daughter, Elaine. Lancelot fell under the spell of an enchantment which made him believe that the maiden Elaine was Queen Guinevere. They lay together till morning and Elaine conceived a son, Galahad. When Guinevere discovered that Lancelot had lain with Elaine, she was deeply distressed and told Lancelot that he was forbidden to come into her presence ever again. Lancelot became mad, and he lived wild and naked in the woods for nearly two years. Finally, Lancelot was taken in by Pelles and cured of his madness by the Holy Grail itself.

Lancelot returned to Arthur's court at Camelot and was reconciled with Guinevere to act once more as the queen's champion. Their passion was rekindled and the love between the two grew, until, one night when King Arthur was away on a hunting trip, Lancelot and Guinevere were discovered together in the queen's quarters. Lancelot killed several knights as he escaped and fled from Camelot, realising that all-out war was inevitable. When Arthur returned, he reluctantly ordered that the adulterous Guinevere be burned at the stake.

At the last moment, as Guinevere was tied to a stake and firewood piled at her feet, Lancelot rode in. As he rescued the queen from the flames, Lancelot cut down many knights, including Sir Gawain's brothers Gareth and Gaheris. Lancelot took Guinevere and rode back to Joyous Guard. Arthur pursued the lovers and laid siege to the castle, surrounded by his loyal knights. A bitter fight ensued, but on the battlefield Lancelot refused to lift a weapon against his king, even though Arthur charged at him with a lance and unseated him. Lancelot's brother, Ector, knocked Arthur from his horse, but

Lancelot refused to kill the king, swearing that he would never harm his lord.

Finally, Arthur agreed to restore the queen's honour and take Guinevere back to Camelot. Lancelot sailed to France, and Arthur pursued him, encouraged by the vengeful Gawain. King Arthur left his treacherous son Mordred in charge of his kingdom, but he seized the throne and the king had to return to fight Mordred. In a final battle at Camlann, Arthur killed the traitor Mordred and then fell himself, mortally wounded.

Sir Lancelot avenged the death of his king by coming to Britain with his cousins Lionel and Bors to drive out Mordred's sons, who had seized Arthur's kingdom. Lionel was killed, and Mordred's two sons were slain. Lancelot learned that Guinevere had joined a nunnery, and he travelled to Amesbury to see her. The two met for one last time in the seclusion of the cloisters. Malory tells us that Guinevere 'swooned thrice' at the sight of Lancelot and that she told him to go and leave her in peace: 'Sir Launcelot, I require thee and beseech thee heartily, for all the love that ever was betwixt us, that thou never see me more in the visage . . . through thee and me is the flower of kings and knights destroyed.'

Lancelot left Guinevere and became a priest. A year later, he had a vision that she was dead. He travelled for two days to Amesbury and found that she had indeed died. The queen was laid to rest, and Lancelot, overcome with grief, refused to eat or drink and mourned at the grave until he died. His body was taken back to his beloved Joyous Guard where, just as the words on the slab in the graveyard had foretold, Lancelot du Lac was laid to rest. In *Le Morte d'Arthur*, Lancelot's brother gives the greatest knight of King Arthur's court a fitting epitaph:

> Ah Lancelot, you were head of all Christian knights . . . never matched of any earthly knight's hand. And you were the most courteous knight that ever bore shield. And you were the truest friend to your lover that ever bestrode horse, and you were the truest lover, of sinful man, that ever loved woman, and you were the kindest man that ever struck with a sword.

SEE ALSO: Camelot; Chivalry; Chrétien de Troyes; Fisher King; Galahad; Guinevere; Lady of the Lake

LAST SUPPER

The Last Supper is believed by Christians to be the very last meal shared by Jesus and his disciples, held on the Thursday night before the Crucifixion of Christ on the Friday — now known as Good Friday. In some Grail romances, the Holy Grail is said to be the vessel of the Last Supper. Robert de Boron tells us that Joseph of Arimathea's miraculous Grail table was built to commemorate the table used by Jesus and the twelve disciples at the Last Supper, and that King Arthur's Round Table is the third in this group of blessed tables.

Because of references to Passover in the Gospels, the Last Supper is traditionally said to have taken place during the Jewish festival. It is often described as a Seder meal, although there is some doubt amongst scholars as to whether this was in fact the case. Randal Helms, in his book *Gospel Fictions*, details why he believes the Last Supper was not the traditional Seder meal:

> Though Mark calls it a Passover meal his description of what happens there, which he found in the kind of tradition Paul also used, is not a description of a Passover meal; no bitter herbs are mentioned, as is required by Numbers 9:11, and no Passover liturgy is recited; indeed, [there is] a tradition that whoever does not mention the lamb, unleavened bread, and bitter herbs at the meal has not fulfilled his Passover obligations.

Tradition holds that the Last Supper took place in a building outside

130

of the walls of Jerusalem – on Mount Zion itself – in an upper room known today as the Cenacle. The original building has been destroyed and rebuilt at least twice since the time of that famous meal. First, the Persians destroyed it, and then, after it had been rebuilt, it was razed to the ground by the Saracens during the crusades. Later, the crusaders rebuilt it, and their building has remained intact until the present day, despite the fact that the city was once again occupied by the Saracens. It fell into the care of Franciscan monks, who purchased the site from the Saracens some time around the year 1335, and they repaired the Cenacle as well as building a new monastery near the site. The Franciscans remained there up until 1552, when the Turks took Jerusalem and all Christians were evicted violently from the city. The sacred room was then used as a mosque, and it was only upon the creation of the State of Israel in the twentieth century that Christians were allowed back into the Cenacle. Today, ownership of the room has passed to the Catholic Church.

At the Last Supper, Jesus told his disciples to remember him by serving wine from the holy chalice. He explained this first by breaking bread and explaining its significance, after which he turned to the matter of the chalice itself. We find this precise moment in I Corinthians:

> The Lord Jesus, on the night he was betrayed, took bread, and when he had given thanks, he broke it and said, 'This is my body, which is for you; do this in remembrance of me.' In the same way, after supper he took the cup, saying, 'This cup is the new covenant in my blood; do this, whenever you drink it, in remembrance of me. For whenever you eat this bread and drink this cup, you proclaim the Lord's death until he comes.'

Later sources stated that this cup was the same vessel in which Joseph of Arimathea (or Mary Magdalene in some accounts) collected the blood of Jesus during the Passion. The Cup of Christ used at the Last Supper became the legendary Holy Grail. Other sources claim that the Grail is not actually the cup but rather the dish from which Jesus ate his last meal of Passover lamb. While these two ideas contradict each other, the fact that both were present at the Last Supper should not be ignored, and the importance of this evening in Grail lore is clearly paramount.

Many depictions of the Last Supper have been painted by artists over the centuries, the most famous of which is undoubtedly Leonardo da Vinci's mural, *Il Cenacolo*, *The Last Supper*, which can still be seen on the wall of the refectory of the convent of Santa Maria delle Grazie in Milan. Leonardo's masterpiece has been scrutinised and analysed in great detail over the years, and one of the points raised by numerous commentators is the fact that there is not a single chalice, or what we might consider a Grail cup, on the table of the Last Supper. Rather, there is a platter in front of Jesus, which in some people's minds confirms that the Grail was a platter and not a cup.

The majority of Arthurian romances, however, describe the Holy Grail as a cup or chalice, and many other depictions of the Last Supper, such as that by seventeenth-century artist Philippe de Champaigne, do show a chalice; this seems to have been the standard way of depicting the famous vessel. While Leonardo might simply have been putting his own spin on the scene and offering his own version of the events that night, it is curious that he chose to omit this detail. Some have even taken this as evidence that Leonardo was trying to show that Mary Magdalene, and not a cup or chalice, was the true Grail. He may in fact be presenting us with a more accurate depiction of the Grail, because Chrétien de Troyes' *Perceval, or the Story of the Grail*, the first Grail romance, describes this sacred vessel as a platter and not as a cup at all.

The scene of the Last Supper, whether in the New Testament sources or in Leonardo's mural, is one full of potential and endless possibilities. It is a defining moment in history and myth, an event that would shape world religions, the beginning of the ritual of Holy Communion and also of the legend of the Holy Grail.

SEE ALSO: Chrétien de Troyes; Holy Grail; Joseph of Arimathea; Mary Magdalene

LAYAMON

During the reign of King Richard I of England, 'the Lionheart' (1189–99), a priest living at Arley Regis by the River Severn in Worcestershire decided that having the tales of Arthur and England's 'outstanding men' available in Latin, Welsh and French was not enough. The priest, Layamon, used the *Roman de Brut* of Wace as his main source, and, 'quill pens he clutched in fingers, composing on his parchment', he translated the stories of the earliest owners of his England into the language of the English common folk, a development of Anglo-Saxon now known as archaised Middle English. Layamon asks that each good man who reads his book say a prayer for his 'father's soul, who first gave him being, and for his mother's soul who bore him as a male-child, and lastly for his own soul, that it may be safer'.

Layamon tells us that he was inspired to recount the noble deeds of the English people, their names and their origin. He makes a distinction between the Saxons and the Britons and, perhaps surprisingly, since he was writing in developed Anglo-Saxon, he portrays Arthur as a great hero who defeats the Saxons. While Wace in his stories has time for gentle things such as love, the more down-to-earth Layamon demonstrates his belief that warriors are so busy slaughtering their enemies and fighting to keep themselves alive that they have little time to enjoy such pleasures. His hero is an Arthur who is forced to take up arms and fight for his existence, a king who is majestic, overpowering and even cruel.

Layamon claims to have been much travelled around England, obtaining books as sources for his work. Any bibliophile will warm to Layamon's description of laying his source works before him, turning over the leaves and looking at them 'lovingly'. He then takes up his pen and begins to write his *Brut*. There are several medieval chronicles referred to as a *Brut* because their subject matter is the history of Britain beginning with the legendary Brutus. While Layamon claims that he drew his story partly from the works of the Venerable Bede, Albinus and Augustine, it is quite apparent that his main source was Wace's *Roman de Brut*.

It has been suggested that Layamon's *Brut* was completed around 1215, the year when King John's Chancery issued Magna Carta in response to pressure from his barons and the threat of civil war. Beginning with the fall of the city of Troy, Layamon's chronicle tells of Brutus, legendary great-grandson of the famous Trojan hero Aeneas, who journeyed across the Mediterranean Sea until he reached the Isle of Avalon, where giants dwelled. These giants are killed and Avalon is renamed Britain in honour of Brutus. The histories of Britain's kings are recounted, including those of King Lear, Cymbeline (Cunobelinus), Hengest and Horsa, Vortigern and Arthur. It ends with the last King of the British, Cadwallader (Cador), towards the end of the seventh century.

Layamon emphasises the elements of the story which most appeal to him. For instance, he has King Arthur as a ruler desiring peace, so that he may reign over an orderly kingdom for many years after his defeat of the Saxons. Considering Layamon was writing during a turbulent period, when England was ruled by the absent, crusading King Richard and then by the notorious King John, a desire for a settled realm is understandable. Yet Arthur, the 'noblest of kings', in Layamon's words, is also a successful warrior, as Layamon's description of the wretched, defeated Scots coming to Arthur to beg for mercy shows:

> Then came towards the host all that were hooded, and three wise bishops, in book well learned; priests and monks, many without number; canons there came, many and good, with the reliques that were noblest in the land, and yearned Arthur's peace, and his compassion. Thither came the women, that dwelt in the land; they carried in their arms their miserable children; they wept before Arthur wondrously much and their fair hair threw to the earth; cut off their locks, and there down laid at the king's feet, before all his people; set their nails to their face, so that afterwards it bled.
>
> *Brut*, Layamon (trans. Eugene Mason)

It is interesting to compare this with Wace's description of the same event (see p. 220). Layamon does give us some details of the Arthur story which are not taken from Wace. For instance, he includes the fact that three female prophets appeared at Arthur's birth to predict that he would become a great man. Jesus had his three wise men, Arthur the same number of wise women!

Although Wace mentions the Round Table, he does not emphasise its importance, whereas Layamon makes a great thing of it, describing a huge, disc-shaped table where many knights can sit in an inner circle facing outwards while a second circle sits on the outer edge facing inwards. It is so important to Layamon's King Arthur that he takes the table with him wherever he travels to avoid anyone claiming precedence, as would happen if seated at a rectangular table. The Round Table is said to be able to accommodate 1,600 people; clearly, then, Layamon's idea of the table was nothing like the version displayed at Winchester Castle today.

Both Wace and Layamon recount the hope that Arthur, the 'once and future king', will some day return to aid his people, although in their accounts they express different levels of belief. Wace is not sure that Arthur is still alive in Avalon: 'Men have ever doubted, and – as I am persuaded – will always doubt whether he liveth or is dead.' Layamon, in contrast, tells us that Arthur will come again to dwell among the Britons.

SEE ALSO: Round Table; Wace

LOHENGRIN

There is a European legacy of tales about the so-called 'Swan Knight'. He became part of the Arthurian story as Lohengrin in Wolfram von Eschenbach's *Parzival*.

The *Cycle de la Croisade*, written in Northern France in the twelfth century, deals with the First Crusade, in particular giving Godfrey of Bouillon, one of its leaders, a mythologised heritage. It contains the story of King Oriant and his wife Beatrix, who are childless until the queen mysteriously gives birth to septuplets, each of whom wears a silver necklace. Oriant's mother, Matabrune, takes the babies, six boys and a girl, to the woods, where they are found by a hermit, who raises them. The malicious Matabrune convinces her son that his wife gave birth to puppies, having been unfaithful, and the unfortunate Beatrix is locked up.

After many years, a servant of Matabrune comes across the children and recognises them by their silver chains. Six children are seized by her men only to turn into swans, leaving only one boy who is away from the house at the time with the hermit. Finally, under constant pressure from Matabrune, Oriant agrees to condemn his wife to death, and she is sentenced to be executed unless a champion arrives to defend her. An angel appears to the hermit and reveals that it is the destiny of the remaining boy, Elias, to save his mother. Although he has no experience in combat, Elias's inherent faith enables him to overcome Matabrune's champion and rescue his mother. Elias's sister and four of his brothers return to their human form, but the last brother is forced to remain a swan, as his magical necklace has been destroyed.

LOHENGRIN

Elias, in a boat drawn by his swan brother, leaves his home and journeys to Nijmegen, where he acts as a champion for the Duchess of Bouillon and then marries her daughter – confusingly also called Beatrix. Elias tells his wife that she must never ask about his identity, and it is foretold that she will have a daughter whose sons will be a king, a duke and a count. Beatrix gives birth to a daughter named Ida, and Elias the Swan Knight defends their land from the Saxons, establishing a peaceful realm. However, disaster strikes on their seventh wedding anniversary, when Beatrix cannot resist asking Elias about his origins. At this point, his swan brother and the boat make a reappearance and he leaves his family, never to return, going home to his own land. Elias takes over the kingdom from his father Oriant and has a successful reign until he decides to become a monk and abdicates in favour of his oldest brother. Just before his death, Elias asks a trusted friend to bring his wife and daughter to him, and he predicts that his daughter will have a son who will be King of Jerusalem.

This story provides a heroic ancestry for Godfrey of Bouillon, who travelled with his brothers to the Holy Land in 1096. His mother was called Ida and her sons with her husband Eustace II of Boulogne were King Baldwin I of Jerusalem, Duke Godfrey of Bouillon and Count Eustace III of Boulogne. In this way the 'prophecy' of the story is fulfilled, although the historical Ida's father, rather than a Swan Knight, was, somewhat more prosaically, Godfrey II of Lower Lorraine. As a leader of the crusade that successfully recaptured Jerusalem in 1099 and as a descendant of the legendary Charlemagne, Godfrey de Bouillon was regarded by later generations as an exemplary Christian knight and hero.

In Wolfram's story, Lohengrin is the son of Parzival and his wife Condwiramurs. While his twin brother Kardeiz is the heir to their father's lands and property, it is Lohengrin who takes on the mantle of the Grail knight. He is sent to the Duchy of Brabant, where the heiress Elsa is under siege from several knights who want to marry her. Lohengrin appears in a boat pulled by a swan and defends Elsa, after which they marry and rule together for many years. It has been a stipulation that Elsa must never ask Lohengrin what his origins are, but, perhaps inevitably, her curiosity gets the better of her. When she asks her husband his name, he explains that he comes from the Grail castle, and, stepping back into his boat, he is drawn away by the swan.

A later version of the story has Elsa goaded into questioning her husband by malicious rumours that he is not of noble blood. This anonymous *Lohengrin*, written in the thirteenth century, extended the story into an epic poem consisting of 767 stanzas. Yet more variation occurs in Richard Wagner's dramatisation of *Lohengrin* as an opera. Here Elsa has been accused of murdering her younger brother Gottfried, and Lohengrin arrives as her champion in answer to her prayers. The couple are married, but, tragically, she asks the forbidden question about who he is, and his role as a guardian of the Grail is revealed. Lohengrin prepares to leave, and his swan is transformed back into the missing Gottfried, who, it transpires, had been bewitched by the wicked Ortrud to prevent him inheriting the kingdom. The dove of the Grail leads Lohengrin away, and, in the finest operatic tradition, Elsa dies of her grief for her lost husband.

SEE ALSO: Percival; Wagner, Richard; Wolfram von Eschenbach

MALORY, SIR THOMAS

Sir Thomas Malory's *Le Morte d'Arthur* is arguably the world's most famous Arthurian work. Malory himself called his collection of eight romances *The Book of King Arthur and his Noble Knights of the Round Table*. William Caxton, the publisher and printer of the stories, right at the end of the reign of King Richard III, in the summer of 1485, decided to give it the pithier but less accurate title *Le Morte d'Arthur*, although it covers much more than the death of Arthur.

Charles Ross, a Professor of Medieval History at the University of Bristol, states in *The Wars of the Roses* that the author of *Le Morte d'Arthur* sat as a Member of Parliament three times and was 'a flagrant law-breaker'. He committed rape (which charge may, in that period, actually signify adultery) and extortion, and with a large gang he attempted to ambush and murder a duke of royal blood. Malory, Ross tells us, rustled cattle and terrorised a monastery. Further, he broke into an abbey and returned on the following day to insult the inhabitants and steal more valuables. Unsurprisingly, Malory ultimately wound up in prison, 'to which,' Ross says, 'we owe the *Morte d'Arthur*', the implication being that while kicking his heels in a cell he began to write to occupy his time.

Malory was born in Newbold Revel, Warwickshire. He was knighted in 1442 and first sat in Parliament in 1445, during the reign of the hopelessly inadequate Henry VI. He served on committees to assess tax exemptions and was accused of, but never tried for, falsely imprisoning a man, wounding him and stealing his goods. It was largely as a result of the weakness of the regime that it was extremely difficult to receive justice when the law had been broken, given that powerful nobles and gentry like Malory retained gangs of tough men willing to do their bidding. A landowner had a duty to protect his holdings and hand over his possessions, enhanced if possible, to his heirs. Laws which existed to make this easy were only effective when they could be enforced. Such enforcement depended on the determination and ability of those responsible to the king to see that his laws were obeyed. Close ties with powerful local magnates were clearly useful; the protection of a mighty lord could help preserve a family's property and allow them to benefit at the expense of others without much fear of retribution.

It may seem surprising that the great poet of *Le Morte d'Arthur* engaged in so much criminal activity, but in the Warwickshire of Malory's day, it would not have been considered so very unusual. Following the death of Richard Beauchamp, Earl of Warwick, in 1439, the area was left with no strong man in control, his heir being a minor. The Duke of Buckingham tried to fill the gap, but factions opposed him and effective local government became chaotic. Sir Thomas Malory, perhaps no better or worse than many of his neighbours, took advantage of this breakdown of control, fought his own local battles and seems to have had little respect for Church or state.

It should be pointed out, in fairness, that such lawlessness did not end with the change of regime when Edward IV took the throne and that it was not limited to the Midlands. Cornwall has been described as 'a chronically disturbed county', with the piratical Sir Henry Bodrugan being perhaps its most infamous son. The Harringtons and Stanleys in Lancashire, Talbots and Berkeleys in Gloucestershire and the Duke of Norfolk and the Paston family are just some entries in a catalogue of disputes that took place around this period, some of which ended in murder.

After 1452, much of Malory's life seems to have been spent in prison, and he waited to come to trial for the next decade. By the summer of 1461, Edward IV of York had deposed Henry VI and became king. His father, Richard, Duke of York, had previously issued a pardon for Malory while he was Protector of England during King Henry's period of madness, but the courts had not accepted it. The new king could now insist, and Malory joined the Yorkist Earl of Warwick on an expedition to reduce some remaining Lancastrian strongholds whose garrisons were still loyal to the old regime. However, circumstances seem to have caused him to change his allegiance. In 1468 and also in 1470, his name appears on lists of malcontents opposed to the Yorkist regime who were so incorrigible that they were excluded from general pardons that had been issued for past offences and crimes. These pardons were sometimes issued to wipe the slate clean in an attempt to reconcile previous offenders to the regime and to rehabilitate them. In 1470, the Lancastrians returned briefly to power, and their friends who were then in jail were freed. Six months later, Malory was dead, buried at Greyfriars, Newgate, London.

The popularity of Malory's tales lies not only in the attraction of the stories but also in the beautiful language in which they are told. It has been said that it is difficult to reconcile a man who is alleged to have committed so many appalling crimes, felonies and breaches of the peace with the creation of a work speaking of chivalric ideals, honour and love. In the context of his time, however, it is not so surprising. In fifteenth-century England, it was normal for a man to elbow aside his competitors, striving only for the aggrandisement of himself and his kin. Malory would have recognised the chivalric qualities of his characters without necessarily believing that they had much practical relevance to his own cavalier lifestyle.

E.K. Chambers writes in his *Malory and Fifteenth-Century Drama, Lyrics and Ballads* that Malory took some of his inspiration from French Arthurian material, including the stories woven about the Sangreal or Sant Graal (Holy Grail). In *Le Morte d'Arthur*, we find a description of Sir Lancelot witnessing a sick knight who is healed by being privileged to touch and kiss the Sangreal, which seems to be the vessel used in the Mass, though in a supernatural setting. Sir Percival and Sir Ector are, by the presence of the Holy Vessel, cured of wounds they have inflicted upon each other, and Sir Bors sees the Sangreal carried by a maiden. Malory emphasises that it is presumptuous for the over-proud to seek the vessel, for a knight who quests for the Grail must be totally virtuous in order to achieve his goal. He also tells us that:

> Merlin made the Round Table in tokening of roundness of the world, for by the Round Table is the world signified by right, for all the world, Christian and heathen repair unto the Round Table, and when they are chosen to be of the fellowship of the Round Table they think them more blessed and more in worship than if they had gotten half the world.

Malory also has Merlin tell the knights who will achieve the Sangreal, in the kind of mysterious language used by seers and prophets, how they should be known:

> there should be three white bulls who should enchieve it . . .
> and the third should be chaste. And that one of the three
> should pass his father as much as the lion passeth the leopard,
> both of strength and hardiness.

Sir Thomas Malory's *Le Morte d'Arthur* was an inspiration to Alfred, Lord Tennyson, William Morris and and a host of nineteenth- and twentieth-century Arthurian writers and filmmakers, bringing the legends to us today. If Malory had been a less violent, more law-abiding and loyal subject, if he had kept his head down and stayed out of trouble, he might never have given the world his vision of King Arthur and his knights.

SEE ALSO: Holy Grail; Lancelot; Percival

MARY MAGDALENE

Mary Magdalene might not normally feature in a book about King Arthur and the Holy Grail, but, with the remarkable success of Dan Brown's novel *The Da Vinci Code*, there has been a great deal of debate about the Holy Grail and whether the term refers not to an object such as a platter or cup but to Mary Magdalene. Dan Brown is not the only author to have put forward such ideas. Michael Baigent, Richard Leigh and Henry Lincoln, in their bestselling book *The Holy Blood and the Holy Grail*, also argued the point that the Grail was nothing less than the bloodline of Jesus and his wife, Mary Magdalene, that, in short, this most sacred of couples had a child. The same concept had also appeared in Liz Greene's novel *The Dreamer of the Vine*.

The idea that it is the bloodline of Jesus that is the true Holy Grail – and specifically that Mary Magdalene was the vessel by which this sacred blood was kept alive – is certainly an intriguing notion and one that is at the very least worthy of investigation. What makes this theory so potent is the idea that if such a child did exist, the descendants of Jesus Christ and Mary Magdalene might actually be walking among us today.

Some versions of the story of the Grail tell that a vessel was used to collect the blood of Jesus during the Crucifixion. Various characters are said to have collected this sacred blood; in some of the stories it is Joseph of Arimathea, but in certain versions it is Mary Magdalene herself. Mary Magdalene reaches out with a cup to collect Christ's blood, to be held safe for eternity. But what if the cup was not the

Grail itself? What if the tale preserved secret knowledge that Mary Magdalene had in fact kept safe the bloodline of Jesus in another way – by bearing his child?

Before we examine whether Mary Magdalene and her possible offspring really could be the Grail, we need to find out a little more about who she really was. Her name means Mary of Magdala, a town on the shores of the Sea of Galilee. There is a tradition that she was of noble blood and even a descendant of the House of David, but it is unclear whether this is truth or speculation. This assumption has been made because early in the history of the Christian Church Mary Magdalene was associated with another Mary mentioned in the New Testament, Mary of Bethany. This woman was one of three children, the other two being Martha and Lazarus. They all inherited great riches after their father, Syrus, died, and, while Martha lived a humble life, Mary of Bethany is said to have assumed an extravagant and colourful lifestyle, one which gained her a reputation as a sinner.

It is clearly this identification of Mary Magdalene with Mary of Bethany that led the Catholic Church to claim that Mary Magdalene was unchaste and a sinner. This in turn gave birth over time to many tales that saw Mary Magdalene branded as a prostitute and a harlot in many people's eyes, a belief that has persisted into modern times. There are very few references to Mary Magdalene in the New Testament or other, apocryphal texts. For someone who has had so much conjecture piled upon her head, she appears very briefly in historical documents.

We first find her in the Gospel of Luke, where she is described as providing Jesus with material goods and possibly providing financial support. This, of course, could confirm the speculation that she did in fact come from a noble house. It is also in Luke that we find a passage detailing how Jesus cured Mary Magdalene of some affliction:

> After this, Jesus travelled about from one town and village to another, proclaiming the good news of the kingdom of God. The Twelve were with him, and also some women who had been cured of evil spirits and diseases: Mary (called Magdalene) from whom seven demons had come out . . .

It seems that these women accompanied Jesus to Jerusalem and this was how Mary Magdalene came to be one of his trusted disciples. The next reference to Mary Magdalene in the New Testament is at the Crucifixion itself and afterwards, as she anoints Christ's body after it is brought down from the cross. Finally, Mary Magdalene is the first witness of the Resurrection of Christ. At first, she does not recognise him, thinking he is the gardener, but when he calls her name she understands. The fact that Mary Magdalene is shown to have been the first to see Jesus after his Resurrection is often cited as a strong indication that Jesus held her in very high esteem or that they were in fact married. This final meeting between Mary and Jesus is the last mention of Mary Magdalene in the New Testament; after this, she falls from the pages of history and all that remains are legends and Gnostic traditions.

The Catholic Church holds that she went to Rome to tell the Emperor Tiberius of the Resurrection of Christ and that she remained there until the arrival of Paul. After Paul's death, Mary is said to have left for Ephesus where she was to spend her final days. However, French tales, collated and compiled some time between the eleventh and thirteenth centuries (the most famous of which is probably *The Golden Legend* by Jacobus de Voraigne) describe how Mary and her brother and sister, Lazarus and Martha (here Mary is again identified with Mary of Bethany), were set adrift by the Jews in a boat with neither oars nor sails with which to navigate the seas. Fate guided them to the shore near Marseilles in France, where after a time Mary Magdalene retreated to live in the caves of Sainte-Baume. Today, a small chapel sitting atop the cliffs there marks what is said to be the spot where angels finally took Mary Magdalene to heaven. Yet another legend relates that Mary Magdalene accompanied St Maximin to another part of France, this time Aix-en-Provence. Many other versions exist, all concluding with Mary Magdalene in France. However, despite the many claims that this is where she ended her days, the place of her burial is unknown, and all we have left to us are the legends.

Gnostic tradition offers a different version of the Magdalene's life after the death and Resurrection of Jesus. The Gospel of Philip – a collection of sayings that was found at Nag Hammadi in Egypt, some of which are claimed to be from the mouth of Jesus himself – mentions Mary Magdalene and sheds some light on the relationship between her and Christ, even if it does not clear up the matter conclusively. Unfortunately, the manuscript is damaged and certain key words are missing so the original meaning can only be guessed at. (These words are indicated by square brackets in the text below.) The inference is clear, however: that Mary Magdalene and Jesus had a close relationship:

> And the companion of [the saviour was] Mary Magdalene.
> [Christ loved] her more than [all] the disciples, [and used to]
> kiss her [often] on her [mouth]. The rest of [the disciples were
> offended by it and expressed disapproval]. They said to him
> 'Why do you love her more than all of us?'

As well as this mention of Mary Magdalene, there is also another passage in which she is referred to as Jesus's 'companion', but no conclusive answer has been reached as to whether this was meant in the sense 'friend and supporter', or whether it was a euphemism for 'wife'.

Potentially more important to us than the Gospel of Philip are the words of Mary Magdalene herself, recorded for posterity in the shape of the Gospel of Mary. Forming part of Papyrus Berolinensis 8502, it was acquired in 1896 in Cairo. It contains three Coptic editions of Gnostic texts, thought to date to the early fifth century. This codex contains the most complete version of *The Gospel of Mary* found to date.

Mary Magdalene's importance is clearly demonstrated in this document, and we see that Jesus had placed the future of his burgeoning church in Mary's hands. When Mary tells the other disciples about the words of Jesus, some clearly doubt her, highlighting the tensions that were present between the disciples after the Resurrection. It appears to be Peter who is the most disturbed at the news of the meeting between Jesus and Mary Magdalene:

> Peter answered and spoke concerning these same things.
> He questioned them about the Saviour: Did He really speak
> privately with a woman and not openly to us? Are we to turn
> about and all listen to her? Did He prefer her to us?

It is not Mary who answers Peter but Levi, and he says:

> But if the Saviour made her worthy, who are you indeed to
> reject her? Surely the Saviour knows her very well.
> That is why He loved her more than us. Rather let us be
> ashamed and put on the perfect Man, and separate as He
> commanded us and preach the gospel, not laying down any
> other rule or other law beyond what the Saviour said.

Many researchers have put forward the argument that at the time of Jesus within the Jewish community it would have been impossible for a rabbi or a spiritual teacher such as Jesus to practise while unmarried, as this went against the divine commandments. However, this argument is flawed because it was not until after the destruction of the Second Temple in Jerusalem in AD 70 that Rabbinic Judaism began to take hold. Consequently, there are said to have been many celibate spiritual leaders in Jesus's day; indeed, John the Baptist himself is an example.

So we are, unfortunately, unable to throw any more light on the matter of whether Jesus and Mary were married and whether Mary Magdalene is in fact alluded to in legends of the Holy Grail. Furthermore, if the Grail is either Mary Magdalene or the bloodline of Jesus sustained through her and her child, then this seems to be at odds with the Holy Grail of the Arthurian romances.

However, there is a way to reconcile the two concepts: in Arthurian myth, the Holy Grail was often guarded by the Fisher King and his family. If we imagine that the Fisher King was a descendant of Jesus and Mary Magdalene, then this royal family was actually the Grail, and the vessel which they had in their possession merely a symbol of this fact. If the Holy Grail really was the bloodline of Mary Magdalene and Jesus, then achieving the Grail was in reality learning the secret that the descendants of Christ still walked the earth.

The Fisher King is sometimes Joseph of Arimathea's brother-in-law, a character called Bron, so here we have a connection with the bloodline of Jesus, as tradition has it that Joseph of Arimathea was a relative of his. The Fisher King's wound is widely thought to be linked to the wounding of Jesus on the Cross by the spear of Longinus. In the French romance *Perlesvaus*, we find the following passage which almost seems to be hinting that both the Grail and the Fisher King could be connected with the matter of holy lineage:

> 'I saw the Grail', says the master, 'before the Fisher King. Joseph [of Arimathea], who was his uncle, collected in it the blood which flowed from the wounds of the Saviour of the World. Know well all your lineage and from what folk you are descended.'

It can be argued that there is a case to be made that the Holy Grail symbolised Mary Magdalene and the bloodline of Jesus in a secret so precious that knowledge of its existence could be alluded to and passed down to us only in the medieval Grail romances. However, the fact remains that all of this is pure speculation.

The Quest for the Holy Grail, and what it means to us, is not over.

Clearly, it still occupies us today. Numerous theologians, academics, priests and Arthurian scholars have spoken out against the theories and concepts within *The Da Vinci Code*. As Norris Lacy says in his article '*The Da Vinci Code*: Dan Brown and the Grail That Never Was', 'Brown's ideas are elaborate, fascinating, and wrong.' He goes on to quote an ironic comment from the book itself: 'We might add only Brown's own admission . . . : "A career hazard of symbologists [is] a tendency to extract hidden meaning from situations that had none."' Nonetheless, for all the evidence against the idea that the Holy Grail is actually Mary Magdalene or the bloodline of Jesus, many people choose to believe the theory.

SEE ALSO: Fisher King; Holy Grail; Joseph of Arimathea

MERLIN

Merlin is often pictured as the archetypal wizard, a befuddled old man with an unkempt white beard, long robes and a tall pointy hat. The real Merlin was a wild man who lived with the wolves and the boars in the woods, a prophet who foretold his own death.

Geoffrey of Monmouth tells us that Merlin's mother was the daughter of the king of Dimetia; she was seduced by an incubus in the shape of a most beautiful young man, who often embraced her eagerly and kissed her, but would suddenly vanish and talk with her without appearing. She says: 'When he had a long time haunted me in this manner, he at last lay with me several times in the shape of a man, and left me with child.'

In Layamon's version of the story, Merlin's mother dreamt each night of the figure of a tall knight, 'the fairest thing that ever was born'. The thing glided before her, and 'glistened of gold'. It often drew near, held her and kissed her, and she became pregnant and gave birth to Merlin, not knowing what his father was.

Robert De Boron's *Merlin* takes this story and embroiders it, explaining that the Devil was filled with wrath by Christ's Harrowing of Hell and sought to undo his work. A gathering of fiends agreed to create their own son of a virgin, an antichrist that would walk the world and do their bidding. A devil was sent to father the child on a virtuous woman, but the plot went awry when Merlin's mother sought the advice of a holy hermit called Blaise. In time, she gives birth to a child and names him Merlin. The miraculous child Merlin can speak as soon as he is weaned and saves his mother from execution, telling her judge: 'I know better my father than thou does yours and thy mother knows better who is thy father than my mother knoweth mine.' The hermit Blaise speaks with the child, saying: 'I have heard thee say, and I believe well that you art the son of the devil. Wherefore I doubt thee sore, lest you deceive and beguile me.' Merlin replied: 'You have heard me say that I was conceived of the devil. So have you heard me say that God has given me mind to know things that are to come.'

Stories of Merlin's life and deeds are told in various early chronicles. From these we learn that shortly after Merlin's birth, the usurper Vortigern seized the crown with the aid of the Saxons and married the Saxon leader Hengest's daughter, but he could not control his treacherous allies, and Hengest, with his pagan warriors, plotted to massacre the British princes when they were to meet to agree a peace. The Saxons went to the meeting carrying long daggers under their garments, and, at the agreed command, they fell upon the Britons, assassinating 460 princes and consuls.

Vortigern fled into the mountains of North Wales and tried to build a tower at Dinas Emrys where he would be safe from the Saxons and the remaining British nobles. Every day, his men built the stone walls up, but every night, the walls fell. According to Geoffrey of Monmouth, Vortigern consulted his magi (magicians or astrologers), who told the king to seek out a child with no father and sprinkle his blood on the foundations of the tower. In the city of Carmarthen, Vortigern's men found the boy Merlin playing ball with some other children. One boy taunted Merlin, saying he had no father, and Merlin was brought before the king. The boy spoke up and ridiculed Vortigern's magi: 'Because you are ignorant what hinders the foundation of the tower, you have recommended the shedding of my blood for cement, as if that would make it stand. But tell me now, what is there under the foundation?' The magi grew afraid and could not answer. Merlin then told Vortigern: 'Command your workmen to dig into the ground and you will find a pond which causes the foundations to sink.' Vortigern's men did indeed find a pond on the hill of Dinas Emrys, just as Merlin had predicted. 'Tell me ye false sycophants, what is under the pond?' said Merlin. Again, the magi were silent. Merlin told Vortigern that at the bottom of the pond he would find two hollow stones, and in them two sleeping dragons. Merlin instructed him that the red dragon symbolised the Britons and the white dragon the Saxons whom Vortigern had invited over, and he prophesied that the red and white dragons were destined to fight until the Boar of Cornwall (Arthur) came to crush the invaders. The wizard then foretold the death of Vortigern.

Soon, Vortigern was besieged in his tower by the British princes Aurelius Ambrosius and Uther Pendragon, who burned down the tower with the usurper inside. Aurelius Ambrosius became king and decided to have a great monument built to commemorate the princes of Britain massacred by the Saxons. Merlin tells the king to send for the Giant's Dance, a structure of mystical stones on a mountain called Killaraus, in Ireland, saying that the stones were brought from the farthest coast of Africa by the giants of old and placed in Ireland when they inhabited that country. Merlin led Uther Pendragon and 15,000 men to Ireland to take the Giant's Dance and 'by craft of his art' he brought the stones to Salisbury plain. They set the stones up to honour the burial place of the fallen princes with an everlasting monument that we now call Stonehenge.

Merlin was also responsible for the creation of the Round Table. As Uther's adviser, he told the king the story of how Joseph of Arimathea set the Grail upon a round table, and that Joseph's table was itself a copy of the table of the Last Supper. The wizard built the Round Table, the third table, in the name of the Holy Trinity. Uther later gave the table to King Leodegrance of Cameliard, the father of Guinevere, and when Arthur and Guinevere married, the Round Table became part of Guinevere's dowry.

When Uther Pendragon laid siege to Tintagel Castle, he again called on Merlin to aid him. Uther desired Igraine, the wife of Duke Gorlois of Cornwall, and the greatest beauty in all Britain. He had fallen passionately in love with her but could not break the castle's defences. Uther was overwhelmed by lust. He feared that his body and mind would break. Merlin transformed Uther so that he could ride into the castle and stay the night with Igraine. She was deceived by the disguise, and that night Arthur was conceived. When Arthur was born, Merlin took the child and entrusted him to Sir Ector, who raised Arthur with his own son Kay, teaching them the ways of knighthood. At 15, Arthur pulled the sword from the stone and became king, with Merlin as his adviser, helping him to defeat 11 kings who rebelled against him. Merlin left the king's court when Arthur married Guinevere, and at this time, it is said, the magician's thoughts turned to love. Merlin wandered the faerie paths of the Forest of Brocéliande, where deep in the green woods he met Viviane, the Lady of the Lake, and fell deeply in love. Viviane persuaded Merlin to teach her the secrets of his magic. In the years that followed,

Merlin would go back to Arthur's court, but always he would return to Viviane. In time, Viviane learned all of Merlin's enchantments and cast a spell to keep the wizard in Brocéliande forever. It is said that Merlin and Viviane still dwell in Brocéliande and that to this day the old enchanter's laughter may be heard in the woods.

This Merlin of Geoffrey of Monmouth and the medieval tales was based upon the poet and prophet called variously Myrddin, Myrddin Wyllt, Merlin the Wild, Merlin Sylvestris, Merlin of the Wood, Merlin Caledonius, Laloecen and Lailoken. The story of Merlin the Wild can be pieced together from lives of saints, fragments of manuscripts and Welsh poems. Merlin the Wild was a seer, gifted with the second sight. He predicted the future for the pagan prince Gwenddolau, who met King Rhydderch in the Battle of Arderydd in AD 573. The dreadful slaughter broke Merlin's mind. Gwenddolau and all his men fell, and Merlin fled into the Forest of Celidon, seized by a strange madness. In the woods, Merlin lived wild, eating hazelnuts and acorns with only the wolves and the pigs for company.

When a holy man named Kentigern came to the forest to preach, Merlin threw stones at him and shouted him down, uttering wild prophecies, and Kentigern was moved to tears by his plight. Merlin predicted his own death, foretelling that he would die a magical threefold death, 'pierced by stake, suffering by stone and by water'. At Stobo, the old pagan Merlin was baptised at an altarstone by Kentigern. That very day, he was attacked by three shepherds as he walked by the banks of the River Tweed. They stoned Merlin and threw him into the river, where he was impaled on fishing spikes and drowned, fulfilling his prophecy.

Merlin has many graves and sleeps beneath many hills. Marlborough in Wiltshire is said to owe its name to Merlin's Barrow, a mound where the wizard sleeps. Legend has it that Merlin sleeps in a hidden cave under Merlin's Hill near Carmarthen, in a cave at Alderley Edge in Cheshire and in a glass tomb in a cave on Bardsey Island, surrounded by the Thirteen Treasures of Britain. A neolithic stone monument in Brocéliande is named Merlin's Tomb, and Merlin's Grave can be found near Drumelzier in the Borders of Scotland.

The thirteenth-century Borders seer Thomas the Rhymer foretold that:

> When Tweed and Powsail meet at Merlin's grave,
> England and Scotland shall one monarch have.

It is said that in 1603, on the day that the Scottish and English crowns were united under King James VI of Scotland and I of England, the River Tweed burst its banks and met the Powsail Burn, thereby indicating the site of Merlin's grave.

Some say that Merlin still lives. In Cheshire, a local folk tale tells that once a farmer with a milk-white horse to sell wandered by Alderley Edge, and as he crossed the sandstone cliffs, he met an old man with a long white beard who offered to buy the horse. However, the farmer decided to take it to market. That night, his horse was still unsold, and he followed the same road home. At Alderley Edge, he was greeted again by the old man, who led him to the cliff-face. Two iron gates appeared in the rock and the mysterious stranger took the farmer and his horse deep into a cave. Within the cave, the farmer saw sleeping knights and their milk-white horses awaiting the day when England would be in greatest need. One soldier was without a horse. The old man showed the farmer a cavern filled with gold and precious gems, and, in a daze, he took some of the gold and staggered out of the cave. The iron gates slammed shut behind him, but when he turned in fright, all he could see was the bare rock wall. The story goes that the old man was the wizard Merlin and that King Arthur and his knights slept within the cliffs. At Alderley Edge, you will find the Wizard's Well. Carved into the rock is an inscription that says:

> Drink of this and take thy fill,
> For the water falls by the wizard's will.

SEE ALSO: Brocéliande; Geoffrey of Monmouth; Joseph of Arimathea; Lady of the Lake; Last Supper; Layamon; Robert de Boron; Round Table

MORDRED

Every story needs a good villain, someone truly evil who dresses all in black, who plots and schemes in secret behind the hero's back. Mordred has become the villain of the tales of King Arthur – a treacherous son who kills his father in his lust for power and revenge.

The tenth-century Latin chronicle *Annales Cambriae* (*Annals of Wales*) records the dreadful Battle of Camlann, 'The strife of Camlann in which Arthur and Medraut fell, and there was death in Britain and in Ireland.' Medraut is the earlier, Welsh name for Mordred. The *Annals* simply note that Arthur and Mordred fell at the Battle of Camlann. There is nothing in the text to suggest they were enemies; they might have fallen in battle fighting side by side against a common foe. Mordred also appears in the Welsh Triads, as Medrawd, where we learn that he went to Arthur's court at Celliwig in Cornwall, where 'he left neither food nor drink', suggesting an abuse of hospitality, dragged Gwenhwyfar (Guinevere) from her royal chair and struck her a blow. We're told that Arthur in turn went to Medrawd's court, where he too 'left neither food nor drink'. We also find in the Triads that Medrawd was married to Gwenhwyfach, the sister of Gwenhwyfar.

Sir Mordred features in Arthurian legend as the youngest son of Morgause (the wife of King Loth of the Lothians and Orkney) and the brother of Sir Gawain. Morgause, sometimes known as Anna, is one of Arthur's sisters. In earlier versions of the story, Mordred is the legitimate son of Loth and Morgause, the nephew of King Arthur.

MORDRED

Some Scottish medieval chronicles said Mordred was the rightful king of Britain, as Arthur was illegitimate. Geoffrey of Monmouth tells us that Arthur entrusted his kingdom to Mordred when he went to war on the Continent. In Arthur's absence, Mordred crowned himself king and took Guinevere for himself. Arthur returned to face his traitorous nephew at Camlann, where the 'accursed traitor was killed and many thousands of his men with him'.

In the *Alliterative Morte Arthure*, Guinevere has borne Mordred children by the time Arthur returns. She has also given Clarent (Arthur's father's sword) to Mordred. When Arthur meets Mordred in battle, hacking off Mordred's sword hand with Excalibur, Mordred deals Arthur a fatal blow before the king finally kills the traitor. Arthur is filled with grief that 'such a false felon should have so fair a death'.

In the *Prose Merlin*, we are told that the wife of King Loth is the sister of King Arthur on his mother's side, and that Loth's wife had five sons, 'Gawein, Agravayn, Gaheret and Gaheries by her husband, and Mordred, that was the youngest, that Kynge Arthur begat'. Mordred was conceived when Arthur was a young squire. Apparently unaware that she was his sister, he coveted Loth's wife, thinking her a great beauty. In his heart he desired her greatly. One night, King Loth slipped from his bed to attend a counsel meeting, and his lady was left alone in their chamber. Arthur saw that the king was gone and slipped under cover of darkness into the lady's bed as she slept. Loth's wife was blameless, believing him to be her husband. That night, Mordred was conceived.

According to Malory's *Le Morte d'Arthur*, Mordred was conceived after Arthur became king. The wife of King Loth of Orkney met Arthur at Caerleon, where she had been sent to spy on the court of King Arthur. She was a fair lady and Arthur desired her; she consented to sleep with him, and Mordred was conceived. King Loth's wife departed and all this time 'King Arthur knew not that King Loth's wife was his sister'. Merlin then tells Arthur: 'You have lain by your sister and on her you have gotten a child that shall destroy you and all the knights of your realm.' Arthur reacts by trying to kill Mordred before he can do any harm by having every baby born on May Day set adrift in a boat at sea. All the babies are drowned except Mordred, and Merlin's prophecy proves true. In the Post-Vulgate *Mort Artu*, as King Arthur lies dying, he says, 'Mordred, in an evil hour did I beget you. You have ruined me and the kingdom of Logres, and you have died for it. Cursed be the hour in which you were born.'

Mordred has frequently been portrayed as a creature of pure malice, a dark shadow in Camelot. In recent years, however, authors' depictions of Mordred have softened. In the novels of Mary Stewart and Phyllis Ann Karr, for example, we find Mordred portrayed more sympathetically. Rather than a two-dimensional villain, Mordred has been seen as a victim of circumstance, entangled in his mother's plots. In some versions of the myths, notably John Boorman's movie *Excalibur*, Mordred's mother is the enchantress Morgan le Fay, who transforms herself into the likeness of Guinevere, tricking Arthur into her arms in an echo of Arthur's own conception, which was brought about through Merlin's deception.

In the ninth-century *Historia Brittonum*, attributed to Nennius, a series of '*miribali*', wonders, are listed. Among these is one in a region which is called Ercing (part of what is now Herefordshire). He describes a tomb next to a spring called Licat Amr, which translates as 'the eye of Amr'. Amr was the name of the man buried in the tomb, 'the son of Arthur the soldier, and Arthur himself killed and buried him in that very place'. The *Historia* says that when men measure the grave they find it sometimes 6 ft long, sometimes 9, sometimes 12, sometimes 15. Whatever length it is on any one occasion, the next time it is measured it will not be found to be the same length. There is no record of what led the soldier Arthur to kill his son; just the tantalising possibility that Amr may be the real figure who became the treacherous Mordred.

SEE ALSO: Arthur, King of the Britons; Cinema and Theatre; Guinevere; Morgan le Fay; Scotland; Wales

MORGAN LE FAY

Morgan le Fay appears in Arthurian legend as a healer, a sorceress, a faerie and even a goddess. She is said to have plotted against her half-brother Arthur and also to have tended his wounds on the enchanted Isle of Avalon.

Morgan le Fay is often portrayed as a wicked enchantress, but in the earliest stories she appears as a skilled healer. After the battle of Camlann the mortally wounded Arthur was brought to the mystical Avalon, the Isle of Apples. Nine sisters lived on the island and one exceeded all her sisters in the art of healing. Her name was Morgan. In Geoffrey of Monmouth's *Vita Merlini* (*The Life of Merlin, c.*1150), Morgan is a renowned healer who has learned the uses of all the herbs so that she can cure the sick. She knows the arts of magic and can change her shape. She can even fly through the air to distant islands, and she is said to have taught mathematics to her sisters. When Arthur was brought to Morgan she placed the king on a golden couch, uncovered his wounds and inspected them for a long time. Finally, she said that he could be healed if he would stay with her and underwent her treatment.

Chrétien de Troyes tells us that Morgan le Fay is a friend of Guigomar, lord of the Isle of Avalon, and that she prepares for her brother a plaster 'of such sovereign virtue that no wound, whether on nerve or joint, provided it were treated with the plaster once a day, could fail to be completely cured and healed within a week'. He also writes that Morgan the Wise made an ointment that could cure any 'delirium of the head'.

In France, 'les dames faées' were 'the enchanted ladies'. In time, 'les faées' became 'les fées', the faeries. Morgan le Fay (Morgan the Faerie) is a supernatural lady who can heal and enchant, bewitch and charm. In the romance *Ogier the Dane*, Morgan le Fay is one of six faeries who appear to bless Ogier when he is born. Morgan's faerie gift is eternal life; Ogier will live forever as her lover on the Isle of Avalon. According to the *Prose Merlin*, Morgan is schooled in a convent, where she learns astronomy, nature, medicine and the seven liberal arts (grammar, rhetoric, logic, arithmetic, geometry, cosmology and music). She is given the name Morgan le Fay because of her gifts as a sorceress. Thomas Malory tells us that Morgan is the half-sister of King Arthur, the daughter of Duke Gorlois of Cornwall and Arthur's mother Igraine. According to him, the young Morgan was educated in a nunnery where she learned so much that she became 'a great clerk of necromancy'. Morgan learned yet more about magic from Merlin and used her arts to plot against Queen Guinevere.

Some stories say that Morgan le Fay was jealous of Guinevere because she had the love of Lancelot, while others relate that she hated the queen because Guinevere put an end to Morgan's love affair with Guigomar, Guinevere's cousin. In *Sir Gawain and the Green Knight*, it is Morgan le Fay who enchants Lord Bertilak de Hautdesert, transforming him into the Green Knight. She hopes that her enchantment will harm Guinevere and that the gruesome sight of the Green Knight holding his head in his hands will make the Queen die of fright. Morgan changes her shape, appearing as an ancient woman in Bertilak's castle. In this tale, Morgan is said to have mastered the magic arts of Merlin and is called 'Morgan the goddess'.

Morgan is sometimes identified with the goddess Modron of Welsh myth. Modron was the daughter of the god Avallach and the mother of Mabon. Modron simply means 'mother' and Mabon 'son'. According to the ancient Welsh tale *Culhwch and Olwen*, when Mabon was three days old he was 'stolen from between his mother and the wall'. He was imprisoned and 'lost beyond the reach of love and war' until two of Arthur's warriors, Kai and Gwrhyr, discovered where he was held captive and rescued him. It has also been suggested that there are similarities between Morgan and the Morrigan, an Irish goddess. The Morrigan is associated with war, appearing over battlefields in the form of a crow. She could transform herself into the form of an animal, appear as a young maiden or turn herself into an old crone. Around 1220, in *Speculum Ecclesiae*, *The Mirror of the Church*, Gerald of Wales refers to Morgan as a '*dea phantastica*', an imaginary goddess.

MORGAN LE FAY

Morgan is also associated with Dahut of Breton legend, the daughter of King Gradlon and princess of the city of Ys. Every night, Dahut would ride out of the city, which was completely surrounded by the sea and protected by a series of locks and dams, to take a new lover. One night, a handsome man with eyes of fire asked Dahut for the key to the city's dams as a love token. Her new lover, the Devil, unlocked the dams and let the waters of the sea flood the city, drowning its inhabitants. King Gradlon rode on his white horse towards the coast of Brittany but was told by God to throw his beloved daughter into the sea. As the city sank beneath the waves, the princess Dahut was turned into the mermaid of Brittany, Marie-Morgane. The Marie-Morgane sits combing her long blonde hair, sweeping sailors to the bottom of the ocean as she sings. Some say that Paris, 'par Ys', is named after the legendary city beneath the waves. In Italy, Morgan le Fay gives her name to the magical faerie islands that appear above the water, the Fata Morgana. In Brittany these mirages are called 'le chateau de Morgan le Fée', 'the castle of Morgan le Fay'.

In Malory's Le Morte d'Arthur, as Arthur lies mortally wounded at Camlann, a little barge with many fair ladies in it comes to take the king to the Isle of Avalon. All the ladies on the barge wear black hoods, and they weep and shriek when they see Arthur. The king is put in the ship and received by three queens, with great mourning. They set Arthur down, he lays his head in one of their laps and that queen says, 'Ah, dear brother, why have ye tarried so long from me?' In the black ship that sails to Avalon are Nimue, the Lady of the Lake, and three queens: the Queen of Northgalis, the Queen of the Waste Lands and Arthur's sister, Queen Morgan le Fay.

SEE ALSO: Arthur, King of the Britons; Avalon; Brocéliande; Faeries; Lady of the Lake; Merlin; Mordred

NANTEOS CUP

An olive-wood cup said to be the Holy Grail was kept for many years at Nanteos Mansion near Aberystwyth in Wales. Local legend stated that the olive-wood cup was the vessel used by Christ at the Last Supper and that it had the miraculous ability to heal the sick.

This supposed Grail cup was reputed to have been brought to Britain by Joseph of Arimathea. It was kept at Glastonbury in Somerset until the sixteenth century and the dissolution of the monasteries under King Henry VIII. Henry had Glastonbury Abbey torn down, but seven monks of Glastonbury escaped with the Grail cup, spiriting it away to Wales. It was hidden by the Cistercian Monks of Strata Florida Abbey in Cardiganshire. According to legend, the last monk of Strata Florida passed the Grail cup on to the trusted Stedman family, which then married into the Powell family. In the 1730s, William Powell built Nanteos Mansion, where the Grail, now known as the Nanteos Cup, remained for centuries, or so the story goes. The name Nanteos is made up of two Welsh words and means 'the stream of the nightingales'.

People travelled to view the cup, believing that water drunk from it had healing properties. It's even said that some pilgrims nibbled on the sacred wooden cup, perhaps explaining why only a tiny fragment has survived. The legend of the Nanteos Cup was popular during the Victorian era. Visitors would arrive at Nanteos Mansion asking to see the Grail, which was by this time kept in a glass case. Tradition has it that Richard Wagner visited Nanteos Mansion and was inspired by the legend of the Nanteos Cup to compose the opera *Parsifal*, although there is no historical evidence to support this story.

When the Nanteos Cup was eventually examined by a representative of the Royal Commission on the Ancient and Historic Monuments of Wales, he concluded that its size and shape were consistent with a medieval mazer bowl. The Nanteos Cup was not carved in olive wood in first-century Palestine; it was a fourteenth-century medieval bowl made from witch elm. Contrary to legend, it is now believed that the cup was discovered by the Powell family in the ruins of Strata Florida Abbey in the mid-nineteenth century. It is likely that the idea that the Nanteos Cup was the Holy Grail became attached to it during the Victorian era following the popular success of Alfred, Lord Tennyson's *Idylls of the King* and the medieval revival led by the Pre-Raphaelites.

The Powell family sold Nanteos Mansion in the 1950s, and the crumbling remains of the Nanteos Cup were moved to a secret bank vault for safe-keeping. Nanteos Mansion is now a rather magnificent hotel. The Georgian mansion is haunted by the Jewel Lady, the ghost of Elizabeth Powell, the wife of William Powell, who built the Mansion. She is said to wander the halls at night searching for the fabulous jewellery she hid there during her lifetime. A phantom horse and carriage is reputed to pull up to the front of the Mansion in the dead of night, and the unearthly sound of a ghostly harp can be heard in the grounds of Nanteos, plucked by the spirit of Gruffydd Evans, who played for the Powells and their guests for 69 years.

SEE ALSO: Glastonbury; Holy Grail; Joseph of Arimathea; Wagner, Richard; Wales

NAZI GRAIL QUEST

In Steven Spielberg's blockbuster movie *Indiana Jones and the Last Crusade*, the archaeologist and adventurer battles the Nazis to find the Holy Grail. The story isn't as far-fetched as it sounds; in the 1920s and '30s, the Nazis were involved in a real quest for the Grail.

Otto Rahn died in mysterious circumstances at the age of thirty-five before the Second World War began. In the ten years before his death, Rahn had travelled across Europe searching for the Holy Grail, studying Wolfram von Eschenbach's *Parzival* and investigating the caves and castles of Cathar heretics. Rahn's quest for the Grail began in the 1920s. The young German writer had originally planned a dissertation on Kyot, the 'renowned scholar' that Wolfram von Eschenbach claimed as the source for his Grail romance. As Rahn studied Wolfram's *Parzival* and Richard Wagner's opera *Parsifal*, he became convinced that Montségur, the last fortress of the Cathar heretics in southern France, was Wolfram's Munsalvaesche and Wagner's Monsalvat – the castle of the Grail.

Otto Rahn's quest for the Holy Grail was centred on the Languedoc region of southern France. Rahn believed that Wolfram's *Parzival* had been influenced by the poetry of the Cathars through the troubadour Kyot. He walked the steep paths up to the ruins of the castle of Montségur and searched the caves and mountains of the Pyrenees for surviving traces of the Cathars, a group of medieval heretics who were brutally suppressed and massacred by the Catholic Church in the thirteenth century. To Rahn, and many other Grail seekers, the castle of Montségur was Wolfram's Munsalvaesche, the Grail castle of Wolfram's *Parzival*. In Munsalvaesche, the Mountain of Salvation, Parzival saw the Grail, a magical stone that had fallen from heaven. Rahn was convinced that the legendary treasure of the Cathars was the Holy Grail.

Otto Rahn saw the Grail as Wolfram's magical emerald jewel, fallen from the Crown of Lucifer as he was cast out of heaven. He wrote two books, *Kreuzzug gegen den Gral* (*Crusade against the Grail*) and *Luzifers Hofgesind* (*Lucifer's Courtiers*), on the fall of Montségur and the destruction of the Cathars. Rahn described the crusade against the Cathars in vivid detail:

> The bells melted in their belfries, the dead burned in the flames, and the cathedral blew up like a volcano. Blood flowed, the dead burned, the town blazed, walls fell, monks sang, crusaders slaughtered, and gypsies pillaged . . . and so began the crusade against the Grail.

Der Wartburgkrieg is a compilation of thirteenth-century German poems. It records a singing contest, at Wartburg Castle, with contestants including Wolfram and the wizard Klingsor. In Strophe 143 we are told that the Crown of Lucifer was made by 60,000 angels. When Lucifer defied God, attempting to force him out of the Kingdom of Heaven, God was angered by his insolence, and there was war in heaven. The rebel angels were cast out, and as the archangel Michael fought with Lucifer, an emerald fell from Lucifer's crown. This emerald fell to earth and became the stone from the stars that Wolfram von Eschenbach called the Grail in *Parzival*.

Otto Rahn claimed that while he was researching the Cathar heresy in the Languedoc, he was told a curious tale by an old shepherd. He told Rahn that the secret treasure of the Cathars of Montségur was the Holy Grail and that this was the stone that had fallen from the Crown of Lucifer. When the walls of Montségur were still standing, the Cathar Perfecti kept the Holy Grail there. The crusade against them drove the last of the Cathars to Montségur, their fortress on Mount Tabor (the name Rahn gave to the peak on which Montségur was built, believing it was the Cathar equivalent of the biblical mountain of mountains), but even this was in danger. The crusaders who besieged the Cathar castle were the armies of Lucifer. They sought the Grail and would kill the Cathars to take it. They wanted to restore 'their Prince's diadem'.

As the siege reached its height, a white dove descended from heaven. With its beak, it split Mount Tabor in two. Esclarmonde de Foix, who was the guardian of the Holy Grail, threw the mystical jewel down into the very depths of the mountain. Mount Tabor closed up once more and the Holy Grail was saved. When the devils of the army of Lucifer took the castle of Montségur, they found that they were too late, the Grail was beyond their grasp. The enraged crusaders put all the Cathar Perfecti to death. Not far from Montségur is the 'Field of the Stake' where the Cathars died on great pyres. All of the Cathars died in the flames except Esclarmonde de Foix. When Esclarmonde knew that the Holy Grail was safe from Lucifer's army, she climbed to the summit of Mount Tabor. There she turned into a pure white dove and flew off toward the mountains of Asia.

In the early 1930s, Rahn returned to Germany and his work came to the attention of Heinrich Himmler, head of the SS. Himmler himself was fascinated by Arthurian legend and the Holy Grail. He created a Nazi Grail castle at Wewelsburg, near the town of Paderborn in Westphalia, Germany. There Himmler's 'knights' of the SS Order met at a round table. Schloss Wewelsburg was a Renaissance castle built at the start of the seventeenth century for the Prince Bishop of Paderborn. It is the only three-cornered castle in Germany. In August 1934, Heinrich Himmler leased Schloss Wewelsburg for 100 years, for the token sum of just one Reichsmark per year. He set about converting the castle into the 'SS-Schule Haus Wewelsburg', a cultural, ideological and spiritual headquarters for the SS order. Himmler's Camelot was built using forced slave labour from concentration camps. Konzentrationslager Niederhagen was established near Wewelsburg to provide a labour force. Over 3,900 prisoners were held at Niederhagen; at least 1,285 of them died there.

Within the North Tower of Wewelsburg was the Obergruppenführersaal, a grand hall with an oak round table that seated 12 of the senior Gruppenführers. These 12 SS 'knights' were hand-picked by Himmler, who acted as their grand master. The esoteric symbol of the Black Sun was inlaid into the floor. Directly beneath the hall was the so-called 'realm of the dead'. Himmler planned that the cremated remains of the SS elite would be kept within this room and that the *Totenkopfrings* (SS death's head rings) of SS officers would be returned to Wewelsburg Castle on their deaths. The 'knights' were also given themed bedrooms within the castle. Himmler's bedroom was devoted to the tenth-century Saxon King Heinrich I, or Henry the Fowler. Himmler is said to have believed that he was King Heinrich reincarnated.

Himmler began to fund Rahn's research and Rahn joined the Ahnenerbe, the Nazi heritage bureau. In the summer of 1936, Rahn joined a Nazi expedition to Iceland. The expedition ship briefly stopped in Edinburgh en route to Iceland, and Rahn took the opportunity to climb Arthur's Seat, a huge hill that offers spectacular views over the city. It has been suggested that the purpose of the expedition to Iceland was to seek evidence for Ultima Thule, the legendary Aryan kingdom. That year, Rahn joined Himmler's SS, and was rapidly promoted to the rank of SS-Unterscharführer.

In 1937, he was assigned to the SS-run concentration camp at Dachau, where he planted a small garden. A year later, having fallen out of favour with the Nazis, he requested that he be dismissed from the SS. It has been theorised that he was of Jewish descent, but testimony from his close family suggests that Rahn was in fact homosexual. In 1939, he fled Berlin fearing for his life. He escaped into the Tyrolean Mountains where he died in the snow by a frozen river.

Conspiracy theories surround the Nazi Grail quest. It has been said that Otto Rahn discovered the Holy Grail as he explored the Cathar caves around Montségur, that the Grail was taken to Himmler's SS castle at Wewelsburg and that Rahn was murdered by the Nazis so he could never reveal the secrets of the Grail. It has also been said that Schloss Wewelsburg was the scene of black-magic rituals, including acts of necromancy where the decapitated heads of SS officers killed on the Eastern Front were temporarily revived and debriefed. It has been claimed that the purpose of the flight of Hitler's deputy, Rudolph Hess, to Scotland in a Messerschmitt was to look for the Holy Grail in Rosslyn Chapel. There are also rumours that trucks loaded with wooden crates full of Cathar artefacts and treasure were taken from the Languedoc by the Nazis. It has even been alleged that Otto Rahn survived, that he escaped across the mountains and lived under a new identity. There is no real evidence to support any of these theories.

Heinrich Himmler intended to carry out massive building works at Wewelsburg. It was estimated that his plans would have cost an incredible 250 million Reichsmarks. Wewelsburg was to become the 'Centre of the New World', an Omphalos for the Thousand-year Reich.

Himmler's plans came to nothing and the Thousand-year Reich lasted just twelve years. Himmler was arrested on 22 May 1945 and later committed suicide by swallowing a potassium cyanide capsule. The last remaining prisoners of Niederhagen concentration camp were liberated by US forces on 2 April 1945.

The Wewelsburg District Museum houses a permanent exhibition entitled 'Wewelsburg 1933–1945: Site of SS Ritual and Terror'. The exhibition was established as a warning to the living and to honour the memory of the victims of KZ Niederhagen.

SEE ALSO: Wagner, Richard; Wolfram von Eschenbach

PATÈNE DE SERPENTINE

Among the medieval treasures of France is the wondrous Patène de Serpentine, a golden vessel that may be the actual Holy Grail. This sacred platter, part of the famous treasure of the Abbey of St Denis, precisely matches Chrétien de Troyes' descriptions of the Grail.

The dish at the centre of the paten (a shallow dish or platter used to carry the sacred Host during the celebration of the Eucharist) is a piece of finely sculpted dark-green serpentine stone. It dates to around the time of Christ, between the first century BC and the first century AD. The stone dish was inlaid with eight tiny golden fish, an early Christian symbol. Two of the fish are now missing, possibly lost during the French Revolution. It is thought that the original serpentine dish may have been a gift to Charlemagne.

During the reign of King Charles the Bald (823–77), a master goldsmith encircled the plain stone dish with a highly decorated gold mount encrusted with precious gems and natural pearls, sapphires, emeralds, moonstones, amethysts, garnets and coloured glass. The craftsmanship is remarkable. Each stone is mounted in gold, and they are set in concentric circles around the serpentine dish. The central circle of 24 small gems and pearls is complemented by 24 miniature stone hearts. The larger circle is made up of 12 larger gems and 12 pearls, set alternately with triquetras and simple fleur-de-lis designs. Around the outer rim is a circle of garnets set in little bands of gold. The Patène de Serpentine was used in the sacred ceremonies of the queens of France at the Abbey of St Denis.

Charles the Bald gave the Patène de Serpentine to the Abbey of

St Denis with a chalice known as the Coupe des Ptolémées, the Cup of the Ptolemys. The cup was likewise fashioned from an ancient object set into a gold mount with precious stones and enamels. It has been said that the Cup of the Ptolemys was the most precious vase in the treasury of St Denis, perhaps in any cabinet in Europe. It is a two-handled goblet exquisitely sculpted from a single white, orange and green agate. It is thought that the Cup was originally sculpted in the workshops of Alexandria around the first or second century AD. It is decorated with scenes of a Bacchic revel, including masks hanging from trees, sphinxes, a panther, goats and birds. In 1804, the Cup of the Ptolemys was stolen. It was recovered without its gold mount and is now on display in the Bibliothèque Nationale de France in Paris.

For hundreds of years, the Patène de Serpentine was part of the Trésor de St Denis, the treasure of the Abbey of St Denis. Abbot Suger, writing in the twelfth century, tells us that the high altar of the abbey was entirely encased in gold; the golden altar frontal was ornamented with sapphires, emeralds, rubies, hyacinths, topazes and pearls. The magnificent Cross of St Eloi stood upon the altar. To the 'great delight' of Abbot Suger, a group of travellers from Jerusalem told him that the marvels of St Denis were greater than the treasures of Constantinople and the ornaments of the Hagia Sophia. The treasures included reliquaries of St Denis, John the Baptist and St Peter the Exorcist, the Chalice of Suger, the Eagle of Suger, the Sardonyx Basin, the Throne of King Dagobert and the Chessmen of Charlemagne. St Denis also housed the regalia of the kings and queens of France: the crowns of St Louis, Charlemagne and Jeanne d'Evreux, the sceptres of Dagobert and Charlemagne and the Sword of Charlemagne.

According to legend, St Denis was the first Bishop of Paris. He was martyred *circa* 270, and his burial place a few miles north of Paris became a place of pilgrimage. King Dagobert founded a Benedictine abbey at St Denis in 630, and over the centuries, successive monarchs made it one of the richest abbeys in all of France. It was said that when Charlemagne built a new church at St Denis, Christ himself assisted at its consecration. Abbot Suger began work on the fabulous Gothic Basilica of St Denis in 1136. For centuries, the abbey was the royal necropolis of France, where the nation's kings and queens were laid to rest. During the French Revolution, the royal tombs were opened and their bodies and bones unceremoniously dumped in a nearby trench. The high altar, the sacred reliquary of St Denis and the head of the saint were all destroyed, and many of the treasures of the abbey were lost forever. Miraculously, the Patène de Serpentine and the Coupe des Ptolémées survived.

Countess Marie de Champagne was the patroness of Chrétien de Troyes, the man who described the Grail in his *Perceval, or the Story of the Grail*. She was the eldest daughter of King Louis VII of France and his queen consort, Eleanor of Aquitaine. Louis VII became King of France in 1137. That year, he married the 15-year-old Eleanor of Aquitaine. As a wedding present, Eleanor gave Louis a fabulous rock-crystal vase decorated with gold and precious stones, which became part of the treasure of the Abbey of St Denis when Louis gave it to Abbot Suger. The Eleanor Vase can now be seen in the Musée du Louvre. Eleanor was a fiery, independent woman, and her behaviour was openly criticised by Abbot Suger and Abbot Bernard of Clairvaux. She was disappointed to find that her husband was an exceptionally pious man, more suited to the priesthood than the marriage bed.

In 1145, Eleanor gave birth to a daughter, Marie. Two years later, Louis and his young queen set out on crusade to Jerusalem. During their journey to the Holy City, the French were ambushed by the Turks, and King Louis was described by the chronicler William of Tyre as fighting with 'his bloody sword, cutting off many heads and hands'. When the French reached the Holy Land, it was alleged, Queen Eleanor was seduced by her uncle, Raymond, Prince of Antioch. William tells us that Eleanor 'disregarded her marriage vows and was unfaithful to her husband'. Louis took his wife to Jerusalem by force and joined Conrad III of Germany and King Baldwin III of Jerusalem as they besieged Damascus. In 1149, Louis abandoned the Holy Land, returning to France and taking Eleanor with him against her wishes. After years of scandal and hostility, the marriage of Louis and Eleanor was annulled in 1152.

Eleanor of Aquitaine married the future King Henry II of England just six weeks after her first marriage was annulled. She went on to become the mother of Richard the Lionheart and King John, while her uncle, Raymond of Antioch, was killed in battle against the Muslims in 1149. He was beheaded by Asad ad-Din Shirkuh bin Shadhi, the uncle of Saladin. Raymond's head was sent to the Syrian leader Nur ad-Din in a silver box, and he in turn sent it to the Caliph of Baghdad.

Marie de Champagne was seven years old when her parents' marriage was annulled. She and her younger sister Alix were declared to be legitimate, and King Louis was awarded custody of his two daughters. Marie was educated at the Abbey of Avenay, and in 1164 she married Henry I, Count of Champagne. Henry and Marie had two sons and two daughters: Henry, who would go on to become Count of Champagne and King of Jerusalem, Theobald, Scholastique and Marie. When her husband joined the Second Crusade, Marie remained in Champagne and acted as regent. Her court at Troyes became a literary centre, where poets and writers explored the nature of love. Young knights and noblewomen, feudal lords and married ladies were entertained by tales of romance and risqué parodies of courtly conduct.

Chrétien de Troyes was one of the writers at the court of Marie de Champagne. In the introduction to *Lancelot, or The Knight of the Cart*, Chrétien tells us that he received the *'matière'*, the material, and the *'sens'*, the style, from his patroness, the Countess of Champagne. It is Marie, he claims, who wishes him to write the romance of Lancelot and Guinevere. The story of a knight utterly devoted to his queen seems to echo Chrétien's own loyalty to Marie. He tells us that he is so devoted to Marie that he would do anything in the world for her, that she surpasses all other ladies who are alive 'as the south wind which blows in May or April is more lovely than any other wind'. To Chrétien, 'The Countess is worth as many queens as a gem is worth of pearls and sards [semi-precious stones].'

In September 1180, Marie's father, King Louis VII, died, and her husband, Henry, Count of Champagne, died the following year, shortly after returning from the Holy Land. For a while, the widowed Marie contemplated marriage to Philip of Alsace, Count of Flanders. It was Count Philip who Chrétien claimed had given him a book that acted as the source for *The Story of the Grail*, 'the finest story ever related in a royal court'.

Chrétien describes the Grail as being of pure refined gold, set with many kinds of precious stones, 'the richest and most costly in sea or earth'. He writes that the stones set in the Grail surpassed all others. The gold mount of the Patène de Serpentine is set with precious stones of the earth, including emeralds and amethysts, and with pearls, the gems of the sea. In the large circle, there are 12 stones and 12 pearls; perhaps for the 12 disciples, the 12 months of the year, the 12 signs of the zodiac or the 12 precious stones and 12 pearl gates of the New Jerusalem, the holy city that will descend from heaven, as described in the Book of Revelation. In Revelation, John of Patmos says that the foundations of the city's wall are adorned with all kinds of precious stones; 12 kinds are listed: jasper, sapphire, chalcedony, emerald, sardonyx, sardius, chrysolite, beryl, topaz, chrysoprasus, jacinth and amethyst. The 12 gates of New Jerusalem are 12 pearls. Each gate is made of one pearl and the street of the city is pure gold.

Wolfram von Eschenbach tells us that the Grail was a magical stone, the *lapsit exillis*, the stone from the heavens. Wolfram's Grail has been interpreted as a small altar stone, possibly a kind of portable altar that was associated with the stone that covered Christ's rock-cut tomb. In the symbolism of the Mass which was established by the time Wolfram was composing *Parzival*, the paten represented the stone before the tomb. The centre of the Patène de Serpentine is, of course, an ancient stone dish.

In Chrétien's *Story of the Grail*, Perceval watches the Grail procession in silence, failing to ask who is served from the Grail. For five years, he wanders without knowing where he is, without loving God or believing in him. Perceval then meets a hermit in a small chapel and discovers the truth about the Grail. The king who is served from the Grail is the hermit's brother, and the brother of Perceval's mother. The Rich Fisherman is the son of the king served from the Grail. The hermit then explains that the Grail does not carry pike, lamprey or salmon; it bears a single consecrated wafer, the sacred Host. A grail was a shallow dish commonly used to serve fish. The hermit specifically tells Perceval that the Grail of the Fisher King does not carry fish – the king is sustained by the Mass wafer. The Patène de Serpentine is inlaid with eight golden fish but it was never used as a serving dish for fish at a feast. Just like the Grail, the Patène de Serpentine bore the Mass wafer, the body of Christ.

On 5 December 1793, the Patène de Serpentine became part of the collection of the Musée du Louvre, where it is on display in the Richelieu Wing, surrounded by medieval treasures including the Eagle of Suger and the Sword of Charlemagne.

SEE ALSO: Chrétien de Troyes; Fisher King; Holy Grail; Jerusalem; Nanteos Cup; Philip, Count of Flanders; Wolfram von Eschenbach

PERCIVAL

When the French poet Chrétien de Troyes wrote *Perceval, ou le conte du graal* (*Perceval, or the Story of the Grail*) in the 1180s, he related the adventures of two knights: Sir Gawain and Perceval. Perceval sees the Grail and is destined to ask the Grail question — 'Who is served from the Grail?' — and thereby heal the Fisher King. Perceval grows through the poem from a naive young man to a chivalrous knight. He learns that he must become more than a worldly knight; he must achieve a spiritual knighthood.

At the start of Chrétien's story, Perceval is a young man who lives in the wilds of Wales in the Gaste Forest (the desolate forest) with his widowed mother. His father was the finest knight 'in all the isles of the sea'. His brothers were knights who died in combat; as the eldest lay dead, the crows and ravens pecked out his eyes. His father died of grief at their loss, and his mother took Perceval to live in the forest to shield him from knighthood. Early one spring day, when the trees were bursting into leaf, Perceval is out hunting with javelins when he hears a group of five knights riding through the forest. At first he thinks the sound must be devils, then, when he sees the knights in their glittering armour, he mistakes them for angels. Perceval decides that he will become a knight, leaves his mother and heads for the court of King Arthur.

During his journey, Perceval comes across a lady in a tent and, having foolishly misunderstood his mother's advice on women, he forces the lady to kiss him, takes a ring from her finger, eats her venison pies and drinks her wine, before leaving her in a state of distress. When her lover, the Haughty Knight of the Heath, finds his lady dishevelled and half undressed, he refuses to believe she was kissed against her will. The Haughty Knight swears to kill Perceval and sets off dragging the lady behind him.

At Arthur's court, Perceval sees a Red Knight who has stolen the king's golden cup. Perceval appears at court in peasant garb and tells King Arthur and his knights that he would like the Red Knight's armour. Sir Kay insults the naive young man and then assaults a damsel and a fool who take his side. Perceval leaves the court and kills the formidable Red Knight with a javelin, needing help from a squire to remove the Red Knight's armour.

Perceval is taught how to be a knight by Gornemant of Gohort. He learns how to fight and act chivalrously, then Gornemant dubs him a knight. He meets the fair lady Blancheflor at her besieged castle of Beaurepaire, where he defeats the knights threatening her before leaving to return to his mother. On his way, he meets a man fishing with a line and rod, and as a result spends a night in the Grail castle, where he watches in silence as the bleeding lance and the Grail are carried through the hall. He fails to ask who is served from the Grail because during his training Gornemant had advised him not to speak too much.

The next morning, Perceval departs from the castle and finds a maiden mourning over the body of a dead knight under an oak tree. The maiden is his cousin, and she tells him that his failure to ask the necessary question will have dire consequences. The knight had been killed by the Haughty Knight of the Heath, who is still searching for Perceval and kills anyone who speaks to his lady. Perceval faces the Haughty Knight and defeats him, freeing the lady. He sends the Haughty Knight to King Arthur, who, with his court, sets out to find Perceval.

Near Arthur's camp, Perceval stares at three drops of blood in the snow, and, in a trance, he sees the face of Blancheflor in the blood. Kay tries to force Perceval to go to the camp, but they fight and Perceval breaks Kay's arm. Gawain manages to persuade Perceval to come to court. There, a hideous damsel appears and scorns him for his failure to ask the question in the Grail castle. She has a nose like a monkey or a cat, eyes as small as a rat, yellow teeth and a beard like a goat. She tells him that if he had asked the question, the Fisher King would finally have been healed. Perceval vows to learn the secrets of the Grail and the lance.

Five years pass, and Perceval has forgotten God. He has beaten 60 knights but fails to find the Grail castle until finally he meets a hermit who hears his confession and then tells him that he is Perceval's uncle, that the Fisher King's father is served from the Grail and that the Fisher King is Perceval's cousin. Perceval's mother, who has died of grief, was the hermit's sister. Perceval stays with the hermit, listening as he tells him to love God and give aid to maidens, widows and orphans, and that the Grail is a holy vessel that carries the sacred Host. At Easter, Perceval receives communion from the hermit, and then his part in Chrétien's *Story of the Grail* suddenly ends.

Perceval first appears in *The Story of the Grail* as a naive creature of the forest, half wild and foolish. While he misunderstands the advice he is given, Sir Gawain appears in Chrétien's Grail romance as the epitome of a worldly knight. Perceval learns how to fight, becoming a knight, but he still needs to understand himself and his destiny in order to ask the Grail question. Perceval seems predestined to move beyond this earthly knighthood to become a new kind of ideal knight – a spiritual knight. He will ask the question and discover the secrets of the Grail.

When Perceval first hears Arthur's knights in the forest, he thinks they are devils, yet when he sees them, he thinks they are angels. In a way, he is right in both respects. The Red Knight steals Arthur's goblet and threatens the court; knights besiege the lady Blancheflor in her castle; and the Haughty Knight abuses his lady and kills a knight at the Grail castle. Knights can be cruel and murderous. As Perceval becomes an effective knight, he forgets God. Yet *The Story of the Grail* shows us that knights may also become angelic, moving beyond worldly chivalry to embrace God and achieve the Grail.

A series of continuators took up Chrétien's unfinished story, picking up themes from his poem and weaving new adventures, and later writers adapted and embellished *The Story of the Grail*. In the Welsh Grail romance *Peredur*, for example, the Grail is a salver that holds the bloody decapitated head of Peredur's cousin. Peredur (Percival) sets out to seek revenge on the Nine Witches of Caer Loyw. Other writers made the Grail the vessel that Christ used at the Last Supper, the vessel that caught his blood at the Crucifixion, and Percival became a knight on a holy quest.

The story of Percival gained popularity across Europe. In the Old Norse *Parcevals Saga*, he returns to his beloved Blankiflúr and marries her. In the Middle Dutch *Moriaen*, Perceval has a son named Moriaen by a Moorish princess. The Middle English *Sir Perceval of Galles* appears in a single manuscript between the *Awentyrs of Arthure* and

PERCIVAL

Three Charms for Toothache. In Wolfram von Eschenbach's *Parzival* and Manessier's Continuation of Chrétien's *Story of the Grail*, Percival becomes the new Grail king. Wolfram expands the story, telling us that the knight has a son named Lohengrin.

In Richard Wagner's opera *Parsifal* the 'pure fool' Parsifal battles the wizard Klingsor to recover the spear that pierced the side of Christ on the cross. Wagner wrote that: '"Parsi fal" means: "parsi" – think of the fire-loving Parsees – "pure"; "fal" means "mad" in a higher sense, in other words a man without erudition, but one of genius.'

Percival has featured in numerous poems, novels and Arthurian movies. Arthur Machen's *The Secret Glory* and Charles William's *War in Heaven* were modern Grail quests. Wolfram's *Parzival* has been adapted for the screen, and elements of Percival's story appear in *The Natural* (the film of Bernard Malamud's novel) and *The Fisher King*. Eric Rohmer brought medieval illumination to life in his film *Perceval le Gallois*, a poetic story-book adaptation of Chrétien's *Story of the Grail*.

Percival is a very real hero. He fails, makes mistakes and learns from them. He has no magical gifts or superhuman abilities. Percival's simple humanity makes the quest for the Grail accessible to us all. No matter how naive, flawed or foolish we are, we can grow and achieve the Grail.

SEE ALSO: Bleeding Lance; Chivalry; Chrétien de Troyes; Fisher King; Gawain; Grail Maiden; Holy Grail; Wolfram von Eschenbach

PHILIP, COUNT OF FLANDERS

Philip of Alsace, Count of Flanders, was a patron of Chrétien de Troyes, whose *Perceval, or the Story of the Grail* was written for him. Twice Count Philip journeyed to the Holy Land on crusade, and his first cousin was King Baldwin IV of Jerusalem, the Leper King.

In 1173, King Louis VII of France held a great council at Paris. Louis and the nobles of France made an oath to the heir to the throne, Henry 'the Young King', that they would assist him in expelling his father, King Henry II, from England. Philip of Flanders was to receive for his homage £1,000 of yearly revenues in England and the whole of Kent, together with Dover and Rochester castles.

Henry the Young King was the son of Henry II and Eleanor of Aquitaine. In 1173, he was 18 years old. He was married to Marguerite, the daughter of Louis VII, the King of France. The Young King rebelled against his father, seeking allies in France. He was joined by his brother Richard, known today as Richard Coeur de Lion, Richard the Lionheart. Their mother, Eleanor of Aquitaine, tried to join her sons' rebellion but was arrested and imprisoned by her husband for the next 15 years.

The contemporary English chronicler Roger of Howden wrote that after Easter 1173:

> the whole of the kingdom of France, and the king, the son of
> the king of England, Richard his brother, earl of Poitou, and
> Geoffrey, earl of Bretagne, and nearly all the earls and barons
> of England, Normandy, Aquitaine, Anjou, and Brittany,

arose against the king of England the father, and laid waste his lands on every side with fire, sword, and rapine: they also laid siege to his castles, and took them by storm, and there was no one to relieve them . . . Then seems to have been fulfilled this prophecy of Merlin which says: 'The cubs shall awake and shall roar aloud, and, leaving the woods, shall seek their prey within the walls of the cities; among those who shall be in their way they shall make great carnage, and shall tear out the tongues of bulls. The necks of them as they roar aloud they shall load with chains, and shall thus renew the times of their forefathers.'

Philip of Flanders was among the nobles of France who joined the revolt of 1173–4. Philip took a leading role in the invasion of Normandy. When the invasion failed, Henry the Young King and Philip of Flanders raised a large army and made plans to cross over to England. The wind was against them, however, and on 8 July 1174, King Henry II landed in England. By September, the revolt was over. Henry II was reconciled with his rebellious sons, though Gerald of Wales tells us that in 1189 when he was near to death he gave his son Richard the kiss of peace, but uttered in a low voice, 'May the Lord never permit me to die until I have taken due vengeance upon you.'

In 1175, Count Philip of Flanders discovered that his wife, Élisabeth of Vermandois, was committing adultery. He had her lover beaten to death. Again, Roger of Howden described events:

> Philip, earl of Flanders, took prisoner a knight named Walter de Fontaines, one sprung of a noble family, and conspicuous before all his compeers in feats of arms; making a charge against him that he had unlawfully known the countess of Flanders. On this, the said Walter, intending to make denial thereof, offered to prove his innocence in any way whatever, affirming that he had never known the countess, nor had ever had it in his thoughts to know her. The earl, however, would not allow him so to clear himself; but in the fury of his wrath gave orders that he should be put to death by being beaten with clubs. Accordingly, the executioners seized him, and, binding him hand and foot, beat him with clubs, and hung him up half dead by the feet, with his head hanging downwards in a filthy sewer, and thus, being suffocated by the stench from the sewer, he ended his life most shockingly.
>
> *Annals of Roger de Hoveden*, trans. Henry T. Riley

Two years later, in 1177, Philip journeyed to the Holy Land and met his cousin King Baldwin IV of Jerusalem. Their grandfather, King Fulk of Jerusalem, was buried in the Church of the Holy Sepulchre. Baldwin and his advisers are said to have been impressed by the Count of Flanders' wealth and high reputation. They offered Philip the role of regent of the Crusader Kingdom, but he declined, telling them that he had travelled to Jerusalem in pilgrimage, not to wage war.

Sybil, the sister of Baldwin IV, was married to William Longsword of Montferrat, the Count of Jaffa and Ascalon, in 1176. William died the following year, leaving Sybil widowed and bearing the heir to the Kingdom of Jerusalem. Whoever married the widowed princess would control the kingship. Count Philip of Flanders demanded that Sybil should be married to one of his vassals. The Haute Cour, the High Court of Jerusalem, rejected Philip's scheme, and Sybil would later marry Guy of Lusignan.

Count Philip left Jerusalem and headed north to besiege the Muslim-held town of Hama, and his force included a large number of Knights Templar. When he failed to capture Hama, he moved to Harenc, where the Muslim garrison paid him a ransom to withdraw. Roger of Howden stated 30 years later that the Templars had urged the Count of Flanders to accept the Muslims' offer.

In 1179, Philip left the Holy Land. Two years later, he rebelled against King Philip II of France, the son of Louis VII. On his return from the crusades, Philip had become the guardian of Philip II when his father fell ill. At the coronation of Philip II at Rheims Cathedral, the count had walked before the king, bearing the sword of the kingdom. Henry the Young King and his brothers Richard and Geoffrey turned against their former ally, Philip of Flanders. They gathered a great force and came to the aid of King Philip II. The brothers forced Philip of Flanders to retreat and attacked his allies the Duke of Burgundy and Marie, the Countess of Champagne.

Marie of Champagne was in fact the half-sister of Henry the Young King, Richard, Geoffrey and King Philip II of France. She was also the patron of Chrétien de Troyes. At the beginning of Chrétien's *Lancelot, or the Knight of the Cart*, the poet tells us that 'the lady of Champagne' wishes him to write a romance. It is thought that at some point between 1181 and 1190 Count Philip of Flanders in turn became the patron of Chrétien de Troyes.

In 1182, according to the seventeenth-century *Martyrs Mirror*, William, Archbishop of Rheims, and Philip of Flanders had many heretics 'most unmercifully burnt'. The text notes that the Count of Alsace put many God-fearing people to death on account of their views against the Roman Church. The following year, Élisabeth of Vermandois died and Philip married Teresa of Portugal, the daughter of King Afonso Henriques.

In 1188, Philip of Flanders, King Philip II of France, and King Henry II of England took up the cross after a meeting with Josias, Archbishop of Tyre, at Gisors, and joined the Third Crusade. Chroniclers said that Josias had been 'filled with the spirit of wisdom' as he preached the word of God to the kings and princes. As the kings Henry II and Philip II took the cross from Josias, a miraculous sign of the cross appeared in the sky. Henry of England and his men wore white crosses, Philip of France and his men wore red crosses, and Count Philip of Flanders and his men wore green crosses.

Count Philip joined the Siege of Acre in 1191, alongside his former enemies Richard the Lionheart and Philip II of France. Baldwin IV, the Leper King, had died in 1185 and Jerusalem had fallen to Saladin in 1187. Sibyl, the Queen of Jerusalem, escaped to Tripoli. Her husband, the king-consort Guy of Lusignan, had led the crusaders at the disastrous Battle of Hattin. Saladin took the True Cross, captured Guy of Lusignan and beheaded the Templar and Hospitaller knights who would not convert to Islam. When Guy was finally released, he marched to Tyre with Sibyl then laid siege to the City of Acre. The Siege of Acre would last two years. In 1190, an epidemic claimed the life of Sibyl. Philip of Alsace, Count of Flanders, died at the siege of Acre on 1 July 1191.

SEE ALSO: Chrétien de Troyes; Jerusalem; Knights Templar

PRE-RAPHAELITES

In 1848, a group of young artists, critics and poets met and formed a 'brotherhood'. The eldest of them, William Holman Hunt, was only 21 years old. Their aim was nothing less than to revolutionise the world of art. They would influence a generation of artists, create some of the world's most popular paintings and draw inspiration from the romances of King Arthur and the Knights of the Round Table.

When the Pre-Raphaelite Brotherhood first formed in London in the middle of the nineteenth century, they had a radical agenda that challenged the art establishment. In four editions of a periodical entitled *The Germ*, they outlined their manifesto. The Pre-Raphaelites would paint directly from nature using vivid, authentic colour. They sought to emulate the great artists who had preceded Raphael. Initially, the Brotherhood had three members: William Holman Hunt, John Everett Millais and Dante Gabriel Rossetti. They decided to keep the Brotherhood secret from the members of the Royal Academy of Arts, where Hunt and Millais were students. By the end of 1848, William Michael Rossetti, James Collinson, Thomas Woolner and Frederic George Stephens had joined.

The first paintings that the Pre-Raphaelite Brotherhood created were enigmatically inscribed with the initials 'PRB'. The artists painted directly from life, finding models and also landscapes and natural forms that inspired their work. The realism of their artworks proved controversial; for example, Charles Dickens claimed that John Everett Millais had painted Christ as a 'hideous, wry-necked, blubbering, red-haired boy'. The Pre-Raphaelite Brotherhood disintegrated in the 1850s, but its ideals began to influence a wider group of artists and poets.

Painters, poets and designers associated with the Pre-Raphaelites include William Morris, Edward Burne-Jones, Christina Rossetti, Jane Morris, John William Waterhouse and Elizabeth Siddal. Throughout the last half of the nineteenth century, as Alfred, Lord Tennyson's *Idylls of the King* proved hugely popular, there was a romantic medieval revival. Burne-Jones, inspired by Tennyson's poems, advised a friend to 'learn "Sir Galahad" by heart; he is to be the patron of our order'. William Morris and Company created interior designs based on motifs and patterns from medieval tapestries and illuminated books. The tragic story of the death of King Arthur and the fall of Camelot suited the mood of the nation as Queen Victoria mourned her husband, Prince Albert.

In Dante Gabriel Rossetti's painting *The Damsel of the Sanct Grael*, the Grail maiden is depicted bearing a golden chalice full of blood or dark-red wine. She carries a basket, wears an emerald green dress and has long, flowing red hair. A dove, symbolising the Holy Ghost, hovers above her head with a censer hanging from its beak. The dove is encircled by a pale-yellow disc, a halo about the Grail maiden's head, like the sun or the moon.

Rossetti also used the motif of the Holy Dove in his painting *The Annunciation*. Here the dove hovers by the Virgin Mary as an angel tells her that she will be the mother of the son of God. *The Damsel of the Sanct Grael* was accompanied by an extract from Sir Thomas Malory's *Le Morte d'Arthur*:

> And there came a dove, and in her bill a little censer of gold, and wherewithal there was such a savour as if all the spicery of the world had been there. So there came a damzel passing fair and young, and she bare a vessel of gold between her hands.

The Lady of Shalott, immortalised in verse by Tennyson, became a favourite subject of the Pre-Raphaelites and their successors. John William Waterhouse painted *The Lady of Shalott* in 1883. In his painting, the Lady Elaine, who has fallen desperately in love with Sir Lancelot, sits in a black barge as it drifts downriver. She does not notice that the tapestry she sits upon drags in the water. She stares forlornly, dying of a broken heart. In William Holman Hunt's *The Lady of Shalott*, he depicts the moment when Elaine first looks from her tower window and sees Sir Lancelot. She stands amid a half-woven tapestry, tangled in the woollen threads. In John Atkinson Grimshaw's *Elaine*, the Lady of Shalott lies dead in her barge, steered by a dark boatman. Her boat is lit by black candles and ornamented with wrought-iron works and a sculpture of a dragon with unfurled wings. Elaine is radiant in death and holds a letter in her right hand. When she arrives at Camelot, Sir Lancelot will read the letter and find that she has died of love for him.

From 1848 to 1864, William Dyce created Arthurian frescos for the Queen's Robing Room in the Palace of Westminster. Edward Burne-Jones depicted the quest for the Holy Grail in a series of tapestries for Morris and Company and painted *Lancelot at the Chapel of the Saint Grael*. In the tapestry *The Attainment: A Vision of the Holy Grail*, Burne-Jones depicts Sir Galahad praying before the Holy Grail. As Sir Bors and Sir Percival look on, Galahad is on bended knee before the Grail, which rests upon an altar, surrounded by angels.

As well as depicting the Arthurian romances in art, the Pre-Raphaelites wrote poems on the subject. William Morris, best known for his decorative wallpaper designs, was an accomplished painter and poet. He designed Arthurian stained-glass windows and painted Jane Burden (who later became his wife) as *Guenevere*. He also wrote of Arthur's queen in his 'The Defence of Guenevere'.

In 2005, a unique edition of Morris's *The Defence of Guenevere and Other Poems* was rediscovered in the library at the State University of New York at Buffalo. The volume contains 21 watercolours by Margaret and Frances Macdonald. In the 1890s, the Macdonald sisters, J. Herbert McNair and Charles Rennie Mackintosh formed the 'Glasgow Four', a celebrated group of artists. Margaret Macdonald's art has been overshadowed by the fame of her husband, Charles Rennie Mackintosh, who once said, 'Margaret has genius, I have only talent.' In 2006, the book was displayed in Glasgow's Hunterian Art Gallery in an exhibition entitled 'Doves and Dreams: The Art of Frances Macdonald and J. Herbert McNair'.

Among the many Arthurian works created by Dante Gabriel Rossetti, including the paintings *Sir Tristram and La Belle Yseult Drinking the Love Potion*, *Arthur's Tomb: The Last Meeting of Lancelot and Guinevere* and *Arthur and the Weeping Queens*, was the poem 'God's Graal':

> The ark of the Lord of Hosts
> Whose name is called by the name of Him
> Who dwelleth between the Cherubim.

PRE-RAPHAELITES

O Thou that in no house dost dwell,
But walk'st in tent and tabernacle.

For God of all strokes will have one
In every battle that is done.

Lancelot lay beside the well:
(God's Graal is good)
Oh my soul is sad to tell
The weary quest and the bitter quell;
For he was the lord of lordlihood,
And sleep on his eyelids fell.

Lancelot lay before the shrine;
(The apple tree's in the wood)
There was set Christ's very sign,
The bread unknown and the unknown wine
That the soul's life for a livelihood
Craves from his wheat and vine.

The Tate Britain gallery in London, Lady Lever Art Gallery in
Liverpool, Birmingham Museum and Art Gallery, and Manchester
Art Gallery all hold major collections of Pre-Raphaelite art.

SEE ALSO: Grail Maiden; Holy Grail; Tennyson, Alfred, Lord

PRESTER JOHN

The story of Prester John, or John the Elder, is one of the most extraordinary legends of the Middle Ages. During that period, a series of letters appeared in Europe telling of the Christian kingdom of Prester John, the land of the 'Three Indies', situated somewhere in the East. Prester John's kingdom was a virtual paradise, a promised land without crime or vice, where the rivers were filled with gold. These letters, purporting to be from Prester John, spoke of barbarian infidels threatening his peace and requested that European warriors come to the relief of this wonderful country.

The title 'prester' is simply a corrupted form of the word 'presbyter', a person who had authority in the early Church, in other words a minister or priest. The first record of the country of Prester John appears in the *Chronicon* of Bishop Otto of Freising, Germany, in 1145, triggered by Bishop Hugh of Jabala (modern Jubayl in Lebanon) who had made a report to the papal court, then in Viterbo, Italy. A letter dating from the middle of the twelfth century addressed to Manuel I Comnenus (reigned 1143–80), Emperor of the Eastern Roman Empire, commonly called the Byzantine Empire, was said to have been written by Prester John. Over the following centuries, more than a hundred versions emerged, variously directed to Emperor Manuel, the King of France and the Pope.

The mysterious letters said that Prester John and his subjects needed knights to help in their battles against those regarded as infidels. There is little doubt that European Christians would have been very interested in the possibility of forging an alliance with a powerful and wealthy Christian king of the East. Pope Alexander III wrote a reply addressed to 'the magnificent king of the Indies, Christ's beloved son' and sent an envoy, Master Philip, to Prester John's kingdom to assess its needs. The ambassador's search was unsuccessful, as in reality the Kingdom of Prester John did not exist.

Prester John himself was said to be descended from one of the three magi, wise men or kings according to the version you believe, who visited Jesus Christ and his parents shortly after his birth. This made John a very special person, of course. He was that rarest of beings: a wise, virtuous and generous monarch who ruled over a land dedicated to Christian virtue and filled with all sorts of wonders, including the Gates of Alexander, built to keep out barbarian tribes, and the fabled Fountain of Youth.

It eventually became generally accepted that the supposed location of Prester John's Kingdom in the East was incorrect, and subsequent 'helpful' versions of the letter appeared that placed the land of Prester John in Abyssinia, now known as Ethiopia. Abyssinia at least had the virtue of being a very ancient Christian kingdom, indeed the very oldest according to Abyssinian claims.

By the middle of the fourteenth century, voyagers and soldiers began to travel to Abyssinia to help its people and in the hope of meeting Prester John. Even as late as the seventeenth century, map-makers were happy to show the kingdom of Prester John as an actual country, although presumably the presbyter would have been a little long in the tooth by then. The positive effect of interest in this fabulous land, with wonders such as the salamander that could live in fire, was that it encouraged travel well outside the usual pilgrim routes. One result of this was that cartography became not a perfect but at least a more accurate science.

There are some elements in this legend that can be linked to fact, though much is pure fantasy. The Assyrian Orthodox Church of western Iraq and Iran was, to twelfth-century Europeans, a faraway Christian Church of the East where a wise priest-king might be found. According to legend, St Thomas the disciple travelled to India, converting people to follow the teachings of his Lord. There exists to this day a group of Christians in southern India known as St Thomas Christians, or Nasrani. These Christians were distant and exotic enough to have been the inhabitants of Prester John's kingdom; they certainly excited the attentions of Portuguese traders and, a little later, colonists in the early sixteenth century. Then there was a John the Presbyter of Syria, who was believed by some to have been the author of the Epistles of John and whose tomb was to be seen in Ephesus in the fourth century. Was this John the Presbyter transmogrified into the fabulous ruler of the twelfth-century letters?

Marco Polo tells us that Prester John and Genghis Khan fought to the death after Genghis sent an embassy to the priest-king asking for the hand in marriage of John's daughter. Prester John replied that he would sooner put his daughter into the fire, as a result of which Genghis Khan swore to take such revenge on Prester John 'that insult never in this world was so dearly paid for'. The two leaders gathered their armies and engaged in a desperate combat that Marco Polo describes as 'the greatest battle that ever was seen'. In the end, Genghis Khan won victory and Prester John was slain.

In Wolfram von Eschenbach's *Parzival*, Parzival's half-brother Feirefîz marries the Grail Queen Repanse de Schoye, and their son is Prester John.

SEE ALSO: Holy Grail; Percival; Wolfram von Eschenbach

ROBERT DE BORON

Virtually nothing is known about the life of Robert de Boron. Around the end of the twelfth century, he composed three Arthurian romances: *Joseph d'Arimathie*, *Merlin* and the *Didot Perceval*. Robert sanctified the Grail, connecting it with Joseph of Arimathea and the vessel of the Last Supper.

We can presume that Robert was a Burgundian, born in the small village of Boron, some 15 miles from Montbéliard, in France. It is generally accepted that Robert wrote his Arthurian romances some time after the monks of Glastonbury Abbey claimed to have discovered the grave of King Arthur and Queen Guinevere in 1191, as Robert associates the Grail with the 'Vales of Avalon', which would seem to be in Somerset.

In Robert's *Joseph d'Arimathie*, also known as *Le Roman de l'Estoire dou Graal* (*The Romance of the History of the Grail*), he reveals that he is in the service of Gautier of Mont Belyal. Gautier of Mont Belyal has been identified as Gautier de Montbéliard, the Lord of Montfaucon, who took the cross and joined the Fourth Crusade. Gautier de Montbéliard joined a group of crusaders who sailed from Marseilles in 1202, and he died in the Holy Land ten years later.

Robert de Boron gives himself the titles of '*meisters*' (clerk) and '*messires*' (knight), and it is possible that he may have accompanied Gautier on crusade. Robert wrote his three Arthurian romances in octosyllabic verse. Only *Joseph d'Arimathie* and 504 lines of *Merlin* survive in verse. Prose versions of all three romances were made by an anonymous writer in the thirteenth century.

It was Robert de Boron who linked the mysterious platter that Chrétien de Troyes introduced in his *Perceval, or the Story of the Grail* with the vessel of the Last Supper which was used to catch the last drops of the blood of Christ.

Professor Daniel C. Scavone of the University of Southern Indiana has suggested in his article 'Joseph of Arimathea, the Holy Grail and the Edessa Icon' that the Edessa icon was the root of the stories of the Holy Grail. This relic was reputed to be the burial shroud of Jesus, the linen winding sheet supplied by Joseph of Arimathea. The bloodstained Edessa icon bore the image of Christ. In 944, the Edessa icon was taken to Constantinople. It was folded into eight sections and stored in a rectangular case with Christ's face visible through a circular aperture.

The Edessa icon disappeared during the Fourth Crusade (although it is thought by some that the famed relic known today as the Shroud of Turin is the Edessa icon). It is believed that the relic was looted by crusading knights during the sacking of Constantinople, the capital of the Byzantine Empire, and seat of the patriarch of the Orthodox Church. *The Chronicle of Novgorod* describes the scene:

> At sunrise they went to the Hagia Sophia and tore down the doors, and cut them to pieces, and the pulpit cased in silver, and twelve silver pillars . . . and twelve crosses which hung over the altar with bosses between them, like trees taller than a man . . . They tore the precious stone and the great pearl from the marvellous altar, and where they put the altar itself is not known.

Pope Innocent III would later condemn the crusaders: 'You vowed to liberate the Holy Land but you rashly turned away from the purity of your vow when you took up arms not against Saracens but Christians.' Robert de Boron's patron, Gautier de Montbéliard, was not among the crusaders who attacked Constantinople, but it is possible that crusaders' tales of the fabulous Edessa icon – a bloodstained relic of the Passion linked with Joseph of Arimathea – may have inspired Robert de Boron's story of Joseph and the Holy Grail.

SEE ALSO: Holy Grail; Joseph of Arimathea

ROSSLYN CHAPEL

In the last ten years, a small Scottish medieval chapel a few miles south of Edinburgh has been brought to the world's attention as the possible resting place of the Holy Grail. When Dan Brown wrote 'The Grail 'neath ancient Roslin waits' in his novel *The Da Vinci Code*, he introduced tens of millions of readers to the mysteries of Rosslyn Chapel. There are many legends surrounding Rosslyn Chapel and Castle: the legend of the murdered apprentice; traditional tales of the ghost dog of Rosslyn and of the White Lady who haunts the ruined castle; and stories of a fabulous secret treasure worth many millions of pounds.

The chapel is said to have been the scene of a bloody murder. When it was being built in the fifteenth century, its founder, Sir William St Clair, third Earl of Orkney and Lord of Rosslyn, requested a magnificent pillar for the Lady Choir. The Master Mason in charge of construction decided that he would have to travel to Rome to study the carvings and architecture of classical antiquity before he could begin to create the pillar. The Master was away for many months, and one night his apprentice had a vivid dream. He dreamed of a wondrous pillar, laced with wreaths of foliage and encircled by dragons. The following day, the apprentice pleaded with Sir William to let him carve the pillar. Sir William agreed, and in the weeks that followed he was amazed by the incredible skill of the young man.

At last, the pillar was completed, but on that very day the Master Mason returned. When the Master saw the apprentice's pillar he was overwhelmed by jealousy and rage. He took hold of a mason's hammer and struck down the apprentice, killing him with a vicious blow to his right temple. The Master Mason was promptly tried and executed for his crime. Three stone heads were carved and placed high in the chapel, looking across to the Apprentice Pillar: the Master Mason, the apprentice's grieving mother and the murdered apprentice, depicted with the fatal gash to his forehead.

It has been claimed that the Holy Grail is hidden inside or beneath Rosslyn's Apprentice Pillar. A series of pseudo-history writers have theorised that the Knights Templar escaped persecution in France in 1307 and took refuge at Rosslyn with the St Clair family. These refugee knights brought with them the Templar treasure, which was hidden at Rosslyn for over a hundred years before the chapel was built as a permanent hiding place full of secret clues waiting to be deciphered. Writers have suggested that the secret treasure is: the Lost Ark of the Covenant; a piece of the True Cross; the embalmed head of Jesus; ancient scrolls containing the lost gospels of Christ; the relics of Mary Magdalene; the real Stone of Destiny; and the Holy Grail. Some writers have speculated that the treasure may have been moved from Rosslyn by the Templars when they allegedly sailed to North America before Columbus and that it may be the mysterious treasure hidden in the Oak Island Money Pit in Nova Scotia.

In reality, there is absolutely no credible evidence to support any of these theories. The Templars did not make a pre-Columbian journey to America, and they would not have found a safe haven at Rosslyn. The St Clairs of Rosslyn had no love for the Knights Templar and in fact testified against them when they were brought to trial in Edinburgh in 1309.

The nearby village of Roslin hit world headlines when Dolly the Sheep was cloned at the Roslin Institute, a few miles from the chapel. Reporters and journalists from around the globe arrived in the small village of Roslin. They visited Rosslyn Chapel and reported on the chapel's mysteries as well as the cloned sheep. In recent years, it has been suggested that the foliate vines that spiral around the Apprentice Pillar actually depict a DNA double helix! In 2003 Rosslyn Chapel again came to the world's attention when it featured in Dan Brown's novel *The Da Vinci Code*. The book claimed that the chapel was built by the Templars, that it was a copy of King Solomon's Temple in Jerusalem and that it had once held the Holy Grail – the body and secret gospel of Mary Magdalene, the bride of Jesus Christ, who bore his child and founded a holy bloodline. Of course, *The Da Vinci Code* was a work of fiction. However, Dan Brown did claim that his descriptions of architecture within the novel were accurate, although he writes that there is a six-pointed star, the Seal of Solomon, worn into the chapel floor. There is no star worn into the floor of the chapel, the Templars had nothing whatsoever to do with Rosslyn, the chapel is not even remotely based on King Solomon's Temple and the remains of Mary Magdalene have never been kept in a 'massive subterranean vault' beneath the building.

The holy bloodline theory was first popularised by Michael Baigent, Richard Leigh and Henry Lincoln in their book *The Holy Blood and the Holy Grail*. They speculated that one of the medieval terms for the Holy Grail, 'Sangreal', actually hid the name 'holy blood'. They theorised that this holy blood was a secret bloodline of the descendants of Jesus and Mary Magdalene.

Rosslyn was not, however, originally linked to the Holy Grail through fanciful connections to the Knights Templar or holy bloodlines; it was linked to the Grail by a writer who saw in Rosslyn Chapel the magic and wonder of the Arthurian Grail romances. In 1952, the historian and esoteric scholar Lewis Spence wrote an article entitled 'Mystical Rosslyn', revealing that 'nothing can shake me from my conviction that Rosslyn was built according to the pattern of the Chapel of the Grail'.

Rosslyn was certainly created by a Scots knight who was surrounded and influenced by tales of King Arthur and the Knights of the Round Table. Sir William St Clair, third Earl of Orkney and Lord of Rosslyn, was a powerful Scots noble who travelled to France as ambassador for the King of Scots and had his castle remodelled in the flamboyant style of a continental chateau. Sir William founded Rosslyn Chapel as the East Quire of an immensely ambitious collegiate church that would have rivalled any of Scotland's cathedrals.

In 1446, Sir William brought the finest stonemasons, carvers and craftsmen to Rosslyn to build his chapel. As the Collegiate Church of St Matthew the Evangelist (as Rosslyn Chapel was originally known) took shape, Sir William brought one of Europe's foremost scholars to Rosslyn to translate the great French books of knighthood and chivalry into Scots. Sir William was patron to Sir Gilbert Hay, and it seems likely that Sir Gilbert became the 'secret architect' of Rosslyn Chapel.

The Arthurian romances were hugely popular among the nobility of fifteenth-century Scotland. Kings, lords, ladies, earls and knights read and listened to tales of King Arthur and Sir Gawain, Lancelot and Guinevere, and the quest for the Holy Grail. The halls of Rosslyn

Castle echoed with the songs of minstrels and tales of noble deeds. Within Rosslyn Chapel, there are carvings of a knight on horseback bearing a lance and of the red and white dragons of a tale of Merlin the Wizard. Sir William even named one of his sons Arthur.

Rosslyn Castle rests upon a rocky hilltop in a bend in the River Esk. The name Rosslyn means simply 'the hill by the waterfall', from two Scots words: 'ross' which is 'hill', and 'lynn' which is 'waterfall'. The medieval castle was literally carved out of the solid rock of the hill, with chambers, halls, kitchens and spiral stairways cut from the stone. Legend has it that the enchanted White Lady of Rosslyn Castle rests in a secret underground chamber behind a blocked-up doorway beneath the dark ruins of the castle. Like Arthur and the Knights of the Round Table, she sleeps within a hollow hill, and like the Grail maiden, she is described as a shining ethereal figure dressed in a gown of pure white, ornamented with jewels, silver and gold. It is said that she guards a hidden treasure worth many millions of pounds and that she can only be awoken by a brave knight, who will undo the evil spell that binds her with a blast on the hunting horn that lies by her side.

Rosslyn Chapel is at the edge of the village of Roslin, a few miles south of Edinburgh. The chapel is open to the public, and there is a gift and book shop and a small café in the visitor centre. Rosslyn Castle is privately owned by the Earl of Rosslyn and is managed by the Landmark Trust. The chapel overlooks Rosslyn Glen, a magical wooded valley which is said to be haunted by a ghostly black knight on horseback and the creatures of faerie. Rosslyn Chapel and Castle have inspired artists and poets, including Sir Walter Scott and William Wordsworth, and still enchant tens of thousands of visitors every year.

SEE ALSO: Gawain; Grail Maiden; Holy Grail; Knights Templar; Mary Magdalene; Merlin; Scotland

ROUND TABLE

The Round Table is for many the most important symbol in the legends of King Arthur. Literally, it is the table around which King Arthur's most favoured knights would sit and meet; but the term 'the Round Table' came to signify not only Arthur's court but also the formidable company of men who met there. We first see the Round Table introduced into the story of Arthur in the *Roman de Brut*, penned by Wace some time around the year 1155: '*Fist Artur la Rounde Table dunt Breton dient mainte fable*' ('Arthur made the Round Table of which the Bretons tell many stories').

Early sources such as the French poet Robert de Boron, who wrote *Joseph d'Arimathie* and *Merlin*, tell us that it was Merlin who convinced Uther Pendragon, King Arthur's father, to build the first Round Table. We also begin to see that this table has enormous significance and is a powerful metaphor not just for King Arthur's court but also for the whole quest for the Holy Grail. Robert's *Merlin* explains that this is to be the last of three holy tables of the Grail, which we are told Christ mentioned to Joseph of Arimathea when he visited him in prison after the Resurrection to tell him of the importance of the Grail. The first of these three tables was the one used at the Last Supper, where Jesus ate with his disciples for the very last time; the second is the table which the Grail itself sits upon and which Joseph of Arimathea will construct himself; and the third is to be the Round Table of Arthur and his knights.

The table is variously described as being able to seat 52, 150, 366 and even 1,600 knights. As the Grail legends developed, it became traditional that there was always one place at the table that had to be left vacant, and this was called the Siege Perilous. This place was designated for the one true Grail knight, and nobody else was permitted to sit there. This applied not only to the other Knights of the Round Table but also to Joseph of Arimathea or even the Fisher King himself, the guardian of the Grail. It was fatal for anyone who was not this sacred and special knight to sit in this place, which gave rise to the dreaded name. According to early versions of the legend, this empty place also signified the seat occupied by the traitor Judas at the Last Supper. Sir Galahad, he who was purest of heart and free of all sin, was destined to occupy the Siege Perilous.

So we see that the Round Table plays a key role in the story of Arthur and the Grail. It is a neat device, a physical object around which we can visualise all of the knights who will play a key role in the search for the Grail. The Round Table, then, is not so much a real table as a symbol of the bond that ties all the knights to one another, to their king, Arthur, and to the Grail itself.

The famous Winchester Round Table hangs in the Great Hall of Winchester Castle. It is 18 ft across and weighs some 1.25 tonnes. The first historical record of this particular table comes from 1464, when it is mentioned in John Hardyng's *Chronicle*. Modern dating methods have confirmed that the table is not of great antiquity. Despite claims that this was the original table around which King Arthur and his knights sat, radiocarbon and dendrochronological (tree-ring dating) studies show that the table is actually medieval. The Winchester Great Hall where it now hangs was completed in the year 1235, and records exist showing that the Great Hall was furnished and decorated over the next 30 years, all under the watchful gaze of King Henry III. It is thought that the Winchester Round Table was built for a great tournament held by King Edward I of England at Winchester in April 1290. Thirteen years previously, Edward had a grand marble tomb built for the supposed remains of Arthur and Guinevere at Glastonbury Abbey. The tournament was to celebrate the forthcoming marriages of King Edward's son and two of his daughters. Sir Thomas Malory insisted that Winchester itself was in fact the site of the legendary Camelot. He probably arrived at this conclusion because the round table was hanging at Winchester when he wrote *Le Morte d'Arthur*.

The Winchester Round Table is painted with alternating bands of white and green, with the names of 24 of Arthur's knights marked in gold around the perimeter. The 25th space is reserved for King

Arthur himself. This decoration of the table probably took place in 1516 upon the orders of King Henry VIII, and we find, perhaps not unsurprisingly, that the place reserved for Arthur is marked by a portrait of Henry VIII.

In the summer of 2006, archaeologists digging in the Upper Ward of Windsor Castle unearthed the foundations of King Edward III's Round Table building, and the excavation was shown as part of the Channel 4 programme *Time Team*'s 'Big Royal Dig'. Accounts record that Edward III built the Round Table at Windsor in 1344. The Windsor Round Table was a circular building 200 ft in diameter. It could hold around 300 knights and ladies for feasting, dancing, stories and theatre. They sat at a vast ring-shaped table within a circular cloister-like building – in effect, an early theatre, built over two centuries before Shakespeare's Globe. The floor was covered with decorated tiles and had a fountain at its centre. The Windsor Round Table building hosted theatrical performances, in which Edward's knights and ladies played the roles of King Arthur, Guinevere and Sir Lancelot in scenes from Arthurian romance.

The whole ethos of the Round Table is that it has no sides and no one sits at the head of it, so all who sit around it are equal. All of Arthur's knights meet as equals – no one is higher or lower at the Round Table. This reflects medieval concerns about status and stability. Knights held a key role in any king's army and were essential to the security of the kingdom. It was common for knights to sit at tables during feasts or councils, and obviously squabbles and fights were bound to break out because some were seen as being favoured by sitting closer to the head of the table. So a round table would have been a very clever device whereby all men became equal and overnight any infighting would cease.

The Round Table, with no position of supremacy or privilege, is still a very potent symbol. Round Tables appear today in parliaments and peace talks where difficult situations between opposing factions must be solved. The Round Table of legend has embedded itself firmly in the psyche of the modern world, and today symbolises fairness, equality and cooperation in overcoming a common problem – a useful tool when you have a quest to achieve.

SEE ALSO: Fisher King; Galahad; Joseph of Arimathea; Last Supper; Malory, Sir Thomas; Percival; Wace

SACRED FEMININE

Although it may not be immediately obvious, the sacred feminine – the Goddess concept – is to be found within the Arthurian legends, particularly in relation to the Holy Grail. At a basic level, a number of the female characters may owe their origins to Celtic mythology and ancient goddess worship. The Lady of the Lake, for example, is thought by some Arthurian scholars to be based on the Celtic water goddess Coventina, while Guinevere is believed to have an association with the Celtic goddess Epona, known as the White Lady. Morgan le Fay may have her origins in a Celtic goddess – Modron, Macha or the Morrigan. In Geoffrey of Monmouth's *Vita Merlini* (*The Life of Merlin*, *c.*1150), Morgan le Fay is depicted as a healer, one of nine sisters who live on the Isle of Avalon. This may have been a remembrance of a first-century group of nine sacred priestesses who lived off the coast of Brittany. These priestesses were famed as healers, seers and shape-shifters; they also had the ability to control the weather – all qualities credited to Morgan le Fay. Like the number three, nine is a potent, magical number, being three times three – 'thrice holy'.

Some writers claim that the story of the Holy Grail has a hidden meaning; the Grail is said to symbolise the Goddess and the quest to restore the lost sacred feminine. The worship of the sacred feminine was at its height in the neolithic period, but goddess fertility images date back to 35000 BC, indicating the duration and importance of goddess worship. It is thought that during the neolithic period the goddess cult was considered central to the vitality and fertility of the land and its people. Working alongside each other the God/Goddess, male/female aspects of the Godhead were seen as essential attributes that balanced and enhanced each other's qualities. As the Goddess possessed qualities of wisdom, caring, nurturing and fertility, so the God encompassed masculine power, virility, vitality and fecundity.

Yahweh, the God of the Old Testament, was associated with a goddess, Asherah, although this connection was later edited out of the Bible during the period when the Goddess cult was suppressed and subsumed by the concept of the all-powerful, vengeful male deity. No longer did the Godhead combine both male and female attributes, and no longer did male and female energy work in unison. Instead, the male deity ruled supreme, breaking the balance and disturbing the equilibrium of the sacred partnership. The natural order of things was to restore the feminine aspect of the Godhead, and it is this search for the lost sacred feminine and her ultimate restoration that can be equated with the knights' quest for the Holy Grail.

In *The Woman with the Alabaster Jar*, Margaret Starbird connects the search for the lost sacred feminine with the bride of the Old Testament's Song of Songs who has become separated from her bridegroom. On a similar theme, Ezekiel 16:3–63 relates how God found His bride-to-be (Jerusalem) when she was only a child (in other words, innocent). He cares for her, protects her and instructs her until she reaches an age when He can marry her. However, once in the world, she becomes unfaithful and corrupted and is lost to her husband, who still loves her and remains faithful to her. Despite her infidelity, God does all He can to return His wife to the comfort and warmth of her loving family. This theme is also woven into the Arthurian romances. When Arthur meets and marries Guinevere she is pure and uncorrupted. However, once married, she meets Lancelot and is unfaithful to her husband, who continues to love her nonetheless.

Another theme that runs through the Arthurian romances is the abduction of Guinevere – representing the period of separation, the absence of the sacred feminine – either by Lancelot, Mordred, Meleagant or Valerin, depending on the version of the story. In the Valerin episode featured in Ulrich von Zatzikhoven's *Lanzelet*, in which Guinevere is abducted twice, Valerin restrains the queen by giving her a sleeping potion. The idea of a 'sleeping beauty' is significant, as it represents the loss or repression of the feminine aspect of the Godhead, with the male searching frantically in order to be reunited with her once more.

When Arthur dies, Guinevere becomes the bereaved widow (as

does the Song of Songs' bride), lamenting the death of her husband. The theme of the bereaved widow is found in ancient religions where the male deity is killed, his female partner deity seeks him out and, once she has found him, tries to revive him (as in the legends of Osiris and Isis, Tammuz and Inanna). Guinevere finds consolation and redemption after Arthur's death, returning to purity by entering a nunnery and living a religious life. The phases Guinevere passes through correspond with those experienced by the Lost Goddess, namely, her fall, repentance and redemption. Moreover, she is also linked to the Goddess in the form of the bereaved widow, and in this respect King Arthur takes on the guise of the sacrificed king/god who will be resurrected, albeit at some time in the future – 'the once and future king'.

In their book *The Grail Legend*, psychologists Emma Jung (the wife of Carl) and Marie-Louise von Franz describe the Grail as 'a mystical symbol for the human self that bears strong traits of the female', which is an interesting analogy bearing in mind that it is thought by many that the Grail, as a cup, is symbolic of the female, representing the womb, reproduction, fertility and plenty. The Grail is borne by a maiden of especial purity and virtue, the Grail maiden. It has the ability to prolong or restore life and to provide food and drink in abundance, like the cauldrons and cornucopias associated with ancient goddesses.

Perhaps the most controversial theory regarding the sacred feminine and the Holy Grail is that of Mary Magdalene's role as the carrier of the *sang real* or holy blood – the offspring of Jesus and the Magdalene. Many supporters of Mary Magdalene see her true, yet expunged, role in the Gospels as that of the counterpart of Jesus and therefore the Lost Goddess herself. As for the sacred feminine, it is therefore thought to be Mary Magdalene's birthright to be restored to her rightful place, for she is the bride of the Song of Songs and the Grail of the Arthurian legends. In *Jesus and the Goddess*, Timothy Freke and Peter Gandy suggest that the loss of the female counterpart in many of the major religions has meant that: 'Women have been denied a sympathetic rapport with the Divine Feminine. Men have been denied a love-affair with a female face of Deity.'

It was the notion of the Grail representing the offspring of the union between Jesus and Mary Magdalene that Dan Brown used in his bestseller *The Da Vinci Code*. The controversy aroused by this idea ensured that tens of millions of people who had never previously considered the Holy Grail as anything other than a lost cup or an unobtainable ideal were introduced to the search for the sacred feminine.

SEE ALSO: Grail Maiden; Guinevere; Holy Grail; Lady of the Lake; Morgan le Fay

SCOTLAND

The idea of a 'Scottish King Arthur' often surprises people, but if there was really a historical Arthur, at least one of his battles was fought in the north, in what is now Scotland. Tales of Arthur and Merlin have been told north of Hadrian's Wall for more than a thousand years. Edinburgh Castle is built on the site of a Dark Age fortress associated with the earliest mention of Arthur. A huge extinct volcano in Edinburgh is named Arthur's Seat, and in the sixteenth century an accused witch confessed to reciting a charm there, 'in name of the Father and the Son and of King Arthur and the Faerie Queen'. Four hundred years later, the Scottish Celtic-revival artist John Duncan would paint such scenes as King Arthur taking Excalibur, Tristan and Isolde, and Merlin and the Fairy Queen.

The real Arthur is believed to have been a Dark Age Briton, a leader of battles who fought against invading Saxons, Angles, Jutes, Picts and Scots. The earliest mention of Arthur appears in the poem *Y Gododdin*, composed by the Welsh bard Aneirin in around AD 600. *Y Gododdin* recounts the story of a warband that gathers at Dinedin, Dark Age Edinburgh. For a year, the warriors of the Gododdin drink and feast before going into battle. They were the descendants of a tribe of Britons that the Romans called the Votadini. They spoke an ancient form of Welsh known as P-Celtic, or Brythonic. Aneirin immortalised the bloody deeds of the warriors of the Gododdin who fought and died in battle at Catraeth. Among the warriors of the Gododdin was Gwawrddur:

> He charged before three hundred of the finest,
> He cut down both centre and wing,
> He excelled in the forefront of the noblest host,
> He gave gifts of horses from the herd in winter.
> He fed black ravens on the rampart of a fortress
> Though he was no Arthur.

Aneirin tells us that Gwawrddur attacked 300, leaving the dead to feed the ravens, but 'ceni bei ef Arthur', 'he was no Arthur'. The name 'Arthur', then, needed no explanation. The Britons already knew of the deeds of Arthur when Aneirin recited Y *Gododdin* over a thousand years ago.

Castle Hill, the extinct volcanic rock where the Gododdin had their fortress, still dominates the heart of Edinburgh. In 1142, David I, King of Scotland, called Edinburgh Castrum Puellarum, the Castle of Maidens. To King David, Edinburgh was the Castle of Maidens, the Arthurian Chateau des Pucelles where Morgan le Fay held court. Geoffrey of Monmouth tells us that Mount Agned, 'now called the Castle of Maidens', was founded by King Ebraucus. Mount Agned was identified as one of the sites of Arthur's battles by the chronicler Nennius.

King Ebraucus also founded Mons Dolorosus and Alclud. In 1171, Mons Dolorosus, the Dolorous Mount, appears in the *Chronicles of Melrose*; the abbot of the Cistercian abbey at Melrose was called 'the abbot of Mons Dolorosus'. Legend has it that Arthur and his knights sleep within the Eildon Hills at Melrose in the Scottish Borders. Alclud is Dumbarton Rock on the Clyde, which, parliamentary records tell us, was called Castrum Arthuri, the Castle of Arthur, in 1367. In the Welsh Arthurian romance *Peredur, Son of Efrawg*, we learn that Peredur is the son of King Ebraucus (the Latinised form of Efrawg). Peredur is the Welsh Percival, the Grail knight.

In the Welsh poem *Pa Gwr*, we hear of Arthur and his men fighting with 'dog-heads' on the mountain of Edinburgh:

> Arthur distributed gifts,
> The blood trickled down.
> In the hail of Awarnach,
> Fighting with a hag,
> He cleft the head of Paiach.
> In the fastnesses of Dissethach,
> In Mynyd Eiddyn [mount of Edinburgh],

He contended with Cynvyn [dog-heads];
By the hundred there they fell . . . '

Hundreds of years after the real Arthur lived, the locations of his 'twelve battles' were listed in Nennius's *Historia Brittonum* (*History of the Britons*). As place names changed over the centuries, the locations of Arthur's battles were lost. Scholars theorise and argue about where the battles took place, but almost all agree that the seventh battle took place in what is now Scotland. The seventh battle 'was in the wood of Celidon, that is, Cat Coit Celidon'. 'Cat Coit Celidon' was the great forest of the Caledonians, a vast native woodland that flourished across what would become southern and central Scotland.

In the depths of the Caledonian Forest, amid the oaks, alder and mountain ash, lived the real Merlin. He was Merlin the Wild, a prophet who had lost his wits after the dreadful Battle of Arderydd. Merlin lived with the wolves and the wild boar, eating nuts and roots and lamenting his fall. He had been the adviser of Prince Gwenddolau, who met King Rhydderch of Strathclyde in battle at Arderydd in AD 573. As Merlin looked on, Gwenddolau and his men were cut down. Merlin lost his mind, and he fled from the battlefield, thereafter living in the wild. King Rhydderch was the patron of Kentigern, a Christian holy man who is said to have preached the Gospel in the woods and there met Merlin the Wild. Kentigern baptised Merlin at a rough-hewn altarstone before the prophet met 'a threefold death', by stake, stone and water. Merlin's grave is still pointed out at Drumelzier on the River Tweed, and the altarstone is said to lie at Altarstone Farm or to be built into the walls of a nearby village church, Stobo Kirk.

The life of Kentigern is as legendary and magical as that of Merlin. Kentigern was the son of the Princess Thanew. He was the grandson of Loth, the pagan king of the Votadini and legendary ruler of the Lothians and Orkney. Loth's fortress lay on the summit of Dunpender, now known as Traprain Law, a massive hill that rises from the flat plains of East Lothian. King Loth was the husband of Arthur's sister Morgause, or Anna. Loth was the father of Sir Gawain, so Kentigern would have been Gawain's nephew.

In some versions of the life of Kentigern, we are told that his father is Ewen, the son of King Urien, who ravishes Princess Thanew. Ewen, Kentigern's father, is the Yvain who appears in the Arthurian romances of Chrétien de Troyes. Arthurian scholars have noted that motifs from the medieval *Vita Kentigerni* (*The Life of St Kentigern*, by the monk Jocelyn of Furness) appear in Chrétien's *Yvain, or the Knight with the Lion*. Yvain meets and marries Laudine, the Lady of the

Fountain. Ewen twice approaches the princess Thanew at a fountain, then ravishes her. Kentigern later helps the Queen of Strathclyde. King Rederech suspects his wife is unfaithful when he sees a ring that he gave her on the hand of another man. The king throws the ring into the River Clyde then demands that his queen show him it. The queen turns to Kentigern, who tells a messenger to catch a fish. Inside the fish is the lost ring. The queen shows it to her husband, and their marriage is saved. In *The Knight with the Lion*, the lady Laudine gives a ring to Yvain. Her handmaiden, Lunete, later asks for the return of the ring, but in the end Yvain and the lady Laudine are reconciled. It appears that a life of Kentigern was one of Chrétien's sources.

St Kentigern, also known as St Mungo, is the patron saint and founder of Glasgow. His tomb is in the crypt of Glasgow Cathedral, on the site of a tiny church he is said to have built. The diocese of Glasgow was restored by David, Earl of Cumberland and of Huntingdon (later King David I), in the twelfth century. David brought together a 'Jury of Inquisition' to decide how large the bishopric of Glasgow had been in the time of Kentigern. The jury was made up of knights, barons, ecclesiastics and the 'old and wise'. They gathered ancient tales, poems and fragments of manuscripts to build up a picture of the life of the saint. Among these texts would have been stories of Merlin the Wild, known as Lailoken.

The Lailoken fragments would become one of Geoffrey of Monmouth's sources. He dedicates his *History of the Kings of Britain* to Robert of Gloucester, the nephew of David I. King David and Robert of Gloucester were allies in the civil war between King Stephen and the Empress Matilda. In 1141, David went to Oxford to support Robert and Matilda. It is possible that Robert introduced David to Geoffrey at Oxford. It was one year later that David, like Geoffrey, called Edinburgh Castrum Puellarum, the Castle of Maidens. Around 1150, Geoffrey would write *Vita Merlini*, *The Life of Merlin*. Geoffrey's *Vita Merlini* tells the story of Merlin who went with Peredur, King of the North Welsh, and Rhydderch, King of the Cumbrians, to make war on Gwenddolau, who ruled the realm of Scotland. The slaughter on the battlefield is so terrible that Merlin laments for three days and refuses food. He is consumed by grief and secretly flees to the woods where he lives hidden like a wild animal.

Jocelyn of Furness wrote *Vita Kentigerni* for the Bishop of Glasgow around 1180. The bishop, also named Jocelyn, had been the Abbot of Melrose, and Jocelyn of Furness had previously written a *Life of St Waltheof*, a former Abbot of Melrose. The Cistercian monks of Melrose Abbey had been granted lands by King David. They kept huge flocks of sheep on their lands and traded the wool with merchants from Flanders. In 1182, Count Philip of Flanders gave a charter to the Cistercians of Melrose Abbey granting them passage through his territories free of all tolls. In *Perceval, or the Story of the Grail*, Chrétien de Troyes tells us that his source was a book that his patron, Count Philip of Flanders, gave to him. Is it possible that Chrétien's source for *The Story of the Grail* was a book that Philip had received from the monks of Melrose? Could Philip of Flanders' trade links with Scotland have brought fragments of the tales of Kentigern, Lailoken or Gawain to France? It is interesting to note that one possible origin of the Grail story is the Dish of Rhydderch. This wondrous serving platter belonged to King Rhydderch, the patron of St Kentigern.

Arthurian place names survive across Scotland: Arthur's Seat, Arthur's Crag, Loch Arthur, Knockarthur, Arthurstone, Suidhe Artair, Arthur's Bridge, Arthurshiels Wood, Ben Arthur, Arthur's Fold, Agaidh Artur, Arthur's Fountain, Arthur's Castle. In the village of Meigle is Vanora's Grave, an ancient mound said to be the burial place of the real Guinevere. Vanora was the Guinevere of Pictish legend, the unfaithful wife of Arthur who was executed for betraying her husband with the Pictish King Mordred. Among the Pictish symbol stones in the museum in Meigle is a huge stone said to show Vanora being torn apart by wild dogs.

A unique stone building called Arthur's O'on (Arthur's Oven) stood above the north bank of the River Carron near Stenhousemuir until the eighteenth century. Arthur's O'on was a large, beehive-shaped building thought to have been a Roman shrine or temple. When it was demolished by a local landowner, the antiquarian Sir John Clerk of Penicuik was so appalled by this act of vandalism that he decided to have an exact replica of Arthur's O'on built at his home as a dovecote.

In recent years, much has been written about Rosslyn Chapel and the Holy Grail. Writers have suggested that the Grail may be hidden within the chapel's famous Apprentice Pillar or in a secret underground chamber. It has been said that Rosslyn may be the chapel that appears in the continuations of Chrétien's *Story of the Grail* in which a mysterious black hand snuffs out the candles.

Govan Old Parish Church is home to a group of Viking hogback tombs and the Govan Sarcophagus. Archaeological excavations have revealed that Govan was an important religious site of the Brythonic

Kingdom of Strathclyde. A boundary ditch ran around the site, and near the church was an artificial mound known as the Doomster Hill. The Govan Sarcophagus is carved from a single block of sandstone, sculpted with knotwork patterns, animals and the figure of a horseman. Some say that it once held the bones of the real Arthur of the Britons.

SEE ALSO: Arthur, King of the Britons; Avalon; Battles of Arthur; Chrétien de Troyes; Cinema and Theatre; Gawain; Geoffrey of Monmouth; Guinevere; Merlin; Mordred; Percival; Philip, Count of Flanders; Rosslyn Chapel

SWORD IN THE STONE

The story of the drawing of the sword from the stone is one of the most important aspects of Arthurian legend. It is this single act that reveals Arthur's royal lineage. In the account Malory gives us in *Le Morte d'Arthur*, the wizard Merlin devises a test to reveal the rightful king, arranging for a tournament to be attended by all the great lords and knights of the realm on New Year's Day. Arthur, the adopted son of Sir Ector, is taken to the tournament with Sir Ector's son Kay, who is to be made a knight at this event. On their way to the tournament, Kay finds that he has forgotten his sword and tells Arthur to ride back to fetch it from their lodgings. Arthur sets off, but finds that the innkeeper and his family have left to watch the tournament, leaving the lodgings locked. Arthur heads back through a churchyard and sees a sword set into a stone. Thinking that this would make the perfect replacement for Kay's sword, Arthur pulls the gleaming steel from the stone and dutifully returns to the tournament. He gives the sword to Kay, who, upon touching it, notices writing etched into the blade: 'Whosoever pulls this Sword from the Stone is the rightwise born King of all England'. On seeing this, Kay takes the sword to his father and claims to have pulled it from the stone himself. Sir Ector demands the truth, and Kay reluctantly tells him that it was Arthur who brought him the sword. Arthur and the sword are taken back to the churchyard, where the sword is replaced in the stone. Kay tries to pull it from the stone but fails, and as the knights and lords look on, Arthur once more pulls the sword from the stone and is hailed as the rightful king.

SWORD IN THE STONE

The fact that the sword was drawn from a stone has led some scholars to suggest that the origin of the story may be traced to Bronze Age sword-making techniques whereby molten metal was poured into a stone or clay mould. When the bronze had hardened, the mould was opened and the sword was literally pulled from the stone. The archaeologist Francis Pryor has suggested that the legends of King Arthur can be traced back to the Bronze and Iron Ages, and Channel 4's *Time Team* has demonstrated Bronze Age sword-making to show where the story might have originated.

In the earliest version of the story, the sword is not pulled from a stone but drawn from an anvil. The original story of the Sword in the Stone is attributed to the twelfth-century French poet Robert de Boron. Robert wrote that after the death of Uther Pendragon, Merlin suggested that a new king should be chosen at Christmas. In the churchyard of a cathedral in London, a mysterious stone was found. On the stone was an anvil with a sword plunged into it. The archbishop sprinkled holy water on the stone and read an inscription stating that the sword would be drawn by the true king, chosen by Jesus Christ. Many knights tried and failed to draw the sword from the stone. Later, at a tournament, Kay decided to join the mêlée, or mock battle. He sent Arthur to get his sword, but it was nowhere to be found. Arthur rode to the churchyard and pulled the sword from the anvil. Antor, the foster father of Arthur in Robert's tale, told the boy all that he knew of Arthur's lineage and promised to support him in his claim to the throne. In front of the assembled barons of the realm, Arthur repeated the feat of extracting the sword and was proclaimed king by the archbishop. The sword symbolised justice, the stone represented Christ.

The anvil also suggests that the story of the Sword in the Stone has its roots in sword-making. The swordsmith's art was kept secret and was seen as magical, as in their forges they made swords from stone, using fire and water to transform raw ore into molten metal and molten metal into shining swords. Swords were often seen as magical weapons. In the Iron Age, they were placed in rivers and lakes as ritual votive offerings. Medieval crusaders often etched crosses into the blades of their swords. Arthur's sword, Excalibur, is supposed to have been forged on the Isle of Avalon, and legends told that other magical swords were forged by elves or trolls.

It has been claimed that the story may in fact be due to a scribal error, with the Latin word '*saxum*', meaning 'stone', being mistaken for 'Saxon'. Perhaps Arthur killed a Saxon and took his sword, but the sword of the Saxon became the sword of or in the *saxum*, the stone. It would have been a simple mistake for a scribe to confuse the two words. Some Arthurian scholars, on the other hand, claim that the Sword in the Stone has its roots in the beliefs of the Alans, a group of nomadic Sarmatians. In the fifth century, the Alans would thrust a sword into the ground during religious rites dedicated to their war god.

Much has been made of the magical nature of the sword, but it is possible that the stone itself was more important. It is the stone that releases the sword, revealing that Arthur is the true king. This makes the stone and not the sword the centrally important item, which is perhaps why this sword itself plays no further part in the mythic cycle, being replaced by the magical Excalibur later. There are precedents for the importance of sacred stones in legends and folklore from around the world. In Nigeria, the magical Queen Stones are said to sing out loud when the rightful queen sits upon them. In the Irish *Lebor Gabála Érenn* (*The Book of the Takings of Ireland*, also known as *The Book of Invasions*), we are told that the Lia Fáil is a sacred stone, one of the treasures of the Tuatha dé Danaan. It was written that the stone would 'utter a cry under every king that should take Ireland'. The Lia Fáil stands on the Hill of Tara in County Meath. Another Stone of Destiny is the Stone of Scone. Legend says that the Stone of Destiny is the stone used as a pillow by Jacob in the Bible, on which the Ark of the Covenant once stood. Jacob's Pillow was taken to Egypt, Spain, then to Ireland and finally Scotland. It is thought by many that King Edward I of England took the Stone of Scone from Scotland in 1296. It was taken to Westminster Abbey and built into the Coronation Chair, on which, for centuries, the kings and queens of England and later Britain have been crowned. The stone became known as the Coronation Stone, and in 1996 it was returned to Scotland. It is now on display in Edinburgh Castle, although many Scots believe that Edward took the wrong stone from Scone and that the real Stone of Destiny is still hidden somewhere in Scotland.

Did the stone of the tales of Arthur echo ancient legends of magical stones associated with kingship? Some say that these stones represented the land. When a man became king, he was symbolically married to the land, to the Goddess of Sovereignty. The Sword in the Stone may be a phallic symbol of the king thrust into the symbol of the goddess.

There is a real Sword in the Stone in Tuscany, Italy. The sword of St Galgano lies in a twelfth-century round chapel set in woods near the village of Chiusdino. Galgano Guidotti was an arrogant, aggressive young knight who lived a violent life full of worldly pleasures until he had a vision of the Archangel Michael. Galgano decided to become a hermit and devote his life to God. He saw a vision of a round church on a hilltop near his village, and, when an angelic voice told him to abandon the life of a knight, he drew his sword and thrust it into the rocky ground. His sword was buried in the stone to its hilt, and from that day forth Galgano lived the life of a simple holy man. Galgano Guidotti died in 1181 at the age of only 33 years. Galgano's story is almost the reverse of Arthur's. As Arthur takes up the sword to lead his people in battle, so Galgano gives up a life of violence to live in peace as a hermit.

The Cistercians built a round chapel, the Cappella di Monte Siepi, around St Galgano's sword in the stone, and it is venerated there to this day. In recent years, the sword, the stone and the chapel have been the subjects of scientific tests. Ground-penetrating radar scans have revealed what may be a burial recess beneath the floor of the chapel. Parts of the round chapel have been shown to date to around 985. It had been assumed by many that the sword itself was a fake, but test drilling has shown that the sword's blade extends deep into the rock and the sword itself has been reliably dated to the late twelfth century.

The image of a sword in a stone evokes a cross upon an altar. The altar stone was the holiest part of a church or cathedral, representing Christ. Some medieval altar stones were inscribed with the quincunx, an arrangement of five crosses representing the five wounds of Christ. It may be that the sword in the stone, which first appears in the churchyard of a cathedral, simply shows that Arthur becomes king by the will of Christ.

In its basic form, the story of the Sword in the Stone provides a device by which Merlin can have Arthur proclaimed the rightful king; however, the story seems to be about much more than that. It appears to have its roots in ancient magical legends about the land, rebirth and perhaps something even older still – the idea of a sacred stone revealing divine kingship and wisdom. The idea may go back as far as Ancient Egypt and beyond.

SEE ALSO: Arthur; Excalibur; Merlin

TALIESIN

When we come to the subject of Taliesin the bard, it is necessary to try to separate the historical figure from the legends and tales that have become attached to him. The *Book of Taliesin* is a collection of poems and esoteric material, although it is not known how much of this material was written by the original poet. A manuscript copy in the National Library of Wales dates to the fourteenth century and is the work of a single scribe, probably from Glamorgan. It is perfectly possible that through the oral rendition of the poems, their original medium, the works of Taliesin were accurately transmitted down the generations until they were finally written down. The *Book of Taliesin* contains poems addressed to several historical kings, including Gwallog of Elmet and Cynan Garwyn, who was king of Powys. Eight of the poems concern Urien of Rheged, including a death lament to his son Owain. Alongside these are other works dealing with more mythological and religious subjects.

Taliesin is mentioned in Nennius' *Historia Brittonum*, which was compiled around AD 800, as one of the five British poets held in high esteem. He may have been the court bard to King Brochwel Ysgithrog of Powys around AD 555 and then to his successor Cynan Garwyn.

The first literary connection between Taliesin and Arthur is found in the eleventh-century *Culhwch and Olwen*. In *Culhwch and Olwen*, one of a collection of stories known as *The Mabinogion*, Taliesin is the chief bard at Arthur's court, while the court magician is Menw. In *The Spoils of Annwn*, a poem in the *Book of Taliesin*, Arthur and his men journey to the faerie otherworld of Annwn to seize a magical cauldron; of the warriors who accompany Arthur in this quest, only seven return alive. In Geoffrey of Monmouth's poem *Vita Merlini*, the bard Taliesin is introduced as having spent time in Brittany and learnt philosophy there. Geoffrey tells us that Taliesin and Merlin accompanied Arthur on his final journey to the Isle of Avalon, where they were welcomed by Morgan le Fay, who greeted the wounded king and promised him a cure if he remained on the island.

Elis Gruffydd, a soldier employed in the English garrison at Calais during the sixteenth century, wrote a monumental history recounting Celtic folklore and ancient British history and giving an account of events up to his own age, including a life story of Taliesin. It is believed that he finished the work in 1552, and it was unusual at the time in being written in Welsh.

In Gruffydd's *Ystoria Taliesin*, we are told that Taliesin had the ability to shape-shift, turning himself into different creatures. As a boy, originally called Gwion, the future Taliesin was a servant to an old woman named Ceridwen. She had a magical cauldron in which she brewed a potion the first three drops of which would impart great wisdom, and which was intended for her son Morfan. As Gwion stirred the contents of the cauldron, some of the hot liquid spilt on his hand, and he licked it off, instantly gaining great knowledge. He realised that Ceridwen would be furious and ran from her, turning himself into a rabbit with his newly acquired magical wisdom. Ceridwen transformed herself into a dog to chase the rabbit, so Gwion became a fish, which was chased by Ceridwen as an otter. The pursuit continued until Gwion, as a grain of corn, was eaten by Ceridwen as a hen, and she became pregnant. When Ceridwen gave birth to her son, despite intending to kill the baby, knowing him to be Gwion, she instead hid the infant in a bag and threw him into the sea. A man fishing for salmon found the child and was astonished by his fairness, which is where the name Taliesin, meaning 'radiant brow', is said to originate. Elphin, the child's new guardian, was later the King of Ceredigion, and Taliesin grew up to be a bard and seer at his court.

A grave on a hilltop near Ceredigion in Wales is known as Bedd Taliesin, and is the legendary gravesite of the bard. The village at the foot of the hill is named Tre Taliesin. Samuel Rush Meyrick, who visited the site while studying the druidic ruins of the county, published *The History and Antiquities of the County of Cardigan* in 1810. In this book, he recounts a local legend about the site: 'The popular superstition respecting this, is that should anyone sleep in this bed for one night, he would the next day become either a poet, or an idiot.' Meyrick is, however, dismissive of this story and doubts that the grave is even that of Taliesin, saying that anyone who considers the matter 'shall readily pronounce such an account to be wholly fabulous'.

More than a thousand years after Taliesin recounted his magical poems to the kings of Wales his name still inspires poets, musicians and storytellers. A monument to Taliesin stands on the shores of Lake Geirionydd in Caernarfonshire. The large vertical stone is surmounted by a cross, which seems to indicate a desire to remove the magical and shamanistic elements from Taliesin and establish him as a Christian. When Alfred, Lord Tennyson wrote his *Idylls of the King*, he described Taliesin as the bard to King Arthur. The great architect Frank Lloyd Wright named the home that he built for himself in Spring Green, Wisconsin, after Taliesin. In 1969, the British rock band Deep Purple released an album called *The Book of Taliesyn*, and the Welsh bard has become a mystical figure of the new-age movement.

SEE ALSO: Avalon; Geoffrey of Monmouth; Merlin; Tennyson, Alfred, Lord

TENNYSON, ALFRED, LORD

Few would deny that Alfred, Lord Tennyson (1809–92) has a rightful claim to be the greatest British poet of the Victorian era. He wrote lyric poetry, patriotic poems, poems of faith and poems of love, all with consummate skill.

His father had been a clergyman, and inevitably the young Alfred was well schooled in the Christian religion by an early age. By the time *In Memorian* was published in 1850, however, he felt able to write:

> There lives more faith in honest doubt,
> Believe me, than in half the creeds.

His youth was largely spent in the countryside, and he developed, as did so many Victorians, a passionate love for his native land, which he rarely felt a desire to leave. Tennyson penned verses to commemorate contemporary military and national triumphs and events, and was drawn to historical events, real and legendary, through which his nation had been forged. Among these stories that of King Arthur struck a chord with him. Tennyson wrote *In Memoriam* between 1833 and 1850 following the death of his beloved friend Arthur Hallam, but these lines from that work perhaps encapsulate his feeling for characters from the past:

> So word by word, and line by line,
> The dead man touch'd me from the past,

> And all at once it seem'd at last
> The living soul was flash'd on mine

Tennyson attended Trinity College, Cambridge, where in 1829 he won the Chancellor's Gold Medal for his poem 'Timbuctoo'. His father died, in debt, two years later and Alfred left university without graduating.

'The Lady of Shalott' appeared in 1832, based on Sir Thomas Malory's story of the Lady Elaine, although Tennyson claimed his inspiration came from an Italian novelette called *Donna di Scalotta*:

> On either side the river lie
> Long fields of barley and of rye,
> That clothe the wold and meet the sky;
> And thro' the field the road runs by
> To many-tower'd Camelot;
> And up and down the people go,
> Gazing where the lilies blow
> Round an island there below,
> The island of Shalott.

In the 1830s, Tennyson began early drafts of his poem 'Morte d'Arthur', and in 1842 his two-volume *Poems* was published, including 'Sir Galahad', 'Sir Launcelot and Queen Guinevere' and 'Morte d'Arthur'. Tennyson's *Idylls of the King* appeared in 1859, selling 10,000 copies in a single month. In *Idylls of the King*, he tells of an ideal destroyed because men break their faith, in contrast to a nation united in support of the established order, which is its own reward:

> And Arthur and his knighthood for a space
> Were all one will, and through that strength the King
> Drew in the petty princedoms under him,
> Fought, and in twelve great battles overcame
> The heathen hordes, and made a realm and reigned.
>
> 'The Coming of Arthur', *Idylls of the King*

The Holy Grail, and Other Poems was published in 1869. Tennyson's Arthurian works drew largely on Sir Thomas Malory for inspiration, and while they were much admired, there was some criticism that, inevitably perhaps, the poet had laid a veneer of Victorian moral attitudes on the medieval tales. Another famous Victorian, William

Morris, was moved to reply to Tennyson's condemnation of Arthur's queen in his poem 'The Defence of Guenevere' (1858). The socialist Morris was in turn criticised in more traditional circles for going beyond the bounds of good taste. Other Arthurian poems were penned by Wordsworth, Longfellow and Swinburne. As a result of the new interest in the Arthurian legends, painters such as the Pre-Raphaelites took up their brushes to produce beautiful works of art, bringing to life the heroes and heroines of the imagined past. Their philosophy was to paint simply, using pure, vivid colours, trying to get as close to the reality of the subject as possible. They greatly admired Tennyson's writing. In the United States, Mark Twain was inspired to write his brilliant satire on the subject of Camelot, *A Connecticut Yankee in King Arthur's Court*.

Having been appointed Poet Laureate in 1850, succeeding Wordsworth, Tennyson eventually accepted a peerage in 1884. After Queen Victoria met with him in 1883, she wrote in her diary:

> After luncheon saw the great Poet Tennyson in dearest Albert's room for nearly an hour; and most interesting it was. He is grown very old – his eyesight much impaired and he is very shaky on his legs. But he was very kind. Asked him to sit down. He talked of the many friends he had lost and what it would be if he did not feel and know that there was another World, where there would be no partings.

Alfred, Lord Tennyson died on 6 October 1892. Victoria wrote that his passing was a great national loss:

> He was a great poet, and his ideas were ever grand, noble, elevating . . . He died with his hand on his Shakespeare, and the moon shining full into the window, and over him. A worthy end to such a remarkable man.

Into the twentieth and twenty-first centuries, countless novels, films, musicals, plays and adventure stories have extended the popular fascination for the Arthurian legends which have been handed down and embellished from generation to generation, and Tennyson's work was a powerful stimulus for all this. Sir Walter Scott also had a deep interest in the popular romantic view of the medieval world. The author of *Ivanhoe* and many other thrilling stories also wrote the poem *Marmion: A Tale of Flodden Field*, in the introduction to which he mentions the adventures of Lancelot of the Lake and a vision he had of the Grail. (Scott positively revelled in long prefaces and introductions.)

While much of Victorian Britain was open to criticism for its harshness and hypocrisy, there was a belief that through morality, hard work and education, society could be improved. The Victorians were ready to accept heroic ideals, and Tennyson's Arthur appealed to them. Their Grail, which they never, of course, acquired, was a dream of Utopia. Tennyson's Camelot was, for a short time, that perfect society:

> . . . And when King Arthur made
> His Table Round, and all men's hearts became
> Clean for a season, surely he had thought
> That now the Holy Grail would come again;
> But sin broke out. Ah, Christ, that it would come,
> And heal the world of all their wickedness!
>
> 'The Holy Grail'

SEE ALSO: Camelot; Guinevere; Holy Grail; Malory, Sir Thomas

VALENCIA HOLY CHALICE

O ver the centuries, there have been many ideas about what the Holy Grail might look like. Would it be the simple wooden or clay cup of a carpenter's son or an ornate and highly decorated golden vessel, a glittering treasure to match its exalted status as Christ's cup?

It is believed by some that the disciple Peter kept the cup, then passed it down through his successors, the heads of the church in Rome, or popes, as they became known. In 258, Pope Sixtus II faced persecution by the Roman authorities, and a tradition exists that the cup was then passed by St Lawrence to a Spanish soldier who took it to his homeland. The 'history' of the cup becomes confused and it becomes impossible to ascertain which real artefact, if any, is being described in the many myths and tales associated with the Cup of Christ.

During the Middle Ages, various relics claimed the honour of being the holy chalice of Christ. There was a silver chalice in a chapel near Jerusalem that is mentioned by a pilgrim in the seventh century. A green bowl in Genoa Cathedral, originally believed to be made of emerald but now identified as Egyptian glass, was said by William of Tyre to have been taken from a mosque at Caesarea in AD 1101. By the thirteenth century, this had come to be identified with the Holy Grail, no doubt to the great pleasure of its custodians, who would have found increasing numbers of pilgrims descending on their cathedral.

In Valencia Cathedral is a cup made from red agate that has been ornately mounted on a golden column, with two golden handles in the form of snakes and an indistinct inscription in Arabic on its base. The base is also of stone, with a gold rim, and set with two emeralds and a number of pearls. In 1399, this chalice was given to King Martin I of Aragon by the monastery of San Juan de la Peña, and it then passed to his successors and was listed in the royal archives. John II, who was also King of Navarre, gave the chalice to Valencia Cathedral in March 1437. Inspection of the cup in the mid-twentieth century determined that it originated in either Egypt or Palestine and dates from between around 350 BC and AD 50. The cathedral has a document claiming to date from AD 262 which says that the chalice was used by St Peter and subsequent popes to celebrate Mass and was removed from Rome for protection. Those who believe that the Valencia Holy Chalice is the Cup of Christ claim that it was venerated in Huesca, northern Spain, until the conquest of the country by the Moors, after which it was hidden in various churches and moved around until it finally reached the monastery of San Juan.

The Valencia Holy Chalice is certainly considered a valuable relic by the Catholic Church. In 1959, Pope John XXIII recognised the chalice, known in Spain as the Santo Cáliz, as an authentic relic and decreed that pilgrims who visited it would receive indulgences. It was used by Pope John Paul II to celebrate Mass in 1982, and his successor Pope Benedict XVI referred to it as 'this most famous chalice' when using it in July 2006. The wording, from the Roman Canon for the Holy Mass, is significant, as *'hunc praclarum calicem'* means 'this venerable chalice' and suggests a deliberate reference to the holy chalice used by Christ, rather than the usual 'the chalice', which, as a generic term, would apply to a cup used to represent the Cup of Christ.

The faint Arabic inscription on the base has been translated in many different ways, and because the characters are crudely carved, they are open to interpretation. In the 1980s, Hans Wilhelm Schaefer, in his book *Kelch und Stein* (*Chalice and Stone*), translated them as 'ALBST SLJS', '*Al-labsit As-silis*' in Arabic or '*lapsit exillis*' in Latin, the name given to the Grail in Wolfram von Eschenbach's *Parzival*. This would certainly provide a very neat link between the Valencia Holy Chalice, the Cup of Christ as seen by the Church and the Holy Grail of Arthurian romance.

SEE ALSO: Holy Grail; Wolfram von Eschenbach

WACE

In Royal Square, St Helier, on the Channel Island of Jersey, there stands a plaque unnoticed by all but a handful of visitors. It commemorates the twelfth-century poet Wace, who first drew breath there as a subject of the Duke of Normandy, who was also the King of England and at the time held a large part of France under his sway. The poet's own proud words are included in the memorial, taken from his *Roman de Rou* (*Story of Rollo*), written during the period between 1160 and 1174, in which he declares in Norman French: 'I am Wace of the Island of Jersey.'

The *Roman de Rou* was a history of the Normans, named after the Viking founder of the Duchy of Normandy, Rollo. It was commissioned by Wace's patron, Henry II of England, Duke of Normandy. Henry was not the most patient of men, and it is typical of him that he became tired of waiting for Wace to complete his task. According to Wace, one Beneeit (who was probably the poet Benoît de Sainte-More), who was working on a rival version, had the task handed over to him. Wace's *Roman de Rou*, possibly due to the cancellation of the commission, was never completed.

At an early age, Wace had been taken to Caen in Normandy, where he received his education and lived most of his adult life. It was there that he took holy orders, eventually becoming a canon at Bayeux. He came to the attention of King Henry II, as Duke, and received due recognition. Wace is thought to have dedicated a book to Eleanor of Aquitaine, King Henry's feisty wife, who had divorced Louis VII of France in 1152. This was the *Roman de Brut* (*Story of Brutus*), which

219

took as its main source the earlier Geoffrey of Monmouth's *Historia Regum Britanniae* (*The History of the Kings of Britain*), which was completed around 1135–7. The *Historia* was, as its title suggests, written in Latin, but Wace realised that while Latin was the language of the Church, his work would be appreciated by a wider audience if he wrote in the common language of the Norman Empire, which he himself referred to as 'the Romance tongue', Norman French. The *Roman de Brut* takes its name from Brutus, the reputed founder of Britain, descended from the survivors of the fall of Troy.

Wace described himself as '*clerc lisant*', literally a 'reading clerk', but his title, '*Maistre*' or 'Master', suggests that he may have taught others. He wrote extensively, translating the works of other writers and producing his own chronicles and saints' lives. His most widely appreciated work was the *Roman de Brut*, which includes the life of King Arthur and was completed by 1155. He does more than simply translate Geoffrey's story in another tongue; rather, he reimagines Geoffrey's themes. Wace has an ability to bring a scene to life:

> Then the bishops and abbots of the realm, with divers monks
> and holy orders, carrying in their hands bodies of the saints
> and many holy relics, came before the king beseeching him to
> show mercy on the Scots. With these went a pitiful company
> of ladies of that country, naked of foot, spoiled of visage,
> with streaming hair and rent raiment, bearing their babes in
> their bosoms.
>
> *Roman de Brut*, Wace (trans. Eugene Mason)

He continues, with the same economy of words, to describe the wretchedness of the petitioners, until Arthur's heart is moved to spare them, to the great relief of the reader, who, because of the language employed, must empathise with the poor Scots. Wace wove in other sources and rejected parts of Geoffrey of Monmouth's inclusions, such as the prophecies of Merlin.

It should not be thought that Wace was the only translator of this period, as Gaimar, an Anglo-Norman, had written *Estoria des Bretons* (*History of the Britons*), during the previous decade, and there are other, unidentified fragments in existence. The Arthurian legends obviously struck a chord with the educated and leisured of society, and there were those who wished to be involved in spreading the tale further.

Geoffrey of Monmouth named King Arthur's sword Caliburn;

however, its more famous name today is, of course, Excalibur, which derives from the Old French Escalibor. The name Excalibur was used by Wace for the first recorded time. There are several conflicting theories about the derivation of the name, including a Latin word for steel and a legendary Irish sword. An early Welsh name for Arthur's sword was Caledvwlch.

Wace's *Roman de Brut* tells the story not only of King Arthur but also of King Lear (later immortalised by William Shakespeare), and he treats them as genuine historical figures. Wace and his contemporaries were writing for an eager audience. He was hard-headed enough to write in one of his chronicles that his works were for the well-to-do, since only they were able to afford to buy books. By 1170, the Prior of Tewkesbury wrote that the fame of Arthur was recognised universally. It may have been mere hyperbole, but his claim that in Byzantium, Egypt, Rome, Carthage and in places as far away as Palestine Arthur's deeds were extolled gives us an idea of the reverence with which the name of Arthur was spoken in Britain and France, much closer to his realm than those far-off exotic lands.

Wace said that the stories told of Arthur were: 'Nor all a lie, nor all true, nor all fable, nor all known, so much have the story-tellers told, and the fablers fabled, in order to embellish their tales, that they have made all seem fable.' Here, surely, Wace has put his finger on the problem of Arthur. So much has been heaped upon his shoulders, even as early as Wace's time, that the hero himself has virtually disappeared, like a statue in an overgrown garden obscured by the shrubs, weeds and wild flowers.

SEE ALSO: Excalibur; Geoffrey of Monmouth; Layamon; Merlin

WAGNER, RICHARD

Richard Wagner's music has excited much criticism and much comment, some serious, some humorous. Gustav Mahler said, after the first performance of *Parsifal*, 'When I came out of the Festspielhaus, unable to speak a word, I knew that I had experienced supreme greatness and supreme suffering, and that this experience, hallowed and unsullied, would stay with me for the rest of my life.' Mark Twain more pithily and very unkindly stated, 'Richard Wagner was a musician who wrote music which is better than it sounds.'

Wilhelm Richard Wagner was born in Leipzig, Germany, in May 1813, his parents' ninth child. His father, a local government officer, died only six months later and his mother remarried after a short time. It has been alleged that her new husband, an actor named Ludwig Geyer, was young Richard's real father, which he himself believed. He was treated by Geyer as a favourite son, and the boy took his stepfather's surname until he was 14.

Wagner acquired some musical skills at an early age, but his ambition was to write and produce drama, and aged only 15, he wrote a verse tragedy. Music began to interest him more, and when he entered Leipzig University to read music at the age of 18, he had already composed several sonatas and overtures. Two years later, Wagner began composing opera and became a musical director. However, his early work was not greatly appreciated, and the young composer fell upon hard times. For most of his life, he was short of money, and on at least one occasion he had to flee from his creditors. He married Minna Planer, an actress, in 1836, and shortly afterwards they moved to Riga (now the capital of Latvia, at the time part of Russian territory) where Wagner became musical director at the opera house. His wife was unfaithful and their union was a cause of great unhappiness.

It was while the couple were living in Paris during 1840 and 1841, and Wagner was working as a writer and arranger of operas written by other composers, that he finished, among other pieces, *Der fliegende Holländer* (*The Flying Dutchman*). For much of the 1840s, the couple lived in Dresden, and Wagner added *Tannhäuser* to his growing portfolio of operas, some of which were successfully staged. Towards the end of the decade, revolutionary fervour began to sweep across Europe, and Wagner's leftist sympathies and friendship with radical writers and agitators saw him involved in an uprising against the government. While some of his associates were not so lucky, Wagner managed to avoid arrest and imprisonment by fleeing to Paris and then to Zurich, Switzerland.

During his next 12 years, he lived as an exile and began some of the works for which he is best remembered today, including *Der Ring des Nibelungen* (*The Ring of the Nibelung*). It was during this period that, under a pseudonym, he wrote a tract, *Jewry in Music*, against Jewish composers, which was later published under his own name, exposing his anti-Semitic leanings.

During the 1850s, Wagner fell in love with Mathilde Wesendonck, a married woman who seems to have been determined not to risk her marriage although she was obviously impressed by Richard. Wagner felt his relationship with Mathilde echoed the famous love affair of the Arthurian knight Tristan and the married Isolde, leading him to compose the opera *Tristan und Isolde*. The affair finished in 1858 after an altercation with his wife, who was clearly unhappy about her husband's fascination with another woman. In 1862, his miserable marriage was finally at an end, and the couple parted for good. Minna died in 1866, still supported, as far as was possible, by her impoverished husband.

In 1861, the political situation had eased to the extent that Wagner was able to go to Prussia. He began working on *Die Meistersinger von Nürnberg*, his happiest opera. He had an affair with and later married Cosima von Bülow, with whom he had three illegitimate children, including a daughter named Isolde. Cosima was the daughter of the great composer Franz Liszt, who had given Wagner's opera *Lohengrin* its first performance in 1850. She was a highly intelligent and capable woman, whose relationship with Wagner was often stormy. After his death, she was for many years the director of the Bayreuth Festival, and in 1924 their son, Siegfried, succeeded her in the post.

The inspiration for Wagner's opera *Parsifal* was Wolfram von Eschenbach's medieval Grail romance *Parzival*. The libretto of *Parsifal* was published in December 1877, but work on the musical score was not completed until 1882, when it was first performed in the Festspielhaus in Bayreuth (which Wagner had made his home town) to 'consecrate' the opera house. Wagner would say that he was first inspired to compose *Parsifal*, his 'Good Friday Music', when he woke one Good Friday morning to find the sun shining brightly and the birds singing. He sat on the roof of his house and felt the peace he had long yearned for; then, at that moment, he remembered reading Wolfram's *Parzival*. He later admitted that it had not really been a Good Friday morning, 'just a pleasant mood in Nature which made me think, "This is how a Good Friday ought to be."'

Wagner's patron was King Ludwig II of Bavaria, sometimes called 'Mad King Ludwig'. Ludwig had Schloss Neuschwanstein, a fairytale castle, built in Bavaria as a castle of the Grail, with its throne room as the Hall of the Holy Grail. The walls were painted with murals depicting scenes from *Parzival*, *Lohengrin*, *Tristan und Isolde*, *Siegfried* and *Tannhäuser*. Wagner wrote of his first meeting with King Ludwig:

> He is unfortunately so beautiful and wise, soulful and lordly, that I fear his life must fade away like a divine dream in this base world . . . You cannot imagine the magic of his regard: if he remains alive it will be a great miracle!

In 1886, King Ludwig was declared insane and was deposed. He was held in the Berg Palace but died the following day in mysterious circumstances, and his body was found in Lake Starnberg.

In the twentieth century, Wagner became a controversial figure because the Nazi leader Adolf Hitler greatly admired the composer's works. In 1939, the poet Peter Viereck claimed that 'Wagner's warped genius' was 'the most important single fountainhead of current Nazi ideology'. Hitler himself said, 'For me Wagner is a god, his music is my religion. I go to his operas as others go to church,' and, 'Whoever wants to understand National Socialism must know Wagner.' Much has been made of Hitler's alleged fascination with Wagner, *Parsifal*, the Holy Grail and the Spear of Destiny. In fact, the Nazis banned performances of Wagner's *Parsifal* in 1939, with Joseph Goebbels commenting that it was 'too pious'. Wagner's granddaughter Friedelind Wagner fled Nazi Germany, making a series of radio broadcasts to Germany against the Nazis, and the Allies used Wagner's music in propaganda broadcasts. The last word on Wagner and the Nazis goes to Woody Allen, who said in *Manhattan Murder Mystery*, 'I can't listen to that much Wagner, you know. I start to get the urge to conquer Poland.'

Richard Wagner died in Venice on 13 February 1883. Cosima had confronted him when she learned that a young English soprano named Carrie Pringle was to visit them. Wagner had grown infatuated with Carrie when she performed as a Flower Maiden in *Parsifal*, and only a few hours after the argument with his wife, Wagner was found dead from a heart attack. He would allow *Parsifal* to be staged only at the Bayreuth Festspielhaus, and for more than 20 years after the composer's death, it was performed nowhere else.

SEE ALSO: Lohengrin; Nazi Grail Quest; Percival; Wolfram von Eschenbach

WALES

Some of the earliest tales of Arthur are Welsh. Arthur's name first appears in the Welsh bard Aneirin's poem *Y Gododdin*. Some say that the name Arthur has its origins in the Welsh words '*art*', meaning 'bear', and '*ur*' which means 'man'.

In north-east Wales, high on a windswept hilltop, are the wondrous ruins of Castell Dinas Bran. Legend tells that beneath the stone walls and fallen towers of the castle lies the Holy Grail. Dinas Bran overlooks the town of Llangollen, home of the International Eisteddfod, in the Dee Valley, Denbighshire. The castle is reached by a tiny, winding single-track road then a steep climb across fields and up the hill. The views and the ruined castle itself are spectacular. Artists and poets including J.M.W. Turner and William Wordsworth have been drawn to the romantic ruins of Castell Dinas Bran. When Wordsworth visited he was inspired to write:

> Relics of kings! Wreck of forgotten wars,
> To winds abandoned and the prying stars.

According to the old tales, after Joseph of Arimathea took the Grail from the Holy Land, in time it passed to his nephew Alain le Gros. Alain was the youngest son of Bron, the Fisher King, who was married to Joseph of Arimathea's sister, Enygeus. Alain and his brothers wandered through Britain, until they came to the Land Beyond. The ruler of the Land Beyond was Calafes, a leper king. He converted to Christianity and was healed by the Grail, whereupon he changed his name to Alphasan. In thanks for his miraculous recovery, King Alphasan built a castle for the Grail, high on a mighty hill. When the castle was finished, a mysterious inscription appeared over the main gates. It said that the castle must be named Corbenic. 'Corbenic' is an old French word that means 'crow' or 'raven'. The Welsh word for 'raven' is 'bran'. 'Dinas' simply means 'hill', so Castell Dinas Bran is 'the castle on the hill of the raven', a Welsh version of Corbenic, the legendary Grail castle.

'Chastiel Bran' appears as a ruined castle in the twelfth-century *Romance of Fulk Fitzwarine*. In the thirteenth century, the ruins were replaced with a new fortress. The impressive ruin that survives today may have been the work of Gruffydd Maelor II, son of Madog ap Gruffydd Maelor, begun in the 1260s, though some say that the castle was founded by an unnamed builder in the 1230s. It was occupied by the princes of Powys Fadog. In 1277, Henry de Lacy, the Earl of Lincoln, laid siege to the castle during Edward I's Welsh campaign. When the invading English army took Dinas Bran, they put it to the torch, and while Henry de Lacy suggested to King Edward that Dinas Bran should be rebuilt and fortified as an English stronghold, Edward refused. In 1282, as Edward began his second bloody campaign into Wales, Dafydd ap Gruffydd, the brother of Llywelyn the Last, held Dinas Bran. Soon after Llywelyn's death, Dafydd was captured by the English and executed.

In *The Romance of Fulk Fitzwarine*, an arrogant Norman knight named Pain Peveril comes to the ruins of Dinas Bran. He is part of a Norman force pushing its way into Wales. Peveril learns that the desolate ruins of Dinas Bran were once the home of King Bran. When he hears that since the death of Bran no one has had the courage to stay a night in the ruined castle, he immediately takes up the challenge. That night, as darkness falls, Peveril and a group of his companions climb the steep hill to the castle. A mighty storm arises, and as the men take shelter, an evil giant appears wielding a huge mace. The giant is the infamous Gogmagog.

Peveril fights with the giant, trying to defend his men with his shield. Gogmagog is startled by his defiance, and the knight leaps forward and thrusts his sword into the giant. Gogmagog falls, but before he dies, he tells Peveril of his battles with King Bran. Bran built the castle on the hilltop to thwart Gogmagog, but the giant drove King Bran and his men away. Gogmagog then tells Peveril that a great treasure, which includes a fabulous golden ox, lies buried within the hill. A nineteenth-century folk tale collected in the Dee Valley also states that there is a vast treasure buried in a cave deep in the hill beneath Dinas Bran. The treasure will be found only by a boy who is followed by a dog with silver eyes.

So we see that Dinas Bran, 'the stronghold of Bran', has also been connected to the giant Welsh king Bran the Blessed, Bendigeid Vran ab Llyr. Bran was the son of the sea god Llyr. Arthurian scholars have noted that he owned a wondrous cauldron, just as Bron, the Fisher King, was a keeper of the Holy Grail. The Fisher King was wounded by the Dolorous Blow, while Bran the Blessed was mortally wounded by a poisoned spear that was thrust into his foot. Bran's gigantic head was cut from his shoulders and eventually buried within the White Hill in London. Bran's head would protect Britain from invasion for as long as it remained under the White Hill. King Arthur, however, had Bran's head dug up. This was one of the Three Unfortunate Disclosures recounted in the Welsh Triads. It did not seem right to Arthur that Britain should be defended by the strength of anyone but him. Today, the Tower of London sits on the White Hill. According to legend, if the ravens of the Tower of London ever leave, the Monarchy will fall. As we have noted, '*bran*' is the Welsh word for 'raven'.

Bran appears in a collection of Welsh tales known as *The Mabinogion*. The tales survive in two medieval manuscripts: *Llyfr Gwyn Rhydderch*, *The White Book of Rhydderch*; and *Llyfr Coch Hergest*, *The Red Book of Hergest*. Arthur appears in the tales known as *Culhwch and Olwen* and *The Dream of Rhonabwy*.

In *Culhwch and Olwen*, the young Culhwch appears at Arthur's court at Celliwig in Cornwall. Culhwch can marry only Olwen, the daughter of Ysbaddaden the giant, but Ysbaddaden sets Culhwch a series of impossible tasks before he will agree to the marriage. Culhwch must release the youth Mabon, hunt the monstrous boar Twrch Trwyth and take the blood of the witch Orddu, daughter of the hag Orwen. With the help of Arthur and his warriors, Culhwch accomplishes all the tasks and weds Olwen. Ysbaddaden is beheaded.

The Dream of Rhonabwy recounts the vision that Rhonabwy has as he sleeps on a yellow ox-skin. In the dream, Arthur and Owein play a board game called *gwyddbwyll*. A red-haired man brings the *gwyddbwyll* set; the pieces are gold and the board is silver. As Arthur and Owein play, Arthur's servants and Owein's ravens fight. A young man with yellow hair and blue eyes tells Owein that his ravens are being attacked by Arthur's squires and servants. Owein asks Arthur to call his men off his ravens. Arthur answers, 'Your move.' Owein orders that his banner be raised. As Arthur and Owein play on, the fighting between Arthur's servants and Owein's ravens grows fiercer. Three times Owein asks Arthur to call off his men, three times Arthur replies, 'Your move.' Owein's ravens fly up and sweep down on Arthur's men, carrying them up into the air and tearing at their heads. A knight in heavy armour tells Arthur that Owein's ravens are slaying his men. Now, Arthur asks Owein to call off his ravens, and Owein answers, 'Your move.' The ravens slaughter Arthur's men and Owein will not call them off. Many of Arthur's best men are slain. Arthur takes the golden pieces from the board and crushes them to dust. Owein orders his banner to be lowered and there is peace.

The White Book of Rhydderch and *The Red Book of Hergest* also contain Welsh adaptations of Chrétien de Troyes' French Arthurian romances. *Owain and Luned*, also known as *The Lady of the Fountain*, is based on *Yvain, or the Knight with the Lion*; *Peredur, Son of Efrawg* is the Welsh *Perceval, or the Story of the Grail*; and *Geraint ab Erbin* is a version of *Érec and Énide*.

The lake into which Bedivere threw Excalibur is sometimes said to be the remote mountain lake, Llyn Llydaw, in the shadow of Mount Snowdon. Alternatively, Excalibur may have been thrown into Llyn Ogwen, also in North Wales. The ancient poem 'The Stanzas of the Graves' records that: 'The grave of Bedwyr [Bedivere] is on the hill of Tryfan,' a Snowdonian peak. Legend tells that Merlin spoke prophecy and saw red and white dragons fighting tooth and claw at Dinas Emrys. Curiously, the hill of Dinas Emrys appears to be made of red stone and white rock. Owein battled a giant at Llyn Dinas, the lake by Dinas Emrys.

Indeed there are Arthurian sites and legends across Wales. St Govan's Chapel in Pembrokeshire is said to be the burial place of Gawain, who became a hermit calling himself Govan. Carmarthen is Caer Myrddin, 'Merlin's town', where the magician was born. A local rhyme says:

> When Myrddin's tree shall tumble down,
> Then shall fall Carmarthen town.

For centuries, a tree known as Merlin's Oak stood in Carmarthen. It died in the mid-nineteenth century, but it was braced and supported until finally it had to be removed. A branch is on display in the Carmarthenshire County Museum. Merlin was trapped by Viviane in Bryn Myrddin, Merlin's Hill, near Carmarthen, and Merlin is thought to lie in a glass tomb in a cave on Bardsey Island, the legendary Avalon.

It is said that anyone who spends a night on the haunted mountain Cader Idris, 'the Seat of Arthur', will be found mad, dead or a poet.

According to Nennius, Arthur's dog Cabal left its footprint in a stone in Wales. Arthur built a cairn named Carn Cabal with the stone at the top. We are told that people would take the stone away only for it to reappear in place the next day. The massive boulder in Gower, Swansea Bay, known as Coetan Arthur, 'Arthur's Stone', is said to have been created when, as Arthur walked to Camlann, he threw a pebble he found in his shoe. In the past, the maidens of Swansea would steal out to Arthur's Stone, leave barley and honey cakes dipped in milk, and crawl around the stone three times in a ritual to test the fidelity of their young men. According to folklore, at full moon a mysterious figure, said to be King Arthur, walks from Arthur's Stone down to the sea.

Arthur is said to have held court at Caerleon, where the Roman amphitheatre is known as King Arthur's Round Table. The town was noted as Arthur's court by Chrétien de Troyes and the twelfth-century poet Marie de France; Caerleon-on-Usk is named as one of Arthur's principal courts in the Welsh Triads; and the medieval *Chronique du Religieux de Saint-Denys* records that King Arthur's Round Table was at Caerleon. One tale from the region goes that a local man, the worse for drink after a night in the Red Lion, was confronted by a soldier, who took him into Caerleon's castle mound. There he found King Arthur and all his knights feasting at tables piled high with gold and silver. Eventually, the man staggered out with a bag of gold. At first light, he was found drunk in a ditch. The gold was gone, and from that day forth the man never touched a drop of drink.

King Edward I of England took more than a bag of faerie gold from Wales. He was presented with the head of Llywelyn ap Gruffydd, the last prince of an independent Wales. Edward had Llywelyn's crown richly adorned and gilded, and it was presented at Westminster Abbey as the Coron Arthur, the Crown of Arthur. The English said that Arthur was dead, that his bones lay in a marble tomb in Glastonbury Abbey. The Welsh knew better. The poem 'Englynion y Beddau' ('The Stanzas of the Graves' or 'Graves of the Warriors of Britain') may have been composed in the tenth century, although the earliest manuscript containing the poem is the thirteenth-century *Llyfr Du Caerfyrddin* (*The Black Book of Carmarthen*). Stanza 44 records the Welsh belief that Arthur still lives. The poem is a long list of the grave sites of heroes and historical figures, but a grave for Arthur cannot be named or found:

A grave for March, a grave for Gwythur,
A grave for Gwgawn Red-sword;
The world's wonder a grave for Arthur.

SEE ALSO: Arthur, King of the Britons; Avalon; Battles of Arthur; Holy Grail; Joseph of Arimathea; Merlin

WOLFRAM VON ESCHENBACH

Wolfram von Eschenbach (*c.*1170–*c.*1220) was a German minnesinger, a composer of epic lyric tales. He is most famous today for his Grail romance *Parzival*. He is considered, alongside Hartmann von Aue and Gottfried von Strassburg, to be one of the greatest Middle High German epic poets. Minnesingers were composers and performers of lyric poetry (*Minnesang*). They were highly regarded in German courts from the twelfth into the fourteenth century. Like the troubadours of France, the minnesingers wrote music and lyrics and sang songs of love and adventure. While some minnesingers were of low degree, others, such as the Holy Roman Emperor Henry VI, were of exalted rank. Themes such as loyalty, constancy, moderation and obedience to authority, all knightly virtues, were common threads in their poems.

We know very little about Wolfram's life outside of his surviving works. He describes himself as a Bavarian, and his birthplace is thought to be the town of Obereschenbach, now known as Wolframs-Eschenbach, near Ansbach, but this is by no means certain. Wolfram's claim to be a soldier has been the subject of controversy among scholars, yet his works display a familiarity with the lives and customs of knights which demonstrates that, if not actually one of them, he lived among them sufficiently closely to absorb their culture.

Wolfram's *Parzival*, composed around 1205, is recognised as a masterwork of the time. Although Wolfram claimed otherwise, he evidently based his epic on Chrétien de Troyes' *Perceval, or the Story of the Grail*. He did, however, deviate from his source and is credited with composing the most complete Grail romance. Other surviving works by Wolfram include eight or nine 'dawn songs', some fragments of a piece entitled *Titurel* and an unfinished *Willehalm*, the story of a crusader called Guillaume d'Orange.

Wolfram is critical of Chrétien de Troyes' *Story of the Grail*, saying that the French poet 'has done this tale an injustice'. Wolfram claims that his source, the true Grail story, came from a renowned Provençal scholar named Kyot. When Kyot was in Toledo, in Moorish Spain, he found a neglected Arabic manuscript. Wolfram tells us that Kyot must have learned Arabic 'without the aid of necromancy', implying that the language was considered so difficult and exotic that most people would need to use magic to learn it. The 'heathen' manuscript was written by a Muslim astronomer named Flegetanis, a descendant of Solomon, who read the secrets of the Grail written in the stars.

In his *The Quest for King Arthur*, David Day states that 'there are Oriental aspects to the Grail quest, and among those who embraced it most enthusiastically were the military brotherhood of the crusader Templar Knights'. Wolfram's purported source for the Grail story might then be supported by this fact, and in telling the history of a crusader knight in Willehalm, Wolfram clearly must have had some understanding of the crusaders' experiences.

It is clear that *Parzival* was well received. It survives in no fewer than 84 manuscripts, painstakingly copied out by hand. Clearly also popular was Wolfram's *Willehalm* that survives in 78 copies. Wolfram claimed, although it is hotly disputed, that he was unable to read and that he did not know a single letter of the alphabet. As a consequence, he would have been forced to dictate his works to scribes. If his claim is true, it would be interesting to know where his knowledge of Latin, astrology, classical and German literature, the Bible and medicine came from. There is little doubt that he showed a superb mastery of language and was unafraid to be original in the form and content of his works.

Parzival was the inspiration for Richard Wagner's three-act opera *Parsifal*. Wagner first read *Parzival* at Marienbad in 1845 and saw the potential of a story describing how Sir Percival, the Arthurian knight, sought the Holy Grail. Wagner's work was first performed at Bayreuth in 1882, the year of its completion. Wagner, like Wolfram, had a way with words and rather than call *Parsival* an opera, he preferred the description '*ein Bühnenweihfestspiel*', 'a festival play to consecrate the stage'.

Wolfram's eponymous hero is so simple that he begins the story not even knowing his own name, but because he is innocent and without guile, he is able to achieve what wiser, more cunning men could not. A similar concept occurs in Matthew 18:3: 'Except ye . . . become as little children, ye shall not enter into the kingdom of heaven.' The pure and innocent heart wins the day. In Chrétien's *Story of the Grail*, Perceval is depicted as being, by very reason of this innocence and freedom from the temptations of the world, a man apart from the rest of the Arthurian court. Wolfram's Parzival, however, becomes the keeper of the Grail — a central, prestigious position — as a consequence of his spiritual development. The Grail itself is not described in detail; Wolfram simply tells us that the Grail surpasses all earthly perfection and that its delights resemble the kingdom of heaven.

SEE ALSO: Chrétien de Troyes; Knights Templar; Percival; Wagner, Richard

SELECT BIBLIOGRAPHY

Alcock, Leslie, *Arthur's Britain*, Pelican Books, 1973

Ashe, Geoffrey, *Avalonian Quest*, Fontana, 1984

Ashe, Geoffrey, *The Landscape of King Arthur*, Henry Holt, 1987

Baigent, Michael, Leigh, Richard, and Lincoln, Henry, *The Holy Blood and The Holy Grail*, Arrow, 1996

Baines, Keith, *Malory's* Le Morte d'Arthur. *King Arthur and the Legend of the Round Table*, Signet Classic, 2001

Barber, Richard (ed.), *The Arthurian Legends: An Illustrated Anthology*, Littlefield and Adams, 1979

Barber, Richard, *The Holy Grail: The History of a Legend*, Penguin Books, 2004

Barber, Richard, *King Arthur: Hero and Legend*, The Boydell Press, 1990

Barron W. R. (ed.), *The Arthur of the English*, University of Wales Press, 1999

Benham, Patrick, *The Avalonians*, Gothic Image, 1993

Biddle, Martin, *King Arthur's Round Table*, B.T. Batsford, 1988

de Boer, Esther, *Mary Magdalene: Beyond the Myth*, Trinity Press International, 1996

Bollard, John K., 'Arthur in the Early Welsh Traditions', in *The Romance of Arthur*, James J. Wilhelm (ed.), Routledge, 1994

Bromwich, Rachel (ed.), *Trioedd Ynys Prydein: The Welsh Triads*, University of Wales Press, 1978

Bromwich, Rachel, Jarman, A.O.H., and Roberts, Brynley F. (eds), *The Arthur of the Welsh*, University of Wales Press, 1991

Brown, Dan, *The Da Vinci Code*, Corgi, 2004

Bryant, Arthur, *The Age of Chivalry*, World Books, 1968

Cavendish, Richard, *King Arthur and the Grail*, Paladin Books, 1980

Clarke, Basil, *Life of Merlin: Vita Merlini*, University of Wales Press, 1973

Day, David, *The Quest for King Arthur*, Diane Publishing Company, 1995

Edwards, Gillian, *Hobgoblin and Sweet Puck*, Geoffrey Bles, 1974

Freke, Timothy, and Gandy, Peter, *Jesus and the Goddess: The Secret Teachings of the Original Christians*, HarperCollins, 2002

Furtado, Antonio L., 'The Crusaders' Grail', 2006 (http://www-di.inf. puc-rio.br/~furtado/the_crusaders_grail.pdf)

Gantz, Jeffrey (trans.), *The Mabinogion*, Dorset, 1985

Geoffrey of Monmouth, *The History of the Kings of Britain*, translated by Lewis Thorpe, Penguin Classics, 1973

Gerritsen, Willem P., Van Melle, Anthony G. (eds), and Guest, Tanis (trans.), *A Dictionary of Medieval Heroes*, The Boydell Press, 1998

Giles, J.A. (ed.), *Six Old English Chronicles*, Henry G. Bohn, 1848

Glennie, J.S., *Arthurian Localities*, Llanerch Press, 1994

Glot, Claudine, and Glot, Hervé, *Brocéliande*, Apogée, 1998

Glot, Claudine, *Hauts lieux de Brocéliande*, Ouest-France, 1996

Grigsby, John, *Warriors of the Wasteland: A Quest for the Pagan Sacrificial Cult Behind the Grail Legends*, Watkins, 2003

Hallam, Elizabeth (ed.), *Chronicles of the Crusades*, Welcome Rain Publishers, 2001

Helms, Randal, *Gospel Fictions*, Prometheus Books, 1989

Hopkins, Andrea, *Chronicles of King Arthur*, Studio, 1994

James, M.R., *The Apocryphal New Testament*, Clarendon Press, 1924

Jones, Gwyn (ed., trans.), Jones, Thomas (trans.), and Jones, Mair (ed.), *The Mabinogion*, Everyman, 1993

Jones, Michael K., *Bosworth 1485: The Psychology of a Battle*, Tempus Publishing Ltd, 2003

Jung, Emma and von Franz, Marie-Louise, *The Grail Legend*, translated by A. Dykes, Hodder & Stoughton, 1971

Lacy, Norris J., 'The Da Vinci Code: Dan Brown and the Grail That Never Was', *Arthuriana* 14.3, 2004

Lacy, Norris J. (ed.), *Lancelot-Grail: The Old French Arthurian Vulgate and Post-Vulgate in Translation*, Garland, 1993

Lacy, Norris J., and Ashe, Geoffrey, *The Arthurian Handbook*, Garland, 1988

Lacy, Norris J. et al. (ed.), *The New Arthurian Encyclopedia*, Garland, 1996

SELECT BIBLIOGRAPHY

Loomis, Roger Sherman, *Arthurian Legend in Medieval Art*, Oxford University Press, 1938

Loomis, Roger Sherman, *The Grail: From Celtic Myth to Christian Symbol*, Constable, 1992

Lupack, Alan, *The Oxford Guide to Arthurian Literature and Legend*, Oxford University Press, 2005

Malory, Sir Thomas, *Le Morte D'Arthur: The Winchester Manuscript*, edited by Helen Cooper, Oxford University Press, 1998

Mancoff, Debra N., *The Arthurian Revival in Victorian Art*, Garland, 1990

Mason, Eugene (trans.), *Wace and Layamon: Arthurian Chronicles*, University of Toronto Press, 1996.

Matarasso, P.M. (trans.), *The Quest of the Holy Grail*, Penguin, 1975

McHardy, Stuart, *On the Trail of the Holy Grail*, Luath Press, 2006

McHardy, Stuart, *The Quest for Arthur*, Luath Press, 2001

Nicholson, Helen, *Love, War and the Grail*, Brill, 2004

Owen, D.D.R. (trans.), *Arthurian Romances: Chrétien de Troyes*, Everyman, 1993

Philip, Neil, *The Penguin Book of English Folktales*, Penguin, 1992

Picknett, Lynn, and Prince, Clive, *The Templar Revelation*, Bantam Press, 1997

Riley, Henry T. (trans), *Annals of Roger de Hoveden*, Bohn's Antiquarian Library, 1853

Ritchie, R.L. Graeme, *Chrétien de Troyes and Scotland*, Oxford, 1952

Ross, Charles, *The Wars of the Roses: A Concise History*, Thames & Hudson, 1986

Scavone, Daniel C., 'Joseph of Arimathea, the Holy Grail and the Edessa Icon', *Arthuriana* 9.4, 1999

Simpson, Roger, *Camelot Regained: The Arthurian Revival and Tennyson 1800–1849*, D.S. Brewer, 1990

Skene, William F. (ed.), *The Four Ancient Books of Wales*, Edmonston, 1868

Snell, F.J., *King Arthur's Country*, Dent, 1926

Starbird, Margaret, *The Woman with the Alabaster Jar*, Bear and Company, 1993

Strachey, Sir Edward, *Le Morte Darthur: Sir Thomas Malory's Book of King Arthur and of his Noble Knights of the Round Table*, Macmillan, 1903

Tolstoy, Nikolai, *The Quest for Merlin*, Hamish Hamilton, 1985

Treharne, R.F., *The Glastonbury Legends: Joseph of Arimathea, the Holy Grail and King Arthur*, Cresset, 1967

Weston, Jessie L. (trans.), *Wolfram von Eschenbach: Parzifal, a Knightly Epic*, Nutt, 1894

Westwood, Jennifer, *Albion: A Guide to Legendary Britain*, Grafton, 1985

Wilhelm, James J. (ed.), *The Romance of Arthur*, Garland, 1994

Camille Hill
270-763-3652

SWEELINCK